Also by Wim J. M. Touw

Without Prejudice (1992), a novel

Guide to American Colleges and Universities (1996),
published by *Education USA* and distributed overseas

Law Street

*America's Dysfunctional
and Sometimes Corrupt
Legal System*

Wim J. M. Touw

iUniverse, Inc.
Bloomington

Law Street
America's Dysfunctional and Sometimes Corrupt Legal System

iUniverse books may be ordered through booksellers or by contacting:

iUniverse
1663 Liberty Drive
Bloomington, IN 47403
www.iuniverse.com
1-800-Authors (1-800-288-4677)

ISBN: 978-1-4620-0873-5 (pbk)
ISBN: 978-1-4620-0874-2 (clth)
ISBN: 978-1-4620-0875-9 (ebk)

Library of Congress Control Number: 2011905250

Printed in the United States of America

iUniverse rev. date: 05/18/2011

To my son Paul for his creativity and his boundless generosity, my daughter Marguerite for her inspiring intellect, my son Courtney for his sterling character, my daughter Jessica for her infectious optimism, and above all for my wife, Brenda, who made it all possible.

Contents

Part III: OVERSIGHT AND REFORM 185

Preface

Many books have been written about the anomalies of the American justice system. These books describe the consequences of bad lawyering, of overzealous prosecutors, of a tort bar run amok,[1] and of archaic legal rules and procedures. They talk about outrageous jury verdicts, the costly damage done by class-action suits, and the harmful effects of malpractice awards. They indeed itemize the ills of the American legal system in a very detailed and often informative way.

What these books do not deal with, however, is what has caused all these anomalies, what is at the root of our dysfunctional, arbitrary, and often unjust legal system. Besides, most of these books deal with tort and lack a critical review of our criminal law system.[2]

The reason these books fail to get to the essence of what has caused our legal system to lose its moorings is that they are practically all written by lawyers. Except for a few insightful books written by nonlawyer Walter K. Olson, they are written by scholars of the American legal system who were taught and trained by the very system they attempt to analyze and criticize. They are on the inside, and, as a consequence, they cannot see the forest for the trees. They are steeped in American legal history, in American case law, and in American rules and procedures, but they have very little knowledge of how all this compares with legal systems in other countries.

---

1   Tort bar is the collective term for lawyers who file civil suits for damages.

2   A tort is a wrong that involves a breach of civil duty owed to someone else. A tort is different from criminal wrongdoing, which involves a breach of duty to the state. Only the state may prosecute a crime, whereas any party who has been injured may bring a lawsuit for tort.

Besides, as members of the bar or prominent members of the legal community, they cannot be too critical. They cannot say that the American legal system is dysfunctional, that it is unjust, that it lacks fairness, or that it is sometimes corrupt. Such judgments would put them at odds with the legal community and their colleagues. It would be politically incorrect for them to say such awful things about the American legal system.

There are a number of legal commentators, moreover, who dislike and discourage comparing the American legal system to legal systems in other countries. Somehow to do so is un-American.[3] They argue that American exceptionalism requires that we let our legal system evolve the American way and that we should do so without studying how other countries have approached some of the same legal problems we face. That idea is as shortsighted as rejecting a new drug because the drug was developed by a Swiss pharmaceutical company or refusing to use software because it wasn't developed in Silicon Valley or in Redmond, Washington. If American business ignored foreign developments or breakthroughs, it would do so at its peril. But where the law is concerned, what is good for the goose is apparently not good for the gander.

Although lawyers have a bad reputation and are often the butt of jokes, public opinion polls suggest that Americans are content with their judicial system. And despite the hunch that the system has its shortcomings, they think it is a fair system and one that is superior when compared to judicial systems in other countries.

The reason Americans think that's the case is that they hear about American exceptionalism from the moment they learn to talk. Since America is an exceptional country, they reason, American laws and the American legal system must also be superior.

As a matter of fact, the American legal system is far from perfect. As this book will explain, high standards of fairness and equal justice for all are frequently lacking, and conflicts of interest and even corrupt legal practices destroy those standards where they do exist. Furthermore, as I will explain in the coming pages, the American legal system has been hijacked by trial attorneys who have succumbed to greed and prosecutors whose actions are dictated by political careers. Rules, procedures, processes,

---

3   James Zirin, partner Sidley Austin LLP, during a NewsTalk online discussion of the pros and cons of a loser-pays model for courts on August 19, 2008, answering the question whether a loser pays system would eliminate frivolous lawsuits and defenses: *"Loser pays is undesirable because it is simply un-American."*

and state and federal laws have, during the last hundred years, been slowly manipulated to serve the profit and growth motives of a thriving industry of legal practitioners in a manner some term The American Way.

I thought long and hard before I reached my verdict about the American legal system. But my education, my experience with judicial systems in other countries, and my interest in American history and the history and evolution of American jurisprudence in particular have left me no choice but to ring the bell to warn that all is not well on the western front—all is not well with the American legal system.

＊ ＊ ＊ ＊ ＊

I was born in the Netherlands. By the time I could read and write I had witnessed horror and despair. In the very early morning of May 10, 1940, I watched German paratroopers, using their novel blitzkrieg strategy, drop out of the sky onto an island in the Maas river, part of the city of Rotterdam where I lived. The island controlled the strategic bridges over the river, which was the reason the Germans occupied the island within hours of invading my country.

The cacophony of grenades exploding everywhere, the rat-tat-tat of machine gunfire, the grief when I watched my own home go up in flames as the result of a Dutch marines counter attack on the German positions, and the utter fear and despair in the eyes of my parents left an indelible imprint on my life.

The five-year German occupation that followed was despotic, murderous, and full of constant fear and total arbitrariness. Watching the Jews first walk the streets with the Star of David sewn on their lapels and then gradually disappear; hearing that the Germans had randomly picked up twenty people walking down the street and executed them on the spot in retaliation for an attack by the Dutch underground and then having to walk for three days by the corpses of the executed people on my way to school; watching people collapse on the sidewalk and die of hunger during the winter of 1944 when the big cities in Holland had run out of food; and then, when the allied food drops began, watching desperate people run into the fields to grab the food and in the process get killed by cans of food falling like rain from the Lancaster aircraft droning overhead—all this utter and unimaginable horror and cruelty instilled in me a thirst for justice and equity at a very young age.

My high school years were fortunate. I attended a school where most of the faculty had PhDs in the subjects they were teaching. It was during those years that I developed my first real interest in and admiration for the United States as the result of an interdisciplinary assignment from my French and history teachers. They made us read, translate, and discuss a number of chapters from an early-nineteenth-century French book entitled *De la Democratie en Amerique* (translated into English under the name *Democracy in America*), a book that, because it could have been written today, made a lasting impression on me.

Because we attended school six days a week, eleven months a year, by the time I graduated from high school I had been in school a full two to three years longer than the average graduating American high school student of today. Later in life, I realized that my high school years—not university—were the most important intellectually formative years of my life.

After two years of service in the military—Holland still had the draft when I graduated from high school—during which I graduated from officer school, I served with NATO in Germany. I subsequently attended the University of Leiden, where I received a candidate of law (iuris candidatus) degree.

Soon afterward I left my native country, first to spend five years in Paris, France, as the Assistant European Director of an American NGO affiliated with the Fulbright Scholarship organization, and then to spend close to three years in Dublin, Ireland, as the Managing Director of Holland-America Line, Ireland Ltd.

In the five years I worked in Paris, I got my first taste of international legal disputes. The Fulbright scholarship organization moved thousands of students, teachers, and professors from Europe to the United States. I was in charge of the chartering of passenger vessels to provide passage for these students and teachers from the French port of Le Havre to New York. Maritime charter contracts traditionally included a clause stating that, in case of a dispute, the parties agreed to arbitration in London. Consequently, I spent a good deal of time in London handling maritime arbitration cases before the London Maritime Arbitrators Association, which in those days were heard at the historic Society of the Inner Temple at the Inns of Court in London.

Falling in love with a young American lady brought me to the shores of the United States where, living in five different states in the east, west, and intermountain west, my wife and I raised four children who all became leaders in business and academia.

My professional career in the United States began as the president of a subsidiary of Transamerica Corporation in San Francisco and continued as the president of a subsidiary of Reader's Digest Inc. in Pleasantville, New York.

While working for Transamerica Corporation, I was a member of a litigation committee that evaluated law suits filed against Transamerica or one of its many subsidiaries, companies such as the insurance company Occidental Life, the car rental company Budget Rent-a-Car, the film studio United Artists, Transamerica Airlines, and Transamerica Title, to name a few. Transamerica did not have in-house counsel, preferring to divide its legal work among independent law firms. As a member of the litigation committee, I learned that the vast majority of suits were nuisance suits that simply abused the system, suits filed by attorneys to force Transamerica or one of its subsidiaries to settle for a certain amount of money just to avoid the nuisance, the administrative burden, and the cost of litigation.

When I worked for Reader's Digest, I was president of their international education subsidiary. In that capacity, I had responsibility for managing relations with what was then called the Civil Aeronautics Board (CAB), one of the most intrusive and controlling regulatory agencies of the US government. The CAB was chartered by Congress to regulate air transportation in general and domestic and international airlines in particular. Since the Digest subsidiary I managed chartered a very large number of passenger aircraft, the CAB ruled the company to be an airline. Twice I had to file suit against the CAB to rescind compliance orders against our company, and twice we prevailed.

In the late seventies I launched my own company in the field of international education and personnel training for multinational companies. Over the years, it grew to include operations and offices in the Americas, Europe, North Africa, the Middle East, and the Far East. As the president and CEO of my company, I never delegated management of our legal affairs. I consequently became involved in the corporate matters of our overseas subsidiaries, international taxation issues, and lawsuits against the company in a number of countries, lawsuits that involved employment matters and a variety of issues, such as, for example, a wrongful death allegation from the parents of a Japanese student who died in an accident, a case that was litigated in both the United States and in Japan.

Having spent the first thirty-four years of my life in Europe and the rest in the United States, I have my feet firmly planted on both sides of the ocean. Having lived in five different American states, having worked for large American corporations on four continents, and having returned to my native country two to three times a year since I left, I have had the privilege of observing life not only in many countries around the world but especially in my adopted country, a country I have come to love with the zeal of a religious convert.

When I write about American law and the American justice system, I do so from a different perspective than the authors of the books I mentioned above. I am not a lawyer, and my legal training in the Netherlands involved old Roman law, old Dutch law, an introduction to modern Dutch law, economics, and civil law. Two of my electives dealt with American state law and maritime law. Consequently, my law school curriculum couldn't have been more different from anything an American law school teaches its students.

All my life I have been a businessman launching and subsequently overseeing operations in many different countries. I have not only become familiar with legal systems that are different from the American legal system; in my professional career I have had to work with different legal systems, and I have had to negotiate or litigate within the framework of different legal systems.

I consequently decided to add my own thoughts to the voices of the various authors who have written about the American legal system. I do not want to limit such thoughts to a recital of the horrors of the system—many other publications have done that job quite adequately. What I would like to do is explain how the American legal system evolved and how it has completely veered away from the original English common law system and why today the system is frequently at odds with established principles of legal fairness and equity as they exist in the rest of the developed world. Like the religious convert I mentioned above, I am unabashedly proud of America. What I have to say about my adopted country's legal system, however, does not fit that description.

This is not a pretty story, and it is not a story that will earn me new friends in the American legal community. But it is a story that must be told. America is an exceptional country—having traveled extensively and worked all over the world, I can attest to that. However, as is the case with every country, America is not without its shortcomings.

This is a story about a serious flaw in American society. This is a story about a legal system that has lost its moral and ethical anchor. This is a story about how a deficient criminal justice system puts innocent people in jail and how, for a good number of its practitioners, lawyering as a profession has turned into lawyering as a business—not just any business, but a dishonest business.

Olympia, Washington
December, 2010
Wim J. M. Touw

Introduction

Few democracies feature coequal executive, legislative, and judiciary branches of government with built-in checks and balances to maintain the separation of powers in the manner suggested by the French political philosopher Baron de Montesquieu (1689–1755) in his 1748 treatise *De l'esprit des loix* (The Spirit of Laws), one of the great works in the history of political theory and jurisprudence and the most important piece of eighteenth-century political writing, which served as an inspiration for the US constitution.

Most democratic systems of government have either a parliamentary style government or a presidential style government. In a parliamentary style government (the system in use in most of Western Europe), the legislative branch, rather than the voters, gives birth to the executive. The legislative branch is therefore supreme. In a presidential style government, the executive is usually elected, allowing a more perfect separation of powers. Furthermore, only the US constitution allows the judiciary both to censor the executive and to declare laws passed by the legislature to be unconstitutional. This is why political scientists generally agree that the American system of government is the perfect embodiment of Montesquieu's political philosophy. In theory, then, the American form of government is the epitome of Montesquieu's political ideas. In practice, that is decidedly not the case.

Montesquieu wrote that "the judiciary is ... the most important of powers, independent and unchecked" and that "the independence of the judiciary has to be real and not apparent." In the United States, the judiciary is not independent. Interestingly, and as is usually the case in dictatorial regimes, it is not the executive branch that exercises undue influence over the US judiciary (although the attorney general, a member of the executive, sometimes attempts to do so). The problem with the legal system in the United States is its culture and its integrity—the system has been hijacked from within.

What permeates the US legal system is a lack of ethics among a large number of its practitioners. Their motivation is not fairness and equity, but money and professional advancement. As this book will show, many attorneys, prosecutors, and judges in both civil and criminal cases are guided by the amount of money they stand to earn or how the outcome of a case affects their careers or influences their chances to be reelected or reappointed.

Furthermore, *LegalReformNow* reports that the US Congress has long been dominated by lawyer-politicians. From 1780 to 1930, two thirds of the Senate and about half of the House of Representatives were lawyers; since then, the percentage has remained fairly stable. At the beginning of the 101st Congress in 1989, 184 members (42 percent) of the US House of Representatives were lawyers (47 percent of Democrats and 35 percent of Republicans). Sixty-three senators (out of one hundred) were lawyers, roughly equally distributed between the two parties. At the beginning of the 102nd Congress in 1991, 244 of the 535 members of both houses (46 percent) claimed attorney as their profession. The same goes for state legislatures, where roughly the same percentages of members are former prosecutors or lawyers. Since members of the bar, in the aggregate, are the largest contributors to the campaigns of members of the state and federal legislatures, the legal profession has an undue influence over those whose task it is to write the laws of the land.[4]

Most Americans are convinced that their legal system is the fairest and most equitable system in the world. In talk shows on radio and television or in articles in newspapers and magazines, the American legal system is often presented as one that is not only fair and balanced, but a system

---

4   In February of 2010 the Center for Responsive Politics (CRP) reports that since 1990, the sums donated to federal political candidates by lawyers— excluding lobbyists—exceed $1 billion. Lawyers as a group have given more to federal candidates than any other industry or profession. Their ability to keep medical malpractice tort reform out of the new health care reform legislation (Obamacare) is not surprising: Congressional campaign contributions by lawyers in the last election cycle were about $25 million more than the combined total of political donations from doctors, pharmaceutical companies, HMOs, hospitals, and nursing homes.

nascent democracies should emulate. The truth is that, compared to other mature democracies, such as Great Britain, the Netherlands, Germany, and the Scandinavian countries, the American legal system is less equitable, frequently inherently unfair, and in many instances dysfunctional. In the tort area it borders on being corrupt.

I should preface what I am about to write by mentioning that numerous prosecutors, attorneys, and judges labor hard every day to make the American legal system fair and equitable. As officers of the court, they admirably defend the innocent as well as the guilty; as judges, they make sure they are the guarantors of judicial process; as counselors, they professionally execute the myriad of transactions required in family and business law.

Furthermore, there are some great minds at work in the American legal profession. Most Supreme Court justices—whether they are interpreters of the constitution and therefore usually appointed by Democratic presidents or strict constitutional constructionists and therefore usually appointed by Republican presidents—and the vast majority of the members of the federal bench are highly impressive legal minds. Equally impressive are many law school professors, whose role it is to shape the legal minds of their students.

Members of the federal bench are, however, not elected—they are appointed for life—whereas state judges are usually elected. Law school professors have tenure and cannot be fired. It is the unusual large number of prosecutors, lawyers, and state judges, however, who do not pursue the loftier and more professional ideals of the law, that render the system lacking in fairness and equity.

When the United States declared its independence, it inherited the British common law system. The founding fathers then adopted a constitution that, together with administrative law, statutory law, and common law (case law), became the source of all law in the country.

The constitution decrees that all powers not preempted by the constitution, federal statutes, or international treaties shall be the prerogative of the sovereign states. Since the constitution only mentions a limited number of areas where the federal government has jurisdiction, all fifty states adopted their own constitutions and their own judicial systems, both civil and criminal.

The individual states all adopted the Anglo Saxon common law system.[5] However, as soon as the federal constitution and later the various state constitutions took effect, new statutes everywhere made the legal system veer away from Anglo Saxon law. Particularly in the twentieth century, when America changed from a rural to an industrial and more urban society, numerous laws were adopted and cases adjudicated that rendered the American legal system today completely distinct and separate from British common law.

It is these new laws, many of them promoted and pushed through the legislatures by the legal profession, that have changed the former Anglo Saxon legal system from one that pursued fairness and equity into one that is frequently unfair and in many instances dysfunctional. It has produced a tort regime that borders on being corrupt and, as some recent high-profile cases and criminal convictions of some of the most famous tort lawyers have shown, is corrupt. Furthermore, the manner in which state judges, and in particular state supreme court judges, are elected makes a travesty of judicial impartiality.

Several elements of American law have done a great deal of damage to the legal system. First and foremost, the practice of electing state judges and prosecutors and the system of plea bargaining has "conflict of interest" written all over it. Furthermore, when viewed from abroad, the jury system in America is a perversion of how a jury system should operate. Finally, in the area of civil law, the absence of the loser-pays rule and the system of pretrial discovery, contingency fees, class-action lawsuits, and punitive and treble damages have changed tort litigation into an often corrupt high-stakes poker game benefiting lawyers rather than an equitable system to establish liability. Most of these elements of the American legal system are unique to the United States and are not part of Anglo Saxon law as practiced in Great Britain or other common law jurisdictions, such as Canada, Australia, New Zealand, or South Africa.

The influence of the bar on American politics is something the founding fathers warned against. In addition to the Declaration of Independence, the Constitution, and the Bill of Rights, the Federalist Papers are part of the Bible of American democracy. The Federalist Papers—unfortunately hardly ever mentioned in civics classes and therefore virtually unknown to many Americans—are a series of eighty-five articles written and published

---

5   Except for the State of Louisiana, which, because it had been a French colony before it became part of the United States, adopted the Napoleonic code and elements of the Spanish civil law system.

in late 1787 and early 1788. They are referred to by their number and were mostly written to support the ratification of the proposed constitution. They are a rich source of what the founding fathers were thinking when they were debating the various clauses in the constitution.

The anonymous articles were mostly written by two towers of wisdom and intelligence: Alexander Hamilton, who later became the first US Secretary of the Treasury (and a brilliant one at that), and James Madison, who became the fourth president. The wisdom contained in the Papers is as applicable today as it was back in 1787.

Federalist No. 10, written by Hamilton and usually regarded as one of the most important ones, warns of the dangers a democracy faces. It addresses the question of how to protect a democracy against factions. Hamilton describes a faction as "a number of citizens, whether amounting to a minority or a majority of the whole, who are united and actuated by some common impulse of passion, or of interest, adverse to the rights of other citizens, or to the permanent or aggregate interests of the community."

Today nascent democracies, particularly in South America, Africa, and countries born out of the former Soviet Union, where factions of wealthy families or corporations or the military have taken control of the country, are witness to the dangers factions can pose to democracies. The labor unions in Greece are a faction that, through their political influence over the country's finances, have brought Greece to near bankruptcy.

In our country, the teachers' unions, with their suffocating hold over the country's public school system, are such a faction. So is the bar. The bar is not as frightening and controlling a faction as the ones mentioned above, but it is a faction with a hold over society nevertheless. The influence of the bar over the choice of which judges will stand for election and its huge campaign contributions to candidates for the state and federal legislatures—resulting in an uncanny ability to get legislation passed that favors lawyers at the expense of the community as a whole—is a clear and present danger to fairness in American society.

This book is written in three parts. The first part is about criminal law, the second is about civil law, and the third is about oversight and reform. Since most Americans are not familiar with the various law systems used by other countries, I should explain that the term civil law is often used to describe law inspired by Roman or Napoleonic law, legal systems that require that all laws be written as a code. Roman law is the basis of the law systems in most western European countries.

Common law, as it exists in the United States, it is derived from Anglo Saxon common law. It is based on historical legal precedent. Common law is law that is not written by elected politicians but by judges.

When I use the term civil law, I refer to an area of US common law that deals with disputes (as opposed to criminal law), and most of the section about civil law deals with tort.

PART I

CRIMINAL LAW

"Make crime pay; become a lawyer."

—Cowboy, humorist, social commentator, radio personality, actor, and author Will Rogers (1879–1935), a Cherokee American Indian who claimed his ancestors did not arrive on the Mayflower—they met the boat

1.

Introduction

On May 6, 2010, I watched NBC's *Nightly News* with Brian Williams. Brian ended the broadcast with his usual human interest story, the nightly NBC make-you-feel-good story. A convicted child rapist by the name of Raymond Towler had been set free after twenty-nine years in jail—DNA evidence had proven him innocent. Brian told his viewers that released inmate 164608 loved pizza and that he was looking forward to sharing a pizza with his relatives and friends. "And come Tuesday, Towler is going to watch the play-offs of his beloved Cleveland Cavaliers as a spectator in the ball park rather than watching the game in front of a dilapidated prison TV," Brian reported

Brian Williams treated the story as if Towler had won a $250 million lottery. Not one word about the agony of an innocent man who had spent twenty-nine years in jail. Not one word about an obviously horrendous miscarriage of justice. Just a message of joy, a story about a happy man walking the streets of Cleveland, Ohio, who enjoyed pizza and was looking forward to watching the ball game.

Compare this to NBC's reporting on the deplorable Iranian human rights violation of three jailed American hikers who strayed from Iraq into Iran (one was recently released). Three innocent Americans in an Iranian jail—an outrage. Apparently no such outrage is warranted when an innocent American is set free from an American prison after having been incarcerated for twenty-nine of the best years of his life

* * * * *

5

The preamble to the Declaration of Independence uses soaring language to get to the essence of American democracy: "We hold these Truths to be self-evident, that all Men are created equal, that they are endowed by their Creator with certain unalienable Rights, that among these are Life, Liberty and the Pursuit of Happiness ..." Life is mentioned first, liberty second. Yet since 1973, more than a thousand people have been executed; of those, it is widely accepted in the legal community that eight were definitely innocent. How many others were innocent is the subject of speculation. Eight innocent human beings lost their lives because of a miscarriage of justice.

Cynics argue that humans are fallible and that, in a large country such as the United States, eight miscarriages of justice is a negligible number of judicial mistakes. However, between 1989 and July 2009 (the latest date for which I was able to find reliable statistics), a period of ten years, 133 people in 26 states, all on death row, have been declared innocent because DNA evidence or research by law school students or pro bono attorneys and professors proved them innocent. In nearly all of these cases, DNA proved conclusively that the crime was committed by someone else.

One woman and 132 men lost their liberty for a considerable length of time (some for more than 25 years) and daily faced the horrendous prospect of execution only to be found innocent. Additionally, 121 convicted Americans serving long prison sentences have been declared innocent, again mostly because of DNA evidence. All together since 1989, 254 convicted felons have left prison after having been declared innocent. And let's not forget that in many, if not most, death penalty or life cases, DNA evidence is not available.[6]

How is this possible, one might ask? How, in one of the oldest and most mature democracies on the face of the earth, in a country where life and liberty are unalienable rights and law and order are prized above all else, in a country where most people are law abiding and 40 percent of the population goes to church, is such a serious miscarriage of justice possible? There is no simple answer to this question.[7] Many causes conspire to bring about the abominable condition of the American criminal system.

---

6   This chapter should not be confused with a debate about the death penalty. It is about a dysfunctional criminal system that allows too many innocent people to be executed or incarcerated.

7   There are a number of books listed in the bibliography that describe the anomalies of the American judicial system. Most of these books confine

When a number of coal miners die in a mine accident, the media doesn't talk about anything else for days, and the outcry lasts for weeks. The House and the Senate hold hearings, and the president eulogizes the victims at their funeral. This is as it should be. But when innocent people end up on death row or are released after years and years in jail, hardly anybody pays attention.

Another aspect of the American criminal system flying under the radar of public opinion is not only what constitutes a criminal offense requiring incarceration, but the length of incarceration of criminal offenders. In this respect, and as is the case with other elements of the American legal system, America is unique. The United States not only incarcerates a larger percentage of its population than any other developed country, it incarcerates many people who, in other jurisdictions, would be guilty of a misdemeanor or would not have broken any law.[8] Furthermore, prison sentences are considerably longer than is the case in other criminal systems. That's why, according to the School of Law of King's College, the United States had, in 2009, 756 people per 100,000 in jail, whereas that number for the Netherlands was 128, for Canada 107, for Germany 95, for Sweden 82, and for Japan 62.

When it comes to crime, American politicians are at their populist worst. Democrat or Republican, when you run for office in America it is a must to demand ever longer prison sentences for ever more crimes. Entire campaigns are won or lost on the issue of crime. The Willy Horton issue dominated the airwaves and presses when Michael Dukakis ran for President against George Bush in 1988.[9] When politicians who have campaigned on the issue of crime are elected to office, they feel honor

---

themselves to civil law and do not deal with the American criminal law system.

8 According to the International Center for Prison Studies at the School of Law of King's College in London, in 2007 there were 2.29 million inmates in the United States and 9.8 million inmates worldwide. The United States held 23.4 percent of the world's inmates. The US total does not include inmates in juvenile detention facilities.

9 Willy Horton was sentenced to life in prison without the possibility of parole. When Michael Dukakis was governor of Massachusetts, he supported weekend furloughs for people serving prison sentences for capital crimes. Horton did not return from one such weekend furlough and committed armed robbery, assault, and rape. When Dukakis ran against George Bush for the presidency, Bush criticized Dukakis for the furlough privileges of inmates.

bound to act on their promises and introduce or vote for legislation that increases the length of prison sentences, and worse, makes it impossible for judges to use their discretion in sentencing.

Take for instance the three-strikes-and-you're-out laws. These laws require that anybody breaking the law a second time receives a double sentence and anybody breaking the law a third time receive a twenty-five year to life sentence.

The application of the three-strikes laws varies from state to state. Some states require all three felony convictions to be for violent crimes in order for the mandatory sentence to be pronounced, while others—most notably California—mandate the enhanced sentence for any third felony conviction so long as the first two felony convictions were deemed to be either violent or serious or both. Furthermore, enforcement of the provision differs from jurisdiction to jurisdiction. Los Angeles County District Attorney Steve Cooley, for instance, does not pursue third strike convictions against offenders whose felony is nonviolent or nonserious in nature.

In the harshest jurisdictions, however, scores of youngsters are languishing in American jails because they have been found twice with small amounts of drugs and are arrested a third time for a minor crime, such as shoplifting goods worth a couple of dollars. Such kids are put away in the most inhumane jails for twenty-five years or more because such sentences are mandated by law. The judge is not allowed any discretion in judging the circumstances or the severity of the crime(s).

Last but not least, a centuries-old principle of criminal law—a principle that is supposedly also a tenet of American criminal law—is that a person is an offender only if that person knows he or she has broken the law. With thousands and thousands of laws, many of them obscure administrative laws or regulatory laws, people in America frequently go to jail because they broke a law they did not have any idea existed.

And new obscure or ill-written laws about subjects some people have never heard of keep piling on. According to a study by the Heritage Foundation and the National Association of Criminal Defense Lawyers released on December 13, 2010, Congress created 450 new crimes between 2000 and 2007. On the federal level, the judiciary committees of Congress have the knowledge and experience to evaluate new crime laws. However in the 2005–2006 congressional year, only half the bills creating new criminal laws in nonviolent, non-drug related matters were reviewed by the judiciary committees. As a result, vague and esoteric laws get on the books that criminalize behavior even legal experts do not understand.

In many cases, high-profile targets of the Justice Department have been remanded to jail based on violations of such laws only to win on appeal. The honest services law is a good example. It is a twenty-eight word sentence added by congress to the federal mail fraud and wire fraud statute (18 USC, 1346) that states, "For the purposes of this chapter, the term, scheme or artifice to defraud includes a scheme or artifice to deprive another of *the intangible right of honest services*" [emphasis added]. No surprise that in 2010 the United States Supreme Court unanimously ruled that this law was vague and therefore unconstitutional.

Finally, when a miscarriage of justice has taken place and evidence has been uncovered proving a prisoner's innocence or casting doubts on a prisoner's guilt, prosecutors, the courts, or governors who, in many states, decide on issues of clemency or parole, routinely create every imaginable obstacle to a prisoner's release. In the next chapter, "The Election of Prosecutors," we will cite many examples of the difficulties innocent prisoners face in winning their release. Frequently years go by before proof of innocence is heard by a court resulting in the release of an innocent prisoner. In case after case, new evidence that, if known during trial, clearly would have changed a jury's verdict or information withheld by the prosecution that, if it had been disclosed during trial, would have resulted in a mistrial, is fought by the prosecution as if it is their mandate under the law to keep a convicted person in jail even when the facts prove the prisoner's innocence. It is as if a prosecutor's job is to maintain the infallibility of the prosecution's actions rather than to serve justice and see to it that innocent people are not incarcerated.

A clear example is the case of Bill Macumber. Convicted of a double homicide, he was sentenced to life without parole and has spent the past thirty-five years in an Arizona jail. For years, however, there has been serious doubt about his conviction, and Macumber has always maintained his innocence. Moreover, another man confessed to the murders several years before Macumber was even arrested—something the jury was not allowed to hear. Macumber would have been eligible for parole in 2000 if he'd agreed to confess his guilt, but he refused. Macumber is seventy-five and seriously ill.

ABC has reported that it has reviewed thousands of pages of documents, reports, and records and has spent months speaking with people close to the case. ABC calls the conviction one of the most doubtful in Arizona history.[10] Last year, the state's board of executive clemency, which rarely recommends the release of prisoners, unanimously recommended that Macumber be released. However, in the fall of 2010, Governor Jan Brewer, running for reelection as Arizona's Governor, denied Macumber's clemency in a one-line sentence without explaining her reason for the refusal. Governor Brewer refuses to answer journalists' questions about why she denied clemency. The unanimous verdict of the major national newspapers is that Macumber was denied clemency because a candidate running for governor cannot be seen as soft on crime. Consequently, Macumber remains in prison to make sure Governor Brewer makes the right impression on the electorate.

---

10 http://www.abcnews.go.com/nightline/billmacumber

2.

The Election of Prosecutors

In the American system of criminal justice, prosecutors play a major role. It is fair to say that they run the system. The most senior and the most important prosecutor is of course the attorney general. He or she is the head of the United States Department of Justice and is the chief law enforcement officer of the United States government. Furthermore, the attorney general is a member of the president's cabinet. The attorney general is not elected but appointed by the president after he or she has obtained advice and consent from the US Senate. Not so with the attorneys general of the various states or the local county or city prosecutors—nearly all are elected.

Consequently, on the federal level, the chief government prosecutor as well as the ninety-three US attorneys (federal prosecutors) in the ninety-three US districts are appointed; on the state and local level, they are usually elected.

The reason prosecutors at the local level are elected is historic. Before the framers of the constitution went to work, a legal framework (prosecutors, judges, a jury system) already existed in the thirteen states that had sent delegates to Philadelphia. As these states had all grown from small communities banding together into states, and these small communities decided everything in community meetings or through elected officials, the communities' prosecutors and later the state prosecutors were always elected.

Because there are few institutional checks on a prosecutor's powers, state attorneys general and local prosecutors are very powerful office holders. Although under virtually every state constitution the legislature has the authority to make laws—not the attorney general or the local prosecutor—when prosecutors convince a judge or jury to enforce a law that has not been written by the legislature and the prosecutor wins the case, under common law the court decision becomes the law.

Consequently, particularly at the state attorneys general level but even at the level of local prosecutors, there is a temptation to make law through victorious prosecutions that become the law of the land. Moreover, there is always the temptation to regulate commerce that extends to other states, to use litigation to impose interstate and national regulations, to impose new rules and regulations, or to impose penalties on out-of-state defenders who are outside the prosecutor's jurisdiction.

In our country, a political career or a career in law enforcement often begins in the prosecutor's office. Get yourself elected to the office of local prosecutor, county attorney, county prosecutor, or district attorney (all titles for the same office in different states), and if you are seen to be doing a good job, you may get yourself elected to other positions higher up the ladder—positions with greater responsibility and greater exposure to the general public, such as legislator in the state assembly or state senate, a top job in the state's executive branch, governor, or even member of the House of Representatives or the US Senate in Washington DC.

Consequently, a prosecutor starting a career in public office wants to be noticed. Getting convictions gets you noticed. In the time-tested populist tradition, getting criminals off the streets and into jail is noble and heroic because it serves the public good. This creates an unfortunate conflict of interest. Innocent people end up in jail or on death row when an unscrupulous prosecutor brings an indictment not to serve justice but to serve his or her career. Unfortunately, as the innocent people who have been executed or spent considerable time on death row shows, this happens all too often.

I am not suggesting that prosecutors knowingly send innocent people to jail. What I am saying is that criminal cases are rarely open and shut. Frequently there are many potential suspects who may have committed the crime, yet police and investigators often jump to a conclusion early on in a case. Even though the conclusion is based on a hunch and some initial and often flimsy evidence, they are convinced they know who is the culprit. The presumption catches on and influences the investigation to such an extent that investigators often only search for evidence that fits the suspect. Prosecutors allow themselves to be easily swayed and cut corners to get on with the case. After all, it is their job to get the accused convicted and put away.

Furthermore, prosecutors have tremendous discretion in choosing which cases to pursue. Taking on a case that produces headlines in the local papers can't hurt the prosecutor's career; hence the tendency to politicize the office.

Finally, when it comes to demanding sentences, prosecutors want to be seen as tough. A prosecutor's compassion can be interpreted as being soft on crime, which hurts election chances. In the previous chapter, I discussed the three-strikes laws that put so many of America's youth in jails for more than twenty-five years even though they have committed only nonviolent crimes. Prosecutors do not have to invoke the three-strikes-and-you're-out laws. They have complete discretion to ask for a sentence they believe fits the crime. Yet they routinely invoke the three-strikes-and-you're-out laws because their election or reelection chances would be hurt by not doing so.

To understand the role of prosecutors in the American legal system, let me quote Robert Jackson, who served as attorney general under President Franklin Roosevelt and later became a member of the Supreme Court of the United States:

"A prosecutor ... has more control over life, liberty and reputation than any other person in America. His discretion is tremendous ... While the prosecutor at his best is one of the most beneficent forces in society, when he acts from malice or other base motives he is one of the worst."

The Duke University Lacrosse Case

A couple of years ago a number of Duke University lacrosse players participated in a stag party featuring an African American stripper. The stripper accused some of the students of raping her. She selected three students in a lineup as the culprits.

Despite the fact that some of these students presented the prosecutor with proof through ATM and mobile phone records that they were elsewhere during the alleged rape, despite the fact that the prosecutor was aware of DNA evidence that irrefutably showed that the students were innocent, and despite the fact that the stripper was drunk that evening and was known to authorities to have severe psychiatric problems, the district attorney indicted the three students for rape. The students were kicked out of school and spent a total of $3.6 million in legal fees to prove their innocence.

When Mr. Nifong, a district attorney (prosecutor) in Durham, North Carolina, brought the indictment against the three students, he was running for reelection. The election was six weeks away, and the polls showed him running behind his major opponent. Durham, the district in question, is predominantly African American. Indicting three privileged, white students from an elite university for raping a black woman would go down well in the district. Indeed, six weeks after the indictment, Mr. Nifong won the election, although barely.

Unfortunately for Mr. Nifong, he had misjudged the accused. The parents of three privileged white students from one of America's premier universities, young men with illustrious careers ahead of them, do not go away quietly when their sons are indicted for rape. Even when these young men are found not guilty by a jury of their peers, escaping a conviction will always be seen as the result of a lack of evidence, not proof of innocence. Consequently, the young men's careers were doomed to be over even if they escaped conviction. The parents fought back and, as mentioned above, collectively spent $3.6 million in legal and other fees (private investigators, DNA labs, collecting mobile phone and ATM records, hiring PR firms, etc.). The North Carolina State attorney general, faced with the parents' findings and an unusual, nationwide public outcry, quashed the indictments and pronounced the students innocent without a trial.

The three Duke students were lucky they had rich parents. The vast majority of indicted criminals are indigent and depend on public defenders to prove their innocence.

Is Mr. Nifong's false indictment of the three students the exception? In his book *The Best Defense*, Professor Alan Dershowitz of Harvard Law School states that prosecutorial misconduct in America is routine.[11]

The media compounds the problem of prosecutors indicting people to advance their careers. I mentioned earlier that prosecuting criminals and removing them from society is viewed by the public as honorable, even heroic. Hence, the temptation of a prosecutor is to indict, particularly in high-profile cases like the Duke lacrosse case. The media suffers from the same temptation. Attention-grabbing headlines that invite the reader to learn about a particular outrage, such as a rape or drugs or murder, unfortunately sell newspapers. However, blowing up a story to make it

---

11   Alan M. Dershowitz. *The Best Defense.* New York: Vintage Books, 1983

sexy, as it is called, or tendentious, as I call it, obviously misleads the public and may lead to wrong convictions.

There used to be a time when many national television broadcasters and newspapers and a good number of responsible local stations and newspapers provided a healthy antidote to such irresponsible reporting. Newspapers like the *New York Times* (often referred to as "the newspaper of record," implying that the *Times* is a highly reliable publication and that its reporting is trustworthy) used to fact-check stories to such an extent that false information had a short story life.

Sadly, times have changed. Even the once stately *New York Times* with its motto "All the News That's Fit to Print" has lost its reputation for thoroughness and reliability. In the Duke lacrosse case, its reporting was reprehensible and shamefully wrong. In the book *Until Proven Innocent: Political Correctness and the Shameful Injustices of the Duke Lacrosse Rape Case,* authors Stuart Taylor Jr. and KC Johnson take the *New York Times* to task for its wrongful and tendentious editorial position.[12] The original reporting in the *Times* by reporter Joe Drape presented the case from both sides and was sympathetic to the students. Since Drape's reporting was in conflict with the position of the editors, Drape was replaced by Duff Wilson, who promoted the prosecution's position. In failing to check the facts, the *Times* became a megaphone not for promoting the truth but for promoting a criminally irresponsible prosecutor out to advance his career at the expense of three innocent students.

Irresponsible broadcasters or newspapers are a megaphone for magnifying falsehoods. In most European jurisdictions, such as Germany, Sweden, or the Netherlands, the media are not allowed to publish the name of the accused until he or she has been convicted. In the States, this is not the case, and the names of accused persons are bandied about without any restrictions. The result is that many innocent people accused of crimes are judged guilty of that crime before having been convicted.

The Debra Sue Carter Case

In 1982 a young cocktail waitress by the name of Debra Sue Carter was murdered in the small town of Ada, Oklahoma. For quite some time, the investigation did not produce a murderer. The police and District Attorney

---

12   Stuart Taylor Jr. and KC Johnson. *Until Proven Innocent: Political Correctness and the Shameful Injustices of the Duke Lacrosse Rape Case.* New York: Thomas Dunne Books, September 2007.

Bill Peterson were under great pressure to find the culprit. On the basis of the flimsiest evidence, they finally settled on Ron Williamson.

Ron Williamson was charged, tried, and sentenced to death and ended up on death row. His trial and numerous appeals were full of lying witnesses, tainted evidence, and unreliable jail house snitches.[13] The district attorney withheld exculpating evidence; the court-appointed attorney(s) were derelict in their duties to mount a decent defense; the elected judge presided over what can only be called a kangaroo court; and the local, small-town jury that produced the guilty verdict was prejudiced in the extreme. On August 30, 1994, twelve years after Debra Carter's murder, the date for Ron Williamson's execution was set.

Then followed the habeas corpus appeal. The petition was submitted in September 1994, a few days before Ron's execution. Ron Williamson was lucky. Janet Chesley, an attorney with the Indigent Defense System in Norman, Oklahoma, who wrote the petition, was an extremely competent lawyer. The petition landed on the desk of Jim Payne, a US magistrate in the federal court office who, because of the inadequacy of Ron's defense, Ron's mental competency, and the unreliability of the evidence presented at trial, immediately developed doubts about the fairness of Ron's trial. Jim Payne met with Federal Judge Frank Seay and recommended a stay of execution. Within five days of being taken to the gallows, Ron Williamson's execution was stayed.

On September 19, 1995, one year after the execution had been stayed, Judge Seay issued a writ of habeas corpus and granted a new trial. At the end of his opinion, Judge Seay added a most unusual paragraph: "When considering my decision in this case, I told a friend, a layman, I believed the facts and the law dictated that I must grant a new trial to a man who had been convicted and sentenced to death. My friend asked, 'Is he a murderer?' I replied simply, 'We won't know until he receives a fair trial.' God help us, if ever in this great country we turn our heads while people who have not had a fair trial are executed. That almost happened in this case."

On April 15, 1996, fourteen years after the murder took place, Ron Williamson went again to trial for the murder of Debra Sue Carter. After presenting newly developed DNA evidence that clearly showed that a certain Glen Gore was the murderer rather than Ron Williamson, the state joined in a motion to dismiss and Ron Williamson walked out of the courtroom a free man. Shortly thereafter Dennis Fritz, a friend of Ron

---

13 A jailhouse snitch is a prison inmate who has become an informer on his cell mates or fellow prisoners.

Williamson who, as an alleged accomplice of Ron, had been sentenced to life, also walked out of jail a free man. Ron had spent twelve years on death row, Dennis twelve years in jail.[14]

Are Mr. Pederson's indictment of Ron Williamson, his bogus trial, and his years on death row the exception? If it is, how did 133 (and who knows how many more) innocent people end up on death row, and how did at least eight innocent people get executed? If it is the exception, how were 244 jailed convicts, some jailed for very long periods of time, exonerated and set free because of DNA testing that proved them innocent? Moreover, if it is the exception, how come hardly a week goes by these days without it being reported that another falsely accused or convicted prisoner is released from jail?

A further question should be asked: Why, if prosecutorial misconduct is widespread, do judges and defense attorneys not put a stop to the resultant miscarriages of justice? The answer is that, as is the case with prosecutors, most state judges are elected. As we will see later, local prosecutors and the local trial bar have enormous influence over these elections. Without their support, it is nearly impossible for a judge to get elected. The result is that judges are beholden to the bar and rarely if ever overrule attorneys. They simply chair the proceedings, provide the maximum amount of leeway to prosecutor and defense attorney, and make sure the participants do not get too far out of line.

Furthermore, in most states, indigent indicted criminals are defended by a full-time public defender who is an experienced criminal defense attorney. However, in the many counties that do not have a public defender, indicted criminals receive court-appointed defense attorneys. Such court-appointed attorneys often have little or no criminal law experience. They frequently have no experience with mistaken eyewitness identification, a common cause of wrongful convictions. They are not familiar with investigations of police misconduct, also a frequent cause of wrongful

---

14 The journey of Ron Williamson through the thicket and morass of the Oklahoma criminal law system was chronicled by the famous author John Grisham in his *New York Times* best-selling book *The Innocent Man* (New York: Doubleday, 2006). Grisham chronicles the entire police investigation and analyzes every court document and every court proceeding. He examines the exceedingly inadequate defense job by the court-appointed defense attorneys and describes the trial and appeals proceedings document by document and minute by minute.

convictions. The fee a court-appointed attorney is paid is usually below the normal hourly attorney rate, and there is no money for expert witnesses or expenses for things like disproving false confessions or unmasking testimony from snitches. Many of these attorneys simply cannot afford to mount a decent defense, and the ones that seek such court-appointed criminal defense work are often at the bottom of the barrel when it comes to the quality of their legal work. Judges usually know full well when defense counsel has provided an inadequate defense. They nevertheless do not instruct the jury accordingly for fear of facing a mistrial or being overturned on appeal.

Finally, criminal sentences in the United States are far more severe than in other developed countries. Surveys show that the average length of sentences in the United States is more than twice as long as sentences in countries like the Netherlands, France, Germany, and Denmark.[15] Moreover, of all the developed nations, only in the United States can a minor receive a life sentence. Also, parole is much less automatic in the United States when compared to parole practices in Western Europe.

Jabbar Collins

On June 9, 2010, prison inmate 95A2646, Jabbar Collins, walked out of Green Haven Prison in Duchess County, New York. Convicted in 1995 for the murder of Brooklyn Rabbi Abraham Pollack, Collins had spent fifteen years of a thirty-three-years-to-life sentence in prison for a murder he did not commit. During his trial, Collins strenuously proclaimed his innocence but was convicted on the basis of the testimony of three witnesses who claimed they had seen Collins at the scene of the murder or were aware Collins had been planning the act.

As Collins began his sentence he vowed that, since it was the lawyers who had put him away, he would have to regain his freedom by becoming a lawyer himself. Collins never became a lawyer. However, every free minute in prison he spent in the prison law library trying to educate himself about the law. A voluminous book entitled *Case Analysis and Fundamentals of Legal Writing* became his intellectual mentor, and texts like *Federal Rules of Criminal Procedure, McKinney's Consolidated Laws of New York,* and *The Legal Research Manual* were his daily reference sources. At the same time,

---

15   The Eighth United Nations Survey on Crime Trends and the Operations of Criminal Justice Systems (2001–2002)

he conducted an intensive and relentless investigation into how it came to pass that he, an innocent man, had been convicted of murdering a rabbi.

Collins hounded state agencies by filing hundreds of requests for information. Many requests remained unanswered, and many were answered months after the request for information had been filed. When a request for information was refused, as was often the case, Collins filed a request for information under the Freedom of Information Act.[16]

During the fifteen years Collins spent collecting data, he learned that the three major witnesses at his trial had not only been coached about what to testify but had been told that failure to say what the prosecutor wanted them to say would lead to serious consequences. Collins learned that the reason he was in jail was prosecutorial misconduct on the part of Michael F. Vecchione, the prosecutor in his case.

Collins elicited information from the three witnesses showing that Vecchione had forced them to testify against Collins by threatening them with prosecution for other minor crimes in which the witnesses had been involved. Collins's records furthermore showed that Vecchione had threatened them with physical violence and had knowingly used false and inaccurate testimony. One of the witnesses claimed that Vecchione had threatened to hit him over the head with a table and put him in jail if he didn't agree to testify against Collins. Collins also found a retired detective who had worked for the prosecutor's office during Collins's case who claimed that one of the witnesses who had testified during trial that he had overheard Collins planning the crime had recanted his story and that Vecchione had not shared this information with the defense attorneys.

In 2005 Collins felt he needed more information and didn't know how or where to find it. That's when he made an attempt to trick Adrian Diaz, who had testified during trial that he had seen Collins with a gun in his waistband after the murder, into talking to him.

"I became Kevin Beekman, a district attorney investigator, for about twenty-five minutes," Mr. Collins told Sean Gardiner, a journalist with the *Wall Street Journal*.[17] The fictitious Mr. Beekman told Diaz that he needed to re-create documents lost in the 9/11 World Trade Center attack. When Diaz agreed to talk about his testimony, Collins routed the call through a phone in his mother's home so it could be recorded. During the phone

---

16　The Freedom of Information Act is a federal law that allows for the full or partial disclosure of previously unreleased information and documents in the government's possession.

17　*Wall Street Journal*, December 24, 2010

conversation, Diaz told Collins that before the trial he had gone to Puerto Rico in violation of his probation for marijuana possession. He had agreed to return and testify against Collins only after prosecutors promised they would make sure his probation wasn't revoked. Prosecutor Vecchione never shared this information with Collins's defense counsel, who could have used the information to undermine the witness by showing he was given an incentive to testify.

Collins learned from another witness by the name of Edwin Oliva that Oliva's records contained a Legal Aid document that referred to a deal being discussed between the judge, the prosecutor, and Oliva's attorney whereby Oliva was allowed to plead to a lesser felony than he had been indicted for in lieu of a sentence of up to three years. The other charge could have kept him in prison longer. Again, none of this information was shared with defense counsel before or during Collins's trial.

In late 2005, Collins contacted Joel Rudin, a civil-rights attorney, who agreed to take on Collins's case, and in March of 2006, Rudin petitioned state Justice Robert Holdman to overturn Mr. Collins's murder conviction on the grounds of exculpatory information prosecutor Vecchione should have shared with the defense counsel. However, Vecchione swore that allegations he had coerced witnesses or failed to turn over potentially exculpatory information were, without exception, untrue.

New York State Justice Holdman dismissed the appeal, declaring the appeal to be "wholly without merit, conclusory, incredible, unsubstantiated, and [because of Collins's impersonation of Kevin Beekman], in significant part, to be predicated on a foundation of fraud." Not only did Judge Holdman deny the request, he barred Collins from filing future requests for information.

Here we have a petition for a rehearing substantiated with a considerable amount of information indicating possible prosecutorial misconduct on the part of Vecchione. Yet a New York State judge turned down the petition because Collins impersonated someone to get at the truth and regain his freedom. Instead of granting at least a hearing into whether Vecchione coerced witnesses (which would be a felony), the judge turned down the request because, while trying to prove his innocence, the petitioner impersonated someone. Justice Holdman's decision shows how some judges protect their prosecutor colleagues at the expense of a potentially innocent person languishing in jail.

Collins appealed Justice Holdman's decision and lost. One last and final legal avenue open to Collins was an appeal in federal court. If he lost there, he would likely spend the rest of his life in jail. With the help of his attorney Collins filed a motion in federal court in Brooklyn seeking to overturn the conviction based on the prosecutor's "knowing presentation, at trial, of false or misleading testimony" and withholding of evidence that might have been used to discredit the main witnesses.

After two more years of legal arguments, federal Judge Dora Irizarry approved Collins's attorney's request for additional material. Information Collins had spent more than ten years trying to gather was now being corroborated by witnesses admitting everything Collins had learned.

At this point, attorneys in the prosecutor's office realized they were facing a problem. Witnesses testifying under oath about what Collins had learned would make it obvious that there had been a colossal miscarriage of justice. Worse, Vecchione might face felony charges. Attempting to solve their problems, they offered to reduce the charge against Collins to manslaughter, allowing his immediate release. Collins, persisting in his innocence, rejected the offer.

Having failed to stop the proceedings in federal court, Collins's prosecutors informed Judge Irizarry that they wouldn't fight Collins's effort to overturn his conviction—instead they now planned to retry him. A retrial would of course get Collins's case out of federal court and move it back to state court, where a sympathetic judge might give them a chance to save their reputation.

Rudin, Collins's attorney, understood that going back to state court would doom Collin's case. He consequently petitioned federal Judge Irizarry to hold a hearing on whether the district attorney should be barred from retrying Collins because the prosecutor's misconduct had been so pervasive.

Judge Irizarry granted the hearing and, as expected, the witnesses whose testimony had led to Collins's conviction recanted their testimony and pointed to Vecchione's threats, his coercion, and his attempts to solicit testimony he knew was false. Judge Irizarry was incredulous and scathing in her condemnation of the prosecution. After the prosecutor's office announced it would not retry Collins, thereby avoiding further damage to the prosecution's case, Judge Irizarry stated that she regretted that her mandate made it impossible for her to pursue charges of prosecutorial misconduct against Vecchione.

Vecchione is today a high-ranking official in charge of the rackets division in the office of Brooklyn District Attorney (prosecutor) Charles Hynes. To illustrate how attorneys protect each other and completely ignore charges of misconduct against other attorneys, in 2007 Michael Vecchione was selected by *Super Lawyers* magazine as a New York super lawyer. *Super Lawyers* magazine names attorneys in each state who receive the highest point totals as chosen by their peers and through independent research. The magazine is published in all fifty states and reaches more than 13 million readers.

Vecchione's conduct with regard to the witnesses in Collins's trial was widely reported in the national press and by the national cable news networks. Nevertheless, Michael Vecchione was never investigated and was never censured.[18] Despite federal judge Irizarry's findings and accusations, the disciplinary arm of the New York Bar Association never looked into the charges against Michael Vecchione. Instead, in 2007, the Bar Association awarded him the Thomas E. Dewey Medal, an award that is presented each year to an outstanding prosecutor in each county in recognition of their excellent work as prosecutors and their contributions to public service.

Mr. Vecchione will finish his career in the DA office and retire with a generous pension. Jabbar Collins, on the other hand, will reach retirement age with a piddling social security pension—piddling because of his inability to pay into the social security trust fund during the fifteen years he was in jail.

The case of Jabbar Collins illustrates not only how serious prosecutorial misconduct can be but the extremes to which prosecutors will go to make sure their convictions are never overturned. Although it may well mean that people who are innocent will remain incarcerated, prosecutors will fight reopening cases even when it becomes abundantly clear that, had the jury known about the new evidence that surfaced after trial, there would have been reasonable doubt in the jury's mind about the defendant's guilt.

Moreover, as I will explain in the chapter about the election of state judges, state judges are too often in the pocket of the prosecution. If it hadn't been for federal judge Irizarry, who, because she serves for life, is independent and therefore dares to stand up to powerful prosecutors, Collins would today still be in jail.

---

18 I should mention that, although the New York bar may have looked into the charges against Vecchione, there is no public record of any investigation. Bar associations strenuously protect their members by sealing investigations against their members. Even in the few states where proceedings against lawyers are public, opinions are rarely available in a searchable format.

The Innocence Project

A wonderful development in the last two decades is the creation of numerous innocence projects, projects dedicated to the utilization of DNA evidence to prove the innocence of individuals who have been wrongly convicted. In 1992 Barry Scheck, who became well known as one of O. J. Simpson's defense lawyers, and Peter Neufeld became the founders of the first Innocence Project at the Benjamin N. Cardozo School of Law, which has been the trailblazer for numerous such innocence projects at other law schools around the country. Hundreds of innocent convicts have walked out of prison because of dedicated innocence projects, mostly staffed by volunteering law students who have taken the time to prove that American justice only too frequently convicts the wrong individual.

Abuse by State Attorneys General

In the late 1980s a rich, brilliant, and ambitious young student graduated from Harvard Law School in the top of his class. He went on to clerk for a short while and then joined one of the most prestigious law firms in New York City. After less than two years at the firm, he joined the Manhattan district attorney's office, the indispensable first step for those aspiring to higher office. He became chief of the labor racketeering unit and spent his time pursuing organized crime. In 1992 he made a name for himself when he led the investigation that ended the Gambino mafia family's control of the Manhattan trucking and garment industries. In 1994 he spent more than $1 million of his family's money to run for the office of New York State attorney general. He lost but won on his second try in 1998.

As attorney general of the State of New York, Eliot Spitzer became one of the most self-righteous prosecutors in America. He wanted to be known as the prosecutor who cleaned up Wall Street not by the rules of legal procedure (i.e., fairness and due process) but by his own rules. His modus operandi was to take aim at public companies and officials, leak allegations to the press, cause the stock price of the companies to fall, threaten a corporate indictment that by itself might lead to bankruptcy, and then negotiate a quick out-of-court settlement. In this manner Spitzer was going to get the big guys, the rich people, and the captains of Wall Street. As I said before, Mr. Spitzer did not indict people—he usually threatened his victims with criminal prosecution unless they settled out of court for huge sums of money.

As an example, in 2005 Mr. Spitzer went on national television to suggest that American International Group (AIG) CEO Mr. Greenberg, one of the most respected titans of the insurance industry, had engaged in criminal activity. Mr. Greenberg had to resign. Six months later, Mr. Spitzer quietly disclosed that he lacked the evidence to file criminal charges.

He did the same thing to Ken Langone, a director of the New York Stock Exchange and a cofounder of hardware behemoth Home Depot. When Langone wouldn't keel over, Spitzer had no choice but to file suit. In early 2008 the charges were found to be without merit by a New York appeals court by a three-to-one vote.

Spitzer went after Dick Grasso, president of the New York Stock Exchange, for an allegedly exorbitant compensation package. Although Grasso's remuneration was indeed disgustingly high, his remuneration had been set by others. In the eyes of the public, however, assailing somebody who earns in one hour what most people earn in a year made Spitzer look like Robin Hood robbing from the rich to benefit the poor.

Former Goldman Sachs chairman John Whitehead, after writing a letter to the editor of the *Wall Street Journal* critical of Spitzer, quoted Spitzer in a subsequent phone conversation as follows: "Mr. Whitehead, it's now a war between us, and you have fired the first shot. I will be coming after you. You will pay the price. This is only the beginning, and you will pay dearly for what you have done. You will wish that you had never written that letter."[19]

Spitzer literally trampled on people but rarely tried a case. When he did, he rarely won. The populist press loved it and branded him as a titan of justice. They prophesied that Mr. Spitzer would not only be the future Governor of New York but most assuredly would become a candidate for the presidency of the United States.

The office of attorney general of the State of New York has few, if any, checks and balances. The occupant of the office is elected, and as long as the person occupying the office is reelected, he or she is beyond reproach. If Eliot Spitzer, in the full light of and spurred on by the national media, can get away with ignoring due process and procedure, what must a local prosecutor think when he or she wants to cut corners and pursue a result-oriented legal strategy rather that one that safeguards fairness and equity?

Following the popular script, in 2006 Mr. Spitzer ran for the office of governor of the State of New York and won in a landslide, with more than

---

19 *Wall Street Journal*, April 22, 2005

60 percent of the vote! His ethics, however, finally caught up with him. When Spitzer was attorney general, he broke up a call-girl ring and sent eighteen people to jail on corruption, money laundering, and prostitution charges. In 2008 Spitzer had to resign as governor because it leaked out that he had spent approximately $80,000 with a high-priced prostitution service over an extended period of time.

The Elliot Spitzer story is certainly not unique. Like Elliot Spitzer, Richard Blumenthal grew up in a well-to-do family, and like Elliot Spitzer, he was a gifted and devoted student. He graduated from Harvard magna cum laude and was a member of Phi Beta Kappa. As an undergraduate at Harvard, he was editorial chairman of the *Harvard Crimson*. Blumenthal also earned a Fiske Fellowship for a year of study at Cambridge before he attended Yale Law School, where he received his law degree and was the editor-in-chief of the *Yale Law Journal*.

After a brief career as a newspaper reporter for the *Washington Post*, Blumenthal served as an administrative assistant to United States Senator Abraham A. Ribicoff, as an aide to Daniel P. Moynihan when Moynihan was assistant to President Richard Nixon, and as a law clerk to Supreme Court Justice Harry A. Blackmun. At the unusually young age of thirty-one, he became United States Attorney for the District of Connecticut, serving from 1977 to 1981. As the chief federal prosecutor of that district, he successfully prosecuted many high-profile cases involving drug traffickers, organized crime, white-collar criminals, civil rights violators, consumer fraud, and environmental pollution. From 1981 to 1986, he was a volunteer counsel for the NAACP Legal Defense Fund. In 1984, when he was thirty-eight, Blumenthal was elected to the Connecticut House of Representatives.

Like Spitzer, Blumenthal developed a stellar résumé that was carefully massaged to position him for higher office. In 1990, all according to script, Blumenthal won his race for the office of attorney general of the State of Connecticut, the first step on the ladder to a governorship, the US Senate, or possibly the highest office in the land.

And again like Spitzer in his quest for higher office, Blumenthal milked his attorney general position for maximum exposure by going after big business, by issuing scores of well-publicized subpoenas in cases that never went to trial, and by selecting politically advantageous prosecutions of high-profile people or companies followed by press conferences featuring Mr. Blumenthal as the angry accuser.

One of the most often repeated platitudes in talking about legal matters is that a person is innocent until proven guilty. This common adage is so strong that TV anchors go to extreme lengths to be politically correct by, for instance, stating that the Christmas Eve bomber who had a bomb in his underpants, pictures of which were shown all around the world, was "alleged" to have attempted to blow up an airplane. Faisal Shahzad, who admitted trying to detonate a car bomb in Times Square, is "alleged'" to have committed a terrorist act.

Maintaining the idea that the accused is innocent until proven guilty, however, doesn't apply to the office of attorney general. Whenever Mr. Blumenthal held a press conference announcing a case, he would smear the accused with alleged facts of the case as if the accused had already been tried and convicted. He did not do so in only some cases; it was his habit to do so in every case he announced. And why not? As I mentioned above when chronicling Elliot Spitzer's career, the attorney general is above the law. Only the voters can touch an attorney general, and when the voters are bombarded by images of press conferences with the attorney general standing up for the rights of the people of Connecticut and the press on the whole goes along with such shenanigans, the people do not know that the attorney general's pronouncements are often nothing more than self-serving allegations.

For example, in 2003 Blumenthal alleged in a press conference that Gina Kolb and her computer supply company had failed to install the proper network interface cards in computers the company sold to the state under a $17.2 million contract. During the press conference, Mr. Blumenthal accused Ms. Kolb and her Computers Plus Center Inc. "of shortchanging and overcharging the state."

The State of Connecticut arrested Mrs. Kolb, claiming seven first-degree larceny charges punishable with up to twenty years in jail.

Mrs. Kolb countersued the State of Connecticut for the false accusations against her company and for having ruined her company. In 2008 Ms Kolb won her case and was awarded $18 million in damages.[20]

In an eminent domain case involving the state taking a working quarry to expand a highway in the town of Brookfield, the owners, who had been paid $4 million, sued the state, claiming incompetent appraisers had cheated them out of reasonable compensation. Blumenthal brought in new appraisers during the suit; they also appraised the property at a low value. Judge Barbara Sheedy finally concluded that the state (Mr. Blumenthal),

---

20 Blumenthal is appealing the verdict.

having picked unqualified appraisers, had been unprofessional and less than scrupulous in the handling of the case.

In 2007 the Competitive Enterprise Institute rated attorney generals in the United States and rated Richard Blumenthal the worst in the nation (Elliot Spitzer came in third from the bottom). Blumenthal was the worst because he failed in every category:

1. using his office to promote personal gain or enrich cronies or relatives,
2. fabricating the law by asking courts to rewrite statutes or stretch constitutional norms,
3. bringing lawsuits that usurp regulatory powers granted to the federal government or other state entities, and
4. seeking to regulate conduct occurring wholly in other states.

Since 1990, Blumenthal has always won reelection as attorney general. However, as could have been expected, in May of 2010 he threw his hat in the ring for higher office when he announced he would run for the senate seat soon to be vacated by Senator Chris Dodd. Blumenthal won the election.

Child Abuse

In 1980 a book was published that had an insidious influence on a spate of criminal cases involving alleged child abuse. The book *Michelle Remembers*, written by Dr. Lawrence Pazder, a Canadian psychiatrist, and his wife Michelle Smith, is a story about Michelle's alleged memories of satanic ritual abuse in the early 1950s, when she was five years old. The alleged abuse occurred at the hands of Michelle's mother and her friends who, supposedly, were members of a satanic cult in Victoria, British Columbia. Smith claims she never remembered the abuse until later in life, when she suddenly recalled being tortured and sexually abused and having to attend rituals in which the blood of murdered babies was used. Pazder claims that Michelle was abused by the Church of Satan, a religious organization predating Christianity.

Initially the book was a best seller. Then, in the late eighties, journalists uncovered numerous inconsistencies, and a large number of witnesses came forward testifying that Michelle's mother was a very sweet person incapable of having performed satanic acts over long periods of time. The events described by Michelle became known as "the hysterical ravings of an uncontrolled imagination." By the early nineties, various authors and specialists in psychiatry came forward debunking the authenticity of the events described in the book.

However, by that time, the book had eaten into the consciousness of parents and especially mothers with young children who believed Michelle's story. More and more people came forward arguing that underground satanic cults were operating all around the United States, primarily in preschools and daycare centers. Feminists and religious conservatives and even law enforcement officials were warning the population to be on guard and to arm themselves against satanic perverts.

As the twenty-eight cases cited below and in appendix I will show, it wasn't long before a number of prosecutors grabbed on to the hysteria and vowed to find these satanic perverts and prosecute them. After all, how honorable can you get? Catching pedophiles and child abusers and throwing them in jail—who could ever find fault with that? Moreover, however flimsy the evidence, however lacking proof, as the cases cited below and in the appendix will show, a prosecutor's remarks in closing arguments before a jury that it is the jury's duty to protect the hapless mothers and defenseless children and get the accused off the street is often all that is needed to get a guilty verdict. Prosecutors salivated at the prospect of getting their hands on such a case. A conviction would not only make them famous in their communities or states, but more importantly, the fame would identify the prosecutor as a decent and honorable public servant, serving society in the most noble way by protecting innocent children from sexual predators.

Consequently guilt became secondary. All that was needed was a parent who claimed his or her child had been abused, and the accused was off to jail. No bail—you can't have people who prey on children walking the streets. The number of people prosecuted for child abuse in the late 1980s and early 1990s who served long jail sentences (often twenty years or more) before they were pronounced innocent makes you wonder whether there were any checks and balances in the system.

Moreover, one simple press conference by a prosecutor detailing the alleged crime, and the life of the accused and the life of his or her family was destroyed. For not only is child molestation viewed as heinous, in prison the child molester is subjected to the worst forms of persecution. The usually male child abuser in prison is in constant fear for his life. In American jails, inmates convicted of robbery wear their convictions as a badge of honor, but a child molester deserves to be tortured; he doesn't belong in the prison population (see the West Side Early Childhood Development Center case below).

A number of legal commentators have argued that there was no relationship between the book *Michelle Remembers* and the child abuse cases of the eighties and nineties. To prove a causal relationship is indeed difficult. However, how else can we explain the terrible spike in such cases during the period immediately after the publication of *Michelle Remembers*?

In all twenty-eight cases detailed below and in the appendix, the accused ended up in jail. Each case involved not just one but two, three, ten, and sometimes many more indicted people. In every one of these cases, the accused were later found innocent. More than one hundred innocent people went to jail, scores of American families were destroyed, an untold number of children grew up without fathers or mothers or became foster children because, in each case, an overzealous prosecutor caused a miscarriage of justice.

Even if there is no relationship between Lawrence Pazder's book and the abuse cases in question, the child abuse convictions of the eighties and nineties detailed below and in the appendix, all ultimately reversed on appeal, stand as a monument to prosecutorial overzealousness and misconduct.

Fells Acre Day Care Center of Malden, Massachusetts

The Fells Acre Day Care Center in Malden, Massachusetts, was the best preschool in the area. Fells Acre had a long waiting list for student admission.

Violet Amirault had raised two children, Gerald and Cheryl, in part on welfare, but Violet had steadfastly educated herself. Fells Acre, which Violet had founded and where Gerald and Cheryl were teachers, brought the family esteem and middle-class status.

In 1984 some parents complained about sexual abuse at the school. Prosecutors put together a case against the Amiraults most law enforcement professionals today describe as a sheer incomprehensible travesty of justice.[21]

---

21 In the late nineties, Judge Borenstein, granting a new trial, held that the children's interrogation was so tainted by grave errors in the investigation process that it could not be used in any new trial. He stated that "These grave errors led to the testimony of the children being forever tainted. The only allegations made by the child witnesses occurred after they were subjected

One four-year-old boy had allegedly been abused by having a big butcher knife put up his rectum, yet miraculously doctors examining the child found no physical evidence, no mark or injury. The list of horrors the accused had allegedly perpetrated was so preposterous as to defy credulity.

The case was based exclusively on the children's testimony. But the children had been cajoled for hours and hours to say what the prosecutors wanted them to say. The coaching of the children had been suggestive and coercive to the point that the children described scenes no child would ever know how to describe without having been coached in the most minute detail as to what to say.

However, the prosecutors had a lethal weapon: the jury. Gerald received a sentence of thirty to forty years, Violet and Cheryl eight to twenty years. Gerald's devoted wife, Patricia, and the couple's three children spent the rest of the 1980s and the 1990s speaking to their husband and father in jail every evening.

1995 produced a glimmer of hope—a new trial was ordered for Violet and Cheryl. Unfortunately the case was to be heard by one of Massachusetts's toughest judges, Judge Robert Barton, a judge known for very long sentences. When Judge Barton became familiar with the facts of the case, he immediately ordered the release of the two women and publicly expressed his contempt for the prosecutors. Superior Court Judge Isaac Borenstein presided over a widely publicized hearing into the case and found that all the children's testimony was tainted. He said that "Every trick in the book had been used to get the children to say what the investigators wanted."[22] The *Massachusetts Lawyers Weekly,* which in its twenty-seven-year history had never taken an editorial position on a case, published a scathing column directed at the prosecutors, "who seemed

---

to the admittedly suggestive interviews and investigative techniques, as well as inappropriate—even if understandable—influence by their families. Moreover, neither behavioral symptoms nor physical evidence which may be consistent with child sexual abuse were revealed until after the children and their families were subjected to these improper interviewing and investigative techniques. *These alleged symptoms were only discussed after the families were overwhelmed by the panic, hysteria and media attention that snowballed this case into national headlines and widespread concern about ritualistic sexual abuse of children.*"

22 *Wall Street Journal.* Rabinowitz, Dorothy *"Martha Coakley's Convictions."* January 14, 2010.

unwilling to admit they might have sent innocent people to jail for crimes that had never occurred." [23]

One would reasonably expect that, at this point in the proceedings against the Amiraults, the prosecutors would give up. Unfortunately, a prosecutor's career depends on victories, not losses, which means that a prosecutor never gives up. The prosecution fought its way up to the Massachusetts Supreme Judicial Court and won a reversal of the women's release.

It is interesting to note that Middlesex County in Massachusetts, where the Amirault case came to trial, is one of the three counties where the Salem trials were conducted in 1692 and 1693. The Salem trials, in which more than 150 citizens were accused of witchcraft, produced 29 convictions. Nineteen (fourteen women and five men) were hanged. The Salem trials have become famous for their religious extremism, false accusations, lack of proof, and absence of due process.

In 1999 in Middlesex County, where the Amiraults' preschool was located and the case against the family was tried, got a new prosecutor. That prosecutor, Ms. Martha Coakley, became well known in January of 2010 when she ran for Teddy Kennedy's old Senate seat and lost. Her defeat meant that the Democrats lost their sixty-seat majority in the senate

When Ms. Coakley became the prosecutor in Middlesex County, she inherited the Amirault case. Again, giving up and letting the Amiraults live the rest of their lives in relative peace was not in the cards. Public opinion by that time having turned strongly in favor of the Amiraults, however, and a penniless Violet having died of cancer at age seventy before she could be hauled back to prison, Ms. Coakley proposed to change Cheryl's sentence to time served. There was, however, a message to the family's attorney: the attorney had to promise he would refrain from representing Cheryl's brother Gerald and take no further legal action on his behalf. In layman's terms, this would be called blackmail. James Sultan, the attorney for the Amiraults, refused.

In 2000 the Massachusetts Board of Pardons and Paroles heard the case of a commutation of Gerald's sentence. After a nine months investigating, the board voted 5–0 to commute the sentence. The board pointed to the lack of evidence in the case and the bizarre allegations on which the Amiraults had been convicted.

---

23 *Massachusetts Lawyers Weekly.* Commonwealth v. Amirault, 399 Mass. 617, 626 (1987)

Any reasonable person would expect the board's decision to finally be the end of the case. However, prosecutors frequently do not answer to reason; they answer to the calls of their careers. For Ms. Coakley, as we now know, that meant the call of becoming a member of the United States Senate. Ms. Coakley started a campaign to convince the governor of Massachusetts to overrule the parole board's decision. Six months after the parole board granted parole to Gerald Amirault, the governor overturned the board's decision. Gerald had to spend two more years in prison before finally being paroled in 2004.

There is a cynical postscript to this story. Ms. Coakley, when running for the United States Senate in 2010 for the seat of the late Senator Ted Kennedy against Republican Scott Brown, who most unexpectedly pulled off a win, argued for the protection of the rights of prisoners in Guantanamo. "The presumption of their innocence should be respected," she argued!

West Side Early Childhood Development Center, Pittsfield, Massachusetts

In 1983 the West Side Early Childhood Development Center (ECDC) hired a nineteen-year-old by the name of Bernard Baran as a teacher's aide. In 1983 many homosexuals had not yet come out of the closet; homosexuality was still seen as a disease, and homosexuals were commonly regarded as dangerous for young children. Bernard Baran happened to be a homosexual.

An uncle of one of the students at the center, who knew Bernard was a homosexual, complained to the school, arguing that homosexuals should not be teaching his nephew. Shortly thereafter, the mother of the child (the uncle's sister) filed a complaint claiming Bernard had molested her son.

In 1984, in the midst of the hysteria about satanic perverts in preschool and daycare centers, Bernard was charged with sexually assaulting a couple of three- and four-year-old children. In 1985, Bernard was sentenced to three concurrent life terms. Bernard, who was slightly built, was easy prey for robbers and murderers who respect each other's crimes but have no tolerance for child abuse. During Bernard's first four years in jail, he was raped and physically assaulted between thirty and forty times, resulting in serious eye injuries and many broken bones.

Bernard's conviction was based on two pieces of evidence. One boy claiming abuse was tested positive for gonorrhea of the throat. Bernard was tested but had never suffered from gonorrhea and had never been treated for the disease. Furthermore, the boy had been a foster child, and his foster mother had previously filed a complaint with the Massachusetts Department of Social Services (DSS) that her boyfriend had molested the child. The DSS substantiated the claim but failed to inform the prosecutor until after Bernard had been convicted. To add insult to injury, the boy's step-father was later alleged to have gonorrhea but was never tested. And in 1988 the Center for Disease Control published a study stating that in more than one third of laboratory samples of children testing positive for gonorrhea, the actual organism turned out to be something else and was harmless.

The second piece of evidence concerned a little girl who claimed she had been sexually abused. The girl's medical examination showed a miniscule tear of her hymen. In 1988 Dr. John McCann of the University of California School of Medicine published a four-year study showing that such hymen irregularities occur in 50 to 60 percent of girls who have not been abused. Moreover, the young girl in question told her therapist after the trial that her mother had urged her to lie so that "she could sue the school for lots of money."

Bernard unsuccessfully appealed his conviction in 1995. In 2006, as a result of action taken by the National Center for Reason and Justice, Massachusetts Superior Court Judge Francis R. Fecteau granted Bernard a new trial. Bernard, after more than twenty-two years in jail, was released from prison on bail.

As I have mentioned before, prosecutors don't give up; it hurts their careers. District Attorney David Capeless waited one year to make the decision to appeal Judge Fecteau's ruling. The appeals court heard the appeal in 2008 and ruled in 2009 that Bernard's original trial had been seriously deficient. One month later, the prosecutor finally dropped all charges against Bernard. After twenty-three years in jail, Bernard Baran was a free man innocent of all charges against him.

The twenty-eight cases of alleged child abuse mentioned above and in the appendix—each of which, without exception, ended up in a miscarriage of justice that condemned innocent people to jail for very long periods of time—have two things in common: an overzealous prosecutor and an erring jury.

Why is it that in so many cases so many prosecutors have pursued so many innocent people? It certainly is a prosecutor's duty to go after criminals, but it is equally important for a prosecutor to see to it that innocent people are protected from having to give up the American dream: life, liberty, and the pursuit of happiness. The latter is apparently not the case.

The cases mentioned above, cases in which innocent people were finally released from jail, are mostly cases where, years after the verdict, DNA science became available to prove a convicted person's innocence. In hundreds and hundreds of cases, there is no DNA available. And if it is available, it frequently has been contaminated by the police or the forensic lab has used it up in the first, inconclusive test. If we have scores of cases where DNA proves conclusively that prosecutors erred, there must be scores of innocent people in jail who do not have DNA to prove prosecutors made a mistake.

The reason so many prosecutors have put so many innocent people in jail is to further their careers. As mentioned before, the success of a prosecutor's career is unfortunately a function of the prosecutor's success in winning convictions. Guilt or innocence does not seem to be the most important issue; the rate of incarceration is what counts. And if incarceration means a supposed pedophile is removed from society and thrown in jail, the populace applauds, and the chances of reelection have improved.

A professional, appointed prosecutor would not have this conflict of interest between the truth and the demands of a political career. This is the reason prosecutors should not be elected but appointed. And in answer to those who claim appointing prosecutors is undemocratic, I say we still elect the people who appoint the prosecutors.

Moreover, if appointing prosecutors works on the federal level, why wouldn't it work on the state level? As is the case with our federal prosecutors—and I am not aware of any serious problems with miscarriages of justice on the federal level—local prosecutors should be professionals, not people for whom the pursuit of justice and fairness is secondary to their careers.

Lastly, a word about the juries who produced all these guilty verdicts of innocent people. As we will see later in the chapter about the use of juries in criminal cases, juries are supposed to be the best defense against an all-powerful government. That's why we have juries—to make sure ordinary citizens are protected from the abuse of power.

The problem is that it doesn't work. American juries do not provide protection against the abuse of power of a prosecutor. To the contrary.

In the chapter entitled "The Use of Juries in Criminal Cases," I examine the manner in which jurors are selected and explain why juries are easily swayed by prosecutors to find the accused guilty. And because juries are so easily swayed, they actually become a tool of the prosecutor's power—an extension of that power—rather than the last line of defense of an accused person who happens to be innocent.

When a prosecutor argues that it is the jury's duty to see to it that pedophiles are removed from society, a juror's concern becomes not determining guilt beyond a reasonable doubt but answering the questions, "What if this accused pedophile is indeed guilty? Despite my doubt about guilt, can I take the risk the guy is guilty and let him return to society?" The prosecutor sees to it that the juror's answer to that question is, "No, I cannot take that risk," which has now replaced the notion of guilt beyond a reasonable doubt.

Finally, the twenty-eight child molestation cases mentioned above and in the appendix are just a few of the literally hundreds of cases that led to convictions that were later overturned. I have cited the child abuse cases to illustrate how prosecutors operate. The same prosecutorial misconduct often occurs in murder cases or in drug cases. Victimsofthestate.org has published a list of well over one thousand cases involving different alleged crimes that resulted in innocent Americans doing jail time before their convictions were overturned. And for every one thousand innocent jailed Americans who were released that we know about, how many innocent Americans are in jail whom we do not know about?

Equally as reprehensible as prosecutorial misconduct to advance a prosecutor's personal career, although much less frequent, is prosecutorial misconduct for purely political purposes: to obstruct or handicap the party in power, to harm the reputation of elected people, or to render them ineffective as servants of the executive branch.

Raymond Donovan, Secretary of Labor

A famous case illustrating such prosecutorial misconduct was New York Bronx District Attorney Mario Marola versus Raymond Donovan, secretary of labor under Ronald Reagan, and six of Donovan's colleagues. Donovan was a controversial labor secretary because he was seen as business friendly. He was the first cabinet member in US history to be indicted when in office and had to resign as a result of the indictment.

The trumped up charge was that Donovan's company had subcontracted construction work to a mafia-controlled company. The trial lasted nine months, and the trial itself became famous because Donovan's defense attorney never called any witnesses: he relied entirely on cross-examination and closing arguments to make the case for the defense. After only minutes of deliberation, the jury cleared Donovan and his six codefendants of all charges. After the trial, walking down the steps of the courthouse, Donovan cried out in despair by shouting into the battery of microphones awaiting him, "Which office do I go to to get my reputation back?"

Every major newspaper in the United States agreed the indictment of Donovan had been brought for the purely political purpose of getting Donovan to resign as secretary of labor.

The United States versus Senator Ted Stevens of Alaska

The attorney general of the United States (AG) is the top law enforcement officer in the country and the government's lawyer. He is a member of the president's cabinet and therefore a member of the executive, as he heads the Justice Department. Yet the judiciary is equal to and separate from the executive and the legislature. Hence the unique position of the AG. With one foot in the executive and one foot in the judiciary, he or she is a hybrid.

Although the AG serves at the pleasure of the president and is therefore a political appointee, the AG administers what is under the Constitution a fiercely independent judiciary. It is for this reason that the AG is expected to act scrupulously within the law and to execute his job in a nonpartisan manner. There has always been an inherent conflict in the role of the AG between serving the president and acting independently and serving justice.

This conflict exploded under Nixon. Two of Nixon's attorneys general resigned rather than obeying Nixon's orders to fire the special Watergate prosecutor, Archibald Cox. Nixon's first AG, John Mitchell, having attempted to protect Nixon in the Watergate scandal and having lied about it, even ended up in jail.

Aside from his other duties, the attorney general is of course the chief federal prosecutor in the country. Together with ninety-three federal prosecutors (called US attorneys) spread around the country, the Justice Department prosecutes all the major federal cases, both criminal and civil, in the land.

A very recent example of prosecutorial misconduct at the highest level, a case of prosecutorial misconduct with serious consequences for the United States Senate, is the case of the United States versus Senator Ted Stevens, the consequences of which are of paramount importance today. The Justice Department has what is called a Public Integrity Section. It is a special office manned with some twenty-five career attorneys. The office is charged with rooting out corruption in high places.

Senator Stevens from Alaska, at the time eighty-five years of age, had served in the US Senate for forty years and was up for reelection in the fall of 2008. Popular in Alaska, his reelection was assured. After the unpopular Bush years, the Republicans were fearful of losing a lot of Senate seats. They were concerned that the Democrats might end up with sixty seats in the Senate, which, under Senate rules, means complete control. Consequently, Republican Senator Stevens's reelection was of paramount importance to the Republican party.

It has always been a tradition in the Justice Department to avoid filing criminal charges against a politician close to an election, as a mere indictment might affect his or her election chances. The Public Integrity Section of the Justice Department nevertheless filed suit against Senator Stevens in the spring of 2008, accusing him of accepting bribes. Senator Stevens was convicted of bribery two weeks before the 2008 election. He lost his Senate seat to a Democrat by 3,724 votes out of 362,500 cast. "Justice done," one would say. "Too bad for the Republicans."

After the verdict, the champagne flowed in the offices of the Public Integrity Section of the Justice Department. Bringing down a sitting senator, particularly one as powerful as Senator Stevens, would be very good for the prosecuting attorneys' careers.

And now the rest of the story. Senator Stevens's legal team suspected professional misconduct on the part of the lawyers of the Justice Department's Public Integrity Section, to wit withholding exculpatory evidence that would prove the senator's innocence.

When they presented their findings, (federal) US District Judge Emmet G. Sullivan was appalled. "In twenty-five years on the bench, I have never seen anything approaching the mishandling and misconduct [of prosecutors] that I have seen in this case." This was about prosecutors in, of all places, the Public Integrity Section of the Justice Department, prosecutors who set the example in the land, prosecutors who should be beyond reproach.

Normally the Justice Department would do an internal investigation when faced with a case like this, but Judge Sullivan declared that he had no confidence in the Justice Department and appointed his own prosecutor to determine whether the six Justice Department lawyers should face criminal contempt charges and go to jail. The case against the attorneys resulted not in their being fired or being disbarred—attorneys protect attorneys—but they were removed from litigation relating to allegations of misconduct.

All charges against Senator Stevens were later dismissed. However, as a result of the trial and false conviction, the Democrats ended up with a filibuster-proof sixty seats in the United States Senate!

The Impeachment of President Clinton

The worst abuse of prosecutorial misconduct in our times was the impeachment of President Clinton. A number of former prosecutors in the Republican-majority-controlled House of Representatives brought the impeachment charge for pure partisan political purposes. For months on end, Clinton, the president of the United States, was totally absorbed by the impeachment and was unable to govern effectively.

Clinton had indeed lied under oath and was later disbarred and paid a fine. However, his misdeeds did not rise to the level that required impeachment, and Clinton prevailed in the Senate trial that follows impeachment.

Does prosecutorial misconduct only happen in the United States? Of course not. Prosecutors in western European legal systems are not without blemish. However, cases involving an innocent person being released from jail after many years of incarceration are rare. Why don't France or Germany or Holland or that other common law country, the United Kingdom, suffer from the same appalling problem of convicting innocent people? Why only the United States?[24]

Part of the answer lies in the fact that in the United States, most prosecutors are elected, and as explained above, running for the office of prosecutor is frequently the first step in a political career. Winning cases, particularly criminal convictions, is such a powerful tool in a political

---

24 It should be mentioned that prosecutors in Japan (professional appointees) have a reputation for using illegal practices. When a Japanese prosecutor loses one case his career is in jeopardy—a loss of two cases is the end of his career. Hence an intolerable pressure to win a conviction.

career that many prosecutors are tempted to resort to a result-oriented legal strategy, a strategy that pursues conviction rather than fairness and equity.

Contributing to this anomaly is the holy alliance between prosecutors and the media and the fact that prosecutors can hold press conferences and make any accusation they want without being held to account. By holding press conferences, prosecutors such as Elliot Spitzer or Richard Blumenthal or Durham County's District Attorney Mike Nifong can accuse people who are supposed to be innocent until proven guilty and get their accusations in print or on the local or national news within minutes. Such prosecutors bombard the media with their publicity-seeking accusations, and the media are only too eager to provide these prosecutors with the megaphone of their news organizations. In many western European jurisdictions, even the names of accused people cannot be published before conviction. However, by holding a simple press conference, any American prosecutor can smear a person to the point where that person has already been convicted in the court of public opinion before even being indicted.

Finally, the practice of prosecutors seeking office in the executive or legislative branches of government, which in the United States is routine, does not exist in most European jurisdictions. European prosecutors are mostly career officers within the judiciary branch of government, where expertise and professionalism count and there is no need to get elected.

The founding fathers were very much aware of the possibility of prosecutors overstepping their boundaries and, in the Fifth Amendment to the Constitution created the grand jury to protect citizens against unlawful prosecution.

In conclusion, because American prosecutors on the state level often use their positions to launch their careers and because they lack any meaningful oversight, the conduct of the prosecutor in American criminal law is often fraught with problems leading to an unconscionable number of miscarriages of justice.

There is no reason why prosecutors on the state level cannot be appointed in the same manner as on the federal level. The governor should nominate candidates selected by a panel consisting of an equal number of prominent legal scholars and laymen, although the governor should be able to nominate anybody not selected by the panel if the governor so desires. The candidate should then go through the process of advice and consent in the state legislature as happens on the federal level during the selection of the attorney general and the US attorneys. Prosecutors should be appointed for six-year terms and, upon completion of their terms, should be reappointed at the option of the governor.

Compensation for Victims of a Miscarriage of Justice

With so many miscarriages of justice, it behooves our society to compensate innocent people for the time they have spent in jail. After all, the American legal community defends its aggressive tort regime and its insatiable quest for damages—and particularly punitive damages—with the argument that it affords the little guy, the poor person, the one without access to the legal system, an opportunity to seek redress for a grievance.

Who then is more entitled to redress for a grievance than the person whose grievance and resulting damages were caused by the very legal system that was created to protect that person? Having lost most of their skills to function in society while incarcerated and without money, transportation, health insurance, or a job, innocent people released from jail face daunting odds to rebuild their lives. One would think that our well-meaning and supposedly altruistic tort regime would have pushed legislation long ago to make sure that victims of inadvertent miscarriages of justice and especially victims of gross negligence on the part of the legal community are properly compensated. Unfortunately, and most embarrassingly, this is not the case.

The Innocence Project at the Benjamin N. Cardozo School of Law reports that of all the victims of miscarriages of justice, only about half have been compensated for the injustice they suffered and the time they spent in prison.[25]

Laws providing compensation for wrongly convicted people exist in twenty-seven states and in Washington DC; twenty-three states provide no compensation whatsoever. Furthermore, many of the laws that do provide for compensation are wholly inadequate to meet society's obligation to help exonerated people recover from their loss. For instance, in states where laws do exist to compensate victims for a miscarriage of justice, the compensation is not, as is the case in Europe, an entitlement. Exonerated persons must first file a lawsuit against the state to claim compensation or find a legislator who is willing to introduce a private bill for compensation in the state's legislature. Such obligations are all a terrible hindrance to a

---

25 The Innocence Project at the Benjamin N. Cardozo School of Law, Yeshiva University, October 2009.

swift resolution of every state's moral obligation to compensate the victims of its erroneous actions.

There is no law in the State of Washington to compensate innocent people who have spent time in jail. Although most people would find this unconscionable, as the story of Alan G. Northrop and Larry W. Davis will show, the State of Washington goes even further to make life miserable for the victims of its imperfect criminal justice system.

In January 1993, a thirty-six-year-old woman in the town of La Center, Washington was sexually assaulted by two men. During the attack the woman was blindfolded and had a chance to glance at her attackers only briefly. She later told the police she would not be able to identify the men—all she remembered was that one of her attackers was blond and the other one dark haired.

When shown a photo lineup of possible suspects, a lineup that included the photos of Alan G. Northrop and Larry W. Davis, she could not identify her assailants. After the police received a tip that the hair color of the assailants matched two gentlemen by the name of Northrop and Davis, the police once again showed the woman a photo lineup, which again included Northrop and Davis. This time the woman identified Northrop and Davis as her assailants.

Northrop and Davis were tried and, despite the fact that there was absolutely no corroborating evidence to go along with the fuzzy memory of the victim, the two men were convicted of first-degree rape and first-degree kidnapping. Northrop was sentenced to twenty-three years and six months, Davis to twenty years and six months.

In 2003 Northrop and Davis had been in prison for ten years when the Innocence Project Northwest at the University of Washington School of Law took on their case and asked the authorities to be allowed to test the DNA of her attackers the victim had produced (hair samples, skin from under her nails, semen, and so on).

The Clark County District Attorney refused to allow the testing. Although two men were languishing in prison, men that just might be innocent and whose innocence could only be proven by the simple act of testing the DNA from the crime scene, the district attorney, as happens time and time again, fought the DNA testing because it might prove that the judicial system was not perfect or that the prosecutor and jury had erred in reaching a verdict.

The Innocence Project sued the State of Washington to force it to allow the testing and won. The result of the test was that Northrop and

Davis could not have been the attackers. In 2010 a motion was filed for a retrial; the original verdicts were reversed, and both men were released after seventeen years in jail for a crime they had not committed.[26]

Because the State of Washington does not pay any compensation to victims of a miscarriage of justice, both men were penniless (and without any skills) when they left prison.

Davis was the father of a couple of children when he entered prison. Because he earned hardly any money while in prison, the mother of his children did not receive child support. Davis, upon release from jail, owed her a considerable amount of money. Consequently, when Davis found a job earning him a few dollars above the minimum wage, the State of Washington—the very entity that had made it impossible for Davis to pay his child support—added insult to injury and garnished Davis's wages to pay the child support he owed the mother of his children.

The State of Washington and the other states without mandatory compensation for victims of miscarriages of justice should proceed forthwith with legislation to correct this terrible wrong in the American legal system.

---

26 Note that it took the Washington School of Law Innocence Project seven years from the time they took on the case of Northrop and Davis to the time the accused were released.

3.

Forensic Evidence and Crime Laboratories

As Robert Jackson, the former attorney general and Supreme Court justice, famously said, "While the prosecutor at his best is one of the most beneficent forces in society, when he acts from malice or other base motives he is one of the worst." Jackson might have added that a prosecutor is at his or her best when that prosecutor pursues cases that have fairness and the public interest at heart, whereas a prosecutor is at his or her worst when he or she pursues cases with the sole purpose of winning convictions and getting publicity and self-aggrandizement.

As we have seen in the previous chapter, many prosecutors act from malice or other base motives. Rule 3.8 of the American Bar Association's Model Rules of Professional Conduct stipulates that prosecutors must "make timely disclosure to the defense of all evidence or information ... that tends to negate the guilt of the accused or mitigates the offense."

Since a prosecutor has many resources at his or her disposal, such as a staff of attorneys, the local police, the sheriff or the FBI, and the crime laboratories analyzing forensic evidence—usually many more resources than the average criminal defendant can marshal—it is incumbent upon a prosecutor to 1) manage those resources in such a manner as to ensure that the evidence they produce is true and untainted and has not been manipulated, and 2) make sure the evidence is at all times immediately shared with the defense. Time and again, prosecutors violate one or both of these two rules, rules that are the bedrock of the American criminal system.

In many cases when a convicted criminal has been released from jail, it is has come to light after the trial—sometimes after ten or twenty years of incarceration—that the prosecutor withheld exculpating evidence from the defense. It is absolutely amazing, even in high-profile cases like the trial of Senator Stevens of Alaska, how often prosecutors violate this basic tenet of a fair and just criminal system. Such prosecutorial conduct (withholding exculpating evidence) is criminal, yet despite searching state bar associations' reports and the records of individual prosecutors who were censured by judges, except for the prosecutor in the Duke lacrosse case, I have not been able to find any cases where prosecutors were ever punished for such illegal behavior.[27]

Equally damaging as those who withhold exculpating evidence are prosecutors who use false, tainted, or manipulated evidence in the pursuit of a criminal case. This happens time and time again. As a matter of fact, as the record of the many miscarriages of justice cited in this book shows, the vast majority of convicted criminals who are set free or whose convictions are later overturned are the victims of false, tainted, or manipulated evidence produced during trial.

Many instances of improper evidence involve bad police work: improperly trained or overzealous police officers may have contaminated a crime scene; police officers may have used coercion in extracting confessions; police officers may have used erroneous investigative methods such as a suggestive lineup identification process; they may have used questionable jail house informers; or they may have used plea bargaining resulting in false testimony. Prosecutors are, however, responsible for the evidence they use in trial and, as the record of exonerated convicts shows, have frequently been too eager to use what they know or should know is tainted evidence to get the conviction they desire.

Much of the evidence prosecutors use during a trial is forensic evidence, evidence that is developed through science. Fingerprints, DNA analysis, and ballistics all produce forensic evidence, and much of that forensic evidence is produced by crime laboratories.

It is consequently incumbent upon prosecutors to use crime laboratories that are reliable and professional. It is incumbent upon prosecutors that they inspect such laboratories to make sure the personnel are professional and have the proper training, that the testing and analysis do not taint the

---

27 Since state bar investigations of misconduct by their members are usually secret and the results of such investigations are rarely made public or available in a searchable format, it is difficult to monitor disciplinary proceedings.

material used, and that management is knowledgeable in the most modern and advanced forensic techniques.

The Houston Police Crime Laboratory (1999)

In 1999 Josiah Sutton went on trial for the rape of a woman who was the only witness in the case. The victim's recollection of what happened was sketchy. However, technicians from the Houston police crime laboratory told the jury that Sutton's DNA and the DNA of the semen found on the woman were a solid match. Josiah Sutton was sentenced to twenty-five years in prison.

In March of 2003, a new DNA test was performed that demonstrated that the semen found on the raped woman was definitely not Sutton's. The retesting of the semen was part of a review of a devastating state audit of the work performed by the Houston police crime laboratory. The problem with faulty lab work in Houston was highly disturbing: more defendants with cases whose forensic evidence came from the Houston police crime laboratory had been executed than from any other crime lab in the country.

The laboratory, experts concluded, was one of the worst in the country. There were no standards, and the standards that were followed were lax and vague. The technicians used by the laboratory were badly trained; they misinterpreted data and had exceedingly bad record keeping. Even the roof of the laboratory had a serious leak problem.

Of the 525 cases involving DNA that required retesting, 7 involved convicts on death row.[28]

The Washington State Patrol's Crime Laboratory

In the fall of 2001, a fifty-eight-year-old suspect in the town of Pacific in Washington who had a prior sex-crime conviction admitted to raping his niece. The fifty-eight-year old suspect was expected to be sentenced to twenty-five years in jail.

However, the Washington State Patrol's crime laboratory in Tacoma reported that the DNA extracted from the girl's underwear was definitely not her uncle's DNA. Lacking sufficient evidence to proceed to trial, prosecutors agreed to a plea bargain whereby the uncle pled to child molestation, which carried a sentence of fifteen years. In January of 2002,

---

28 *New York Times*, March 11, 2003

a retest was done that concluded without any doubt that the fifty-eight-year-old uncle was the rapist.

An investigation that followed concluded that forensic scientists at the Tacoma laboratory had contaminated tests or made other mistakes in twenty-three cases involving major crimes during the preceding three years.[29]

The Massachusetts State Police Crime Laboratory

In the fall of 2006, auditors from the US Justice Department's Office of the Inspector General concluded that the Massachusetts State Police crime laboratory had entered incomplete genetic profiles into its database in twelve cases out of a sample of one hundred suspects who had left DNA evidence at a crime scene. The profiles were useless, which meant that crime suspects who could have been convicted on the basis of DNA evidence were allowed to go free.

Furthermore, it took the laboratory eight months to report a match between evidence obtained at a crime scene and the DNA of a convicted felon whose DNA had been entered in the database.

The administrator of the laboratory was dismissed.[30]

The Baltimore Crime Laboratory

On August 21, 2008, the *Baltimore Sun* reported that Baltimore crime lab analysts had been contaminating evidence with their own DNA—a revelation that led to the dismissal of the city police department's crime lab director. Defense attorneys and forensic experts questioned the professionalism of the state's biggest and busiest crime lab.

On January 9, 2009, the same newspaper published a letter from the police department's chief attorney, Mark H. Grimes, which stated that the Baltimore police refused to release a report prepared by an outside group detailing problems in Baltimore's crime lab, arguing that revealing the contents would be "contrary to the public's interest."

---

29 *Seattle Post-Intelligencer* staff, July 22, 2004
30 Compliance with Standards Governing Combined DNA Index System Activities at the Massachusetts State Police Crime Laboratory, Sudbury, Massachusetts. Audit Report GR-70-06-012, September 2006, Office of the Inspector General.

The Houston Crime Laboratory (2010)

On January 13, 2010, an independent audit reported that out of 548 analyses of fingerprints prepared by the Houston crime lab, there were irregularities in more than half. As a result of the audit, two analysts were put on leave and a third resigned.

The information about serious irregularities in the Houston crime lab came after many such problems had been reported during the previous ten years. Houston recently paid a man who had spent seventeen years in prison on rape charges $5 million after the charges against him were overturned as a result of faulty crime lab evidence.

The Maine State Police Computer Crime Unit

On February 23, 2010, MSNBC reported that 250 files of child pornography cases were languishing in a bin in the Maine State Police computer crime unit in Vassalboro, Maine.

The San Francisco Police Department's Crime Laboratory

On April 25, 2010, the *San Francisco Examiner* reported that problems that occurred at the Houston crime lab were identical to the problems of the San Francisco Police Department's crime lab. "Both labs are underfunded, and lab employees maintain close ties to police and prosecutors."

The Austin Police DNA Laboratory

On July 8, 2010, the StandDown Texas Project, which identifies and advocates best practices in the criminal justice system, announced that Austin's police DNA lab would be the subject of an independent review, potentially affecting thousands of criminal cases, following complaints about the lab's operations by a former employee.

Travis county prosecutors have begun notifying hundreds of defense attorneys about allegations by the former DNA analyst Cecily Hamilton, which included allowing workers to perform tasks they were not capable of doing.

Prosecutors are still seeking to confirm the number of cases—they think it could reach two thousand—and how many are resolved or are still pending. The cases involve all classes of felonies in which DNA evidence is collected, including murders and sexual assaults.

The North Carolina State Bureau of Investigation (SBI)

On August 19, 2010, the Death Penalty Information Center reported that a government-ordered audit of the North Carolina State Bureau of Investigation (SBI) found that the agency falsely reported blood evidence in dozens of cases, including three that ended in executions. The inquiry, ordered by Attorney General Roy Cooper, found that SBI agents improperly aided prosecutors over a sixteen-year period, calling into question convictions in 230 criminal cases. Duane Deaver, a veteran SBI analyst who performed the work in five particularly troubling cases, was suspended pending further investigation. According to the audit, SBI lab reports omitted or overstated important information about test results that would have been favorable to the defense. The report blames the flaws on "poorly crafted policy, inattention to reporting methods which permitted too much analyst subjectivity; and ineffective management and oversight." The state supreme court ruled in 1992 that lab notes are evidence that should be made available to the defense. According to the report, however, "that did not happen for several reasons, including a mindset, led by a section chief, that the lab's main customer was law enforcement."

Of the questionable cases, the report says, eighty of the defendants are still in prison, three have been executed, four are on death row, and five died in prison.

Examining crime lab problems all over the United States, it is no wonder there are so many miscarriages of justice. With the release of exonerated prisoners a regular feature of the news these days, the question arises, how many innocent Americans have been executed for crimes they did not commit, and how many innocent prisoners are today languishing in state or federal prisons?

Prosecutors are responsible for the evidence they use to get a conviction, which means that numerous prosecutors have been derelict in their duties and negligent by allowing crime labs to produce unreliable or false forensic evidence. If prosecutors were appointed career professionals, unconcerned about reelection or their political careers, the scourge of wrongful convictions, which are endemic in the American criminal system, would not be the problem it clearly is today.

One final word about DNA. I mentioned earlier that many convicted inmates have proven their innocence through DNA. Since the DNA Finger Print Act of 2003, the US government has been taking DNA samples from everyone who is arrested or detained. Consequently, the national DNA database receives over one million DNA profiles each year. And since the inception of the program, more than one hundred thousand matches have been made between biological evidence in a crime and DNA information in the database. These matches have resulted in numerous arrests and convictions.

The good news is that some states allow convicted criminals post-conviction access to testing. In the last three years, Texas has overturned thirty-eight convictions as a result of DNA evidence, and Illinois has overturned twenty-nine—a total of sixty-seven wrongfully convicted human beings have walked out of jail in just two states. Any reasonable person would of course allow DNA testing in any convictions where inmates or their defense attorneys request the data.

And now the bad news. Alaska, Massachusetts, and Oklahoma do not give inmates the statutory rights to obtain DNA evidence after conviction, and some states allow testing in only limited circumstances—Kentucky allows testing only in death row cases, not for life cases. Consequently, an innocent inmate in Kentucky is better off with a death sentence—being on death row will allow him or her to prove innocence. With a life sentence, that person may have to remain in jail forever.

It is no surprise that prosecutors are against allowing DNA tests after a conviction. As happens only too frequently, these tests may lead to convicted inmates proving their innocence, which would call attention to the fact that the prosecutor convicted the wrong person.[31] Prosecutors are afraid of the truth—it might damage their careers. In cases where inmates have been convicted of capital crimes, the use of DNA to complement the evidence used during trial has reversed wrongful convictions in a large number of cases. America should get on with post-conviction DNA testing not just in some states but in all states.

---

31 See the case of Alan G. Northrop and Larry W. Davis described at the end of chapter 2, "The Election of Prosecutors."

4.

The Grand Jury

The Fifth Amendment to the Constitution reads, "No person shall be held to answer for a capital, or otherwise infamous crime, unless on a presentment or indictment of a Grand Jury ..."[32]

A grand jury is a group of citizens chosen to hear arguments about whether an individual should be charged with a crime. The use of a grand jury in common law goes back to times in England even before King James allowed its use to be codified in the Magna Carta (1215). Today its use survives only in the United States of America; all other common law jurisdictions have abolished the institution.

As I mentioned before, in the early days of our country, small communities decided everything in community meetings or through elected officials. A complaint, whether it related to a criminal matter or the conduct of a public official, would be brought before a group of citizens where at least twelve votes were required to bring an indictment before the case could be prosecuted. The group of citizens charged with reviewing indictments was called the grand jury and was formed to screen out false or malicious accusations. In the Bill of Rights (the Fifth Amendment) the founding fathers made the use of grand juries the law of the land to protect the citizens from potential abuse by the government.

The constitutional mandate for the use of grand juries applies to federal law only—the Supreme Court has decided that the Fifth Amendment does

---

32 In addition to establishing the grand jury, the Fifth Amendment also protects citizens from double jeopardy and self incrimination (having to bear witness against oneself).

not apply to state law. Consequently, only twenty-two states require the use of grand juries to indict a person for capital or otherwise infamous crimes, which usually means crimes which carry the death penalty or otherwise severe punishment. Most states have replaced the grand jury process with a preliminary hearing before a judge to ascertain whether the prosecution has a prima facie (legally acceptable) case to be brought to trial.

The problem with the use of grand juries is that, as is the case with so many other elements of American criminal and civil procedure, over the years the process has turned into a charade, a sham. The purpose of a grand jury, which is a supposedly wholly independent body, has always been twofold: 1) the investigation of crimes and the initiation of criminal prosecution and 2) the protection of the citizens against overzealous prosecutors. Because prosecutors play a dominant role in the affairs of the grand jury, and defendants do not have the right to demand to be heard by a grand jury, and because in general the members of a grand jury do not consist of a cross section of the population but of laymen utterly ignorant of the judicial process, grand juries usually decide to follow a course of action advocated by the prosecutor. The role of the prosecutor is so central to grand jury proceedings that one of its functions, namely to protect citizens against prosecutors who propose to bring unfounded criminal charges, has lost its meaning. Furthermore, although grand jury proceedings are secret to protect citizens who are the subjects of grand jury inquiries from unwarranted publicity, prosecutors time and again will issue press releases or hold press conferences discussing matters that are concurrently pending before a grand jury.

In the United States prosecutors are above the law. Even constitutional guarantees against unjust prosecution are typically flaunted by a prosecutor who, in the words of Robert Jackson "acts from malice or other base motives." Unfortunately, that is too often the case.

5.

Plea Bargains

In a plea bargain, a prosecutor and a defendant in a criminal case agree to settle the case against the defendant. The defendant agrees to plead guilty (and often to provide testimony against another person) in exchange for a reduced punishment or the prosecutor agreeing to charge a lesser crime.

The system has great advantages; it lessens the caseload before the courts and often allows the prosecutor to obtain additional information about the alleged crime and the involvement of others. In the United States plea bargaining is a daily occurrence, and more than 90 percent of criminal cases are settled pursuant to a plea bargain.

It is important to note that, as is the case with so many other elements of American criminal and civil procedure, the use of plea bargains in the United States is unique. Other common law countries do not use plea bargains, or if they do, they do so in very limited circumstances. For instance, in England, the source of Anglo Saxon common law, plea bargaining is permitted only to the extent that the prosecutor and the defense can agree that the defendant will plead guilty to some charges with the prosecutor dropping the remainder. In England, punishment or the reduction of punishment can never be part of a plea bargain—only the courts can decide punishment. Although prosecutors in the United States cannot guarantee a reduced sentence in a plea bargain, they pledge to petition the court to do so. In most cases judges comply.

In the United States, the system of plea bargaining is rife with plea bargainers providing prosecutors with erroneous information in a play for the judge's sympathy or a negotiated reduced sentence. Time and again, criminals finger their accomplices and are later shown to have lied.

If prosecutors or judges would provide decent checks and balances for the practice of plea bargaining, plea bargains might be a useful tool in criminal procedure. However, in most instances prosecutors are only too eager to embrace testimony resulting from a plea bargain. It is usually the prosecutor who suggests the plea bargain, and it is the prosecutor who uses the often tainted but easily obtained testimony from a plea bargain or a jailhouse snitch as a substitute for time-consuming conventional—and often more reliable—police work.

In white-collar crimes prosecutors often use plea bargains in order to catch the higher ups. They indict a number of executives in a company and, in order to garner information on the ones higher up, negotiate with the least senior ones to urge them to tell all with the promise of a lesser sentence.

Again, this plea bargain process has "conflict of interest" written all over it. Indicted businessmen are well aware of conditions in American prisons. Conditions are inhumane, rape of male prisoners is not uncommon, and compared to most countries in Europe, American prison sentences are much longer while prison facilities in the United States are by far inferior. An indicted person, even if he or she is innocent, will do anything to avoid prison or to shorten the length of prison time as much as possible.

I just used the words "even if he or she is innocent." Yes, even people who are innocent will at times consider a plea bargain. In highly complex cases or very emotional cases, such as the Enron case (a very complex multibillion dollar debacle and a highly emotional one since thousands of middle-class citizens lost their life savings), the risk of a prosecutor twisting the facts before a jury is so great, the risk that a prejudiced jury might find an innocent person guilty is so frightening, the fear of having to go to an American prison is so severe that, yes, even innocent people will at times resort to a plea bargain. Indicting a person under such circumstances often amounts to legalized blackmail. More about such indictments may be found in the chapter entitled "The Justice Department and the Strong Arm of Regulatory Agencies."

6.

The Use of Juries in Criminal Cases

There are two chapters in this book dealing with the American jury system. This chapter deals with the role of juries in criminal cases. The chapter in Part II deals with the use of juries in civil cases.

When researching the history of the jury system, one is surprised by the conflicting information about the origins of the use of juries to decide criminal cases or settle civil disputes. The Romans are often mentioned as the ones who introduced juries into British law when they occupied the southern part of the British isles. Scandinavia (the Vikings) and the Danes in particular are also mentioned. Others claim juries originated in the Lafif in the Maliki School of classical Islamic law and jurisprudence, which was developed between the eighth and eleventh centuries in the medieval Islamic world. The bestselling author Ken Follett, in his well-researched novel *World Without End,* claims that the Anglo Saxon jury system had its origins in Norman law and was brought to England by invaders from France in the eleventh century.[33]

What is clear, however, is that juries in ancient Greece and Rome and as used by the Vikings and the Normans were mostly conceived as a protection against the frequently arbitrary power of rulers. The Magna Carta forced King James I in 1215 to limit his rights and provide his subjects with protection against his arbitrary rule. It forced him and his heirs to respect various legal procedures and accept that his will was subject to the law. The charter included a clause establishing juries as

---

33 Ken Follett. *World Without End.* New York: Penguin Putnam Inc, 2007.

protection against abuse by the executive that found its way into the American Constitution.

Article 39 of the Magna Carta reads: "No free man shall be captured, and or imprisoned, or diseased of his freehold, and or of his liberties, or of his free customs, or be outlawed, or exiled, or in any way destroyed, nor will we proceed against him by force or proceed against him by arms, but by the lawful judgment of his peers ..."

Since the Magna Carta, the English have used juries to take the fate of subjects out of the hands of rulers when deciding civil and criminal cases.

Why does the United States still use juries, and what is wrong with the American jury system? Just look at the O. J. Simpson trial and that jury verdict, and one gets only a glimpse of what's wrong with the American jury system.

In high-profile cases, no doctors, no lawyers, no professors—in other words, no professionals—serve on juries. The reason? They have degrees. They are too well educated and too intelligent, and consequently they are a threat to the prosecutor or the defense attorney. The same goes for businessmen, entrepreneurs, shop keepers, and self-employed people—they are routinely dismissed from the jury pool on grounds of financial hardship or because they are indispensable to the local community.

What most Americans also do not know is that in other countries where juries are sometimes still used, the American system of voir dire, whereby the judge or the attorneys examine prospective jurors under oath to determine their competence or suitability, which allows attorneys to eliminate scores of jurors, often for no apparent reason, does not exist. In England, jurors are usually seated in the order they appear on the voter rolls.

Although the American Constitution entitles a criminal to a jury of his or her peers, in America one's peers do not serve on juries. Only a very special segment of society serves on juries: usually low- to moderate-income citizens, people without advanced university degrees, salaried people whose employers are by law prevented from objecting to their employees' jury duty, blue-collar workers, and so on.[34]

And in trials that last a very long time (some last more than a year), it should be obvious that jurors who can be away from their jobs for that long are not average citizens. Since certain employees are automatically excused from their jobs for jury duty with pay, jurors are often government employees or low-level employees of large companies that can be easily replaced.

Moreover, to jurists outside of the United States, putting one's fate in the hands of untrained laymen, as occurs daily in the United States, appears bizarre and capricious and seems to risk a serious miscarriage of justice. As the record of wrong convictions shows, such miscarriages of justice happen only too frequently.

And then there is the subject of race. In the United States, race is historically a very sensitive subject. It is difficult to publicly discuss racial issues—whatever you say about race, many politicians or commentators will immediately brand you a racist.

In the last presidential election, 92 percent of African Americans voted for Obama rather than John McCain. Did they do so because they are racist or simply because they were proud that one of their fellow black Americans was making a plausible run for the White House? When you agree it was the latter, as I do, you also agree that, where Obama's candidacy is concerned, black Americans are prejudiced in favor of Obama.

And so it is with supposedly impartial juries. Race plays a role in that people are prejudiced in favor of either whites or blacks. An impartial jury is a misnomer. Just consider the mostly black O. J. Simpson jury that ruled him innocent or the entirely white jury that exonerated a number

---

34 Although the jury pool from which they were selected was 40 percent white, 28 percent African American, 17 percent Hispanic, and 15 percent Asian, the O. J. Simpson jury had nine African Americans, one Hispanic, and two whites, hardly a cross section of O. J.'s peers. They all stated during jury selection that they did not read newspapers—they got their news from tabloid TV shows. They were all Democrats, and nine of the twelve thought that O. J. was less likely to be a murderer because he was a professional athlete. Their stated professions were as follows: vendor, hospital employee, gasoline company clerk, Pepsi delivery truck driver, mail carrier, phone company representative, computer repair technician, environmental health specialist, postal clerk, postal employee, automobile claims adjuster, and house cleaner.

of white police officers in the Rodney King trial (Rodney King is an African American) despite incriminating video tapes of Rodney King being brutally beaten by police officers, tapes that were repeatedly shown on national television. Also note that the vast majority of black criminals in the American South were, before the civil rights act, frequently tried before mostly white juries.[35]

On Thursday, July 16, 2009, Henry Lewis Gates Jr., who lives in Cambridge, Massachusetts, came home from a trip to China. It was two o'clock in the morning. Gates couldn't find his key, and he and his driver attempted to force the front door. A neighbor observed the two men trying to break into Mr. Gates's home and called the police.

When the police arrived, Gates had already forced his way into his home. The police officer, not knowing whether Gates was a burglar, asked Gates to step outside and identify himself. Gates, who is African American, refused and started screaming at the police officer, who is white, that he was racially profiling Gates. Gates demanded that the police officer give him his name and badge number and loudly advised the officer that the police department would be hearing from him, that the officer didn't know who he was dealing with, and so on. He then proceeded to insult the police officer's mother and kept on screaming that, if he was white, this would never have happened to him.

After the officer was satisfied that Gates was the owner of the home, he turned to leave. Gates proceeded to follow him while increasing the amount of verbal abuse he was directing at the officer. The officer had now been joined by two other police officers, one of Hispanic origin, one African American, who testified to the accuracy of this story. The next day the news media and blogosphere reported at their highest pitch that Professor Henry Lewis Gates Jr., a respected scholar in Black Studies at Harvard University, had been arrested for disorderly conduct.

On Wednesday evening, July 22, 2009, a few days after Gates's arrest, President Obama held a prime-time nationwide news conference on the subject of health care. In the final question, a reporter asked the president

---

35 The civil rights act of 1964 outlawed major forms of discrimination against blacks, including unequal application of voter registration. Since juries were selected from citizens on the voter rolls and, before the civil rights act, blacks in the south were often underrepresented on voter rolls, blacks were underrepresented on juries. Even today voter registration among African Americans is below the average of other subgroups in American society.

about the Gates arrest. The president answered: "I don't know not having been there and not seeing all the facts what role race played in that [Gates case]. But I think it is fair to say, number one, any of us would be pretty angry; number two the Cambridge police department acted stupidly in arresting somebody when there was already proof they were in their own home; and, number three, what I think we know separate and apart from this incident is that there is a long history in this country of Afro-Americans and Latinos being stopped by law enforcement disproportionately. That's a fact."

Three more pieces of information: 1) Lewis Gates happened to be a friend of the president; 2) police officer Joseph Crowley is a highly decorated officer who teaches race relations and the avoidance of racial profiling at the Police Academy; 3) ever since the incident the president has been at great pains to backtrack on his press conference statements, saying his words had not been properly "calibrated."

Did race play a role in the way the president answered the question, and had the professor been white, would the president have called the Cambridge police department stupid?

If even the president of the United States—and of all presidents, this president, a cool intellectual who is known for his deliberation on racial issues and who usually carefully weighs everything he says—if even the president of the United States mouths off in such an irresponsible manner in an off-the-cuff remark about race relations, a remark that has cost him a good deal of goodwill, how can a largely uneducated jury be expected to be racially neutral?

Finally, America's heartland consists of many closely knit communities where everybody knows everybody, where being born on the wrong side of the railroad tracks often marks you for life, and where religion and the Bible are sometimes so important that a teacher's mention of evolution can be the kiss of death.

Finding impartial juries in these communities is nigh impossible. Consequently, defense counsel in criminal cases often requests a change of venue, which is just as often denied. This rural community problem and the kind of people who normally serve on juries are some of the reasons why so many juries are so easily swayed by ambitious or unscrupulous prosecutors and why so many innocent people end up in jail or on death row.

Lawyer friends with whom I have discussed my objections against the American jury system tell me that I am an elitist with an arrogant disdain for the common man's wisdom and intelligence (they usually say so in more gentle terms). My answer is that I have no objection whatsoever to those with a modest education or those who linger on the lower rungs of the social ladder being *included* in juries. I object to the fact that everybody else is *excluded*. When they argue that putting educated people on juries makes it impossible to get a unanimous verdict, I answer that they have just made the argument for me that juries are an antiquated way to decide guilt or innocence or to settle disputes.

Will America ever change its jury system as the Brits have done by abolishing the use of juries in civil cases to adjust to a more modern society? Possibly. Legislation would be needed to create adjuncts to the district courts, free-standing courts with jurisdiction over certain issues like bankruptcy courts, which decide without the use of juries. The question is whether such courts would pass muster with the Supreme Court, as they might well be in violation of the constitutional right to a jury.

Moreover, juries are the bread and butter of the American legal system (yearly there are approximately 150,000 jury trials in state courts and 5,000 in federal courts). When I suggest to the average American that there is something wrong with the jury system, people look at me as if I am from outer space. Particularly in criminal cases, Americans truly believe there is no better system to decide on guilt or innocence than the use of juries—to suggest otherwise is akin to blasphemy. The use of juries to decide guilt or innocence in criminal cases has its use, but only if everybody is required to serve on juries—and then only in capital cases. To use juries to decide guilt or innocence in minor cases is anachronistic, inefficient, and doesn't particularly improve fairness in our criminal justice system.

7.

The Justice Department and the Strong Arm of Regulatory Agencies

The Justice Department is part of the executive branch of government. The attorney general, who heads the Justice Department, is the chief law enforcement officer of the government. He is a member of the president's cabinet. The attorney general exercises his or her duties with the help of ninety-three US attorneys. There are ninety-three federal judicial districts in the United States, and each is assigned a US attorney who prosecutes criminal cases brought by the government and defends the United States in civil cases. US attorneys serve at the pleasure of the president and need advice and consent from the United States Senate to be confirmed. Although they are supposed to follow normal legal procedures and are supposed to be nonpolitical and adhere to an ethics manual, they are largely independent; they have their own separate budgets, and they hire their own assistant US attorneys.

In addition to the Justice Department's 112,000 employees, among which are thousands of lawyers, there are numerous regulatory agencies that operate independently from the executive branch of government and the Justice Department. Because of the complexity of certain regulatory and supervisory tasks; the need to proceed rapidly in certain situations, which congress cannot do; and to avoid political interference in politically sensitive areas of business and commerce, congress has established these regulatory agencies to regulate and supervise such areas as interstate commerce, aviation, food and drug policy, the supervision of financial markets and communications, and other services of important economic interest.

These agencies adopt their own rules and regulations, which have the force of law. They have their own enforcement staffs and they have the power to indict and prosecute violators. As such, they act as the prosecutors in their areas of public authority. These agencies are anthills crawling with lawyers operating independently from the Justice Department. They frequently strongarm or elbow companies or organizations they regulate or supervise, or if unsuccessful at browbeating their subjects, they file suit in federal court to force compliance.

On earlier pages I observed that local prosecutors and state attorneys general like Eliot Spitzer frequently exercise their duties without regard to proper process and procedure. I argued that these prosecutors indict people not in a court of law but by announcing their investigations against people who are supposed to be innocent until proven guilty on national television—they indict, try, and convict people in the court of public opinion before such people have had any chance to mount a defense. This way of dealing with alleged violators can be found all too frequently in the Justice Department, and attorneys in many of the regulatory agencies take the same approach.

For certain people or companies, an indictment can be the kiss of death. An auditing firm accused of criminal behavior would instantly lose its clients, a health maintenance company accused of fraud would instantly lose its patients, and certain financial institutions would see a run on their deposits and a rapid loss of clients if accused of malfeasance. Consequently, prosecutors have immense power, and when they abuse that power, they can inflict enormous damage.

Arthur Anderson LLP

Arthur Anderson LLP, with 28,000 employees, was until a few years ago the largest and most respected auditing firm in the world. Arthur Anderson was the auditor of Enron Corp., the energy company with 85,000 employees that had to declare bankruptcy as a result of fraud and the questionable accounting practices they used to cover that fraud.

Arthur Anderson was accused by the Justice Department of having maliciously and fraudulently destroyed documents related to the Enron case. Instead of indicting the individuals involved in the document destruction, the Justice Department decided to indict the company. As a result of that indictment, Arthur Anderson had no choice but to surrender its CPA license, resulting in the demise of the entire company and 28,000 employees losing their jobs. Although the case was litigated all the way up to the Supreme Court, where Arthur Anderson finally prevailed, the company was destroyed in the process.

KPMG

A case that has recently been adjudicated concerns another one of the original Big Five accounting firms, namely KPMG (after the demise of Arthur Anderson, they are now the Big Four).[36] KPMG was accused by the US government of having devised and sold illegal tax shelters.

Unlike Arthur Anderson, KPMG was not indicted. Instead the government indicted the thirteen executives responsible for the creation of the tax shelters. After the immense debacle of the destruction of Arthur Anderson, not indicting KPMG was indeed a wise thing to do. However, the government still threatened KPMG with an indictment of the company unless KPMG cooperated with the government in the case against the thirteen employees.

It is normal for employment contracts of senior executives to contain a clause stating that, when such an employee is indicted in the normal course of working for the company, the company will pay the legal expenses for the employee. Court documents show that the government told KPMG that, in order to avoid a company indictment, KPMG had to refrain from paying its employees' legal expenses. In normal parlance, such actions are called blackmail. Indeed KPMG, in order to avoid the route Arthur Anderson had traveled, had no choice but to refrain from further payment of its employees' legal bills.

Federal Judge Lewis Kaplan of the US district court in Manhattan dismissed the entire case against the thirteen KPMG employees, calling the prevention of KPMG paying for its employees' legal bills prosecutorial misconduct. Here again the prosecutors are trying to run roughshod over the rights of individuals and companies who are supposed to be innocent until convicted in a court of law.

---

36 Deloitte Touche Tohmatsu, PricewaterhouseCoopers, Ernst & Young, and KPMG.

In his ruling to dismiss the government's case against KPMG, Judge Kaplan states, "Those who commit crimes—regardless of whether they wear white or blue collars—must be brought to justice. The government, however, has let its zeal get in the way of its judgment. It has violated the Constitution it is sworn to defend." Note the words "let its zeal get in the way of its judgment." In this case zeal, not fairness or equity, was clearly guiding the prosecutors.

The reason the KPMG case is so important is that the government has time and again been accused of prosecutorial misconduct, particularly since federal prosecutors adopted certain tactics after a wave of corporate scandals in the wake of the Enron scandal. These tactics are described in a now-famous Justice Department memo called the Thompson memorandum. In this memorandum, issued in 2003, the Justice Department sanctions actions by federal prosecutors that include threatening companies with indictment unless they cooperate by, for instance, cutting off payment of legal fees for their employees. Judge Kaplan has now, for the first time, denounced these tactics in the strongest possible terms. Recently, eleven of the thirteen KPMG employees who fought the Justice Department's indictment were cleared of all charges. Sadly, the other two, who would have been innocent as well, had earlier succumbed to a plea bargain.

Prosecutors in America routinely employ tactics that are in conflict with fair and equitable legal procedures. Ethics and internationally accepted legal norms are thrown to the wind in order to quickly reach a desired legal objective. Judges are way too tolerant of such practices, and regrettably, justices like Judge Kaplan who are courageous and willing to punish the government for nonjudicial behavior are few and far between.

PART II

CIVIL LAW

In 1787, Edmund Burke, a famous member of the British parliament (and a staunch defender of the American revolution), looked up at the parliamentary press gallery during one of his speeches and referred to the members of the press as the fourth estate. That's why today we often refer to the media as the fourth estate.

Burke must not have known that in 1580 Michel de Montaigne, one of the most influential authors of the Renaissance, wrote that the French government should rein in the fourth estate. Montaigne did not refer to the press, however. He referred to "the lawyers who are selling justice to the rich and denying it to the rightful litigants who did not bribe their way to a verdict."

Consequently, when we talk about the fourth estate, we should not be talking about the press but about lawyers.

1.

Introduction

Particularly in France, and to a lesser extent in other European countries, capitalism still has a bad connotation. I remember my third or fourth grade teacher in the Netherlands trying to convince us wide-eyed kids that capitalism was immoral. I distinctly remember him using as example the Rockefellers, who during the late nineteen hundreds allegedly sold the Chinese very cheap kerosene lamps that could only burn on Rockefeller's Standard Oil kerosene. He claimed that when most Chinese had bought the lamps, Rockefeller increased the price of kerosene so high many Chinese people could not afford the fuel. Even Karl Marx was still popular in those days.

Today, many political campaigns, such as Segolene Royal's in the last French presidential election; some newspapers, such as the *Guardian* in Britain; and popular songs by famous artists like Bruce Springsteen in the United States continue to perpetuate the populist adage that money is the root of all evil. Business in general, especially big business and businessmen, are routinely portrayed as greedy, materialistic schemers who exploit the working class and rob the environment. Profit as a motive allegedly poisons society.

Such accusations ignore the fact that the desire to earn a living or to amass wealth, even greed, are instinctive human traits that, if exercised within boundaries and properly supervised, benefit mankind.

There are many different ways to compensate people in our modern capitalistic world. Wages, salaries, commissions, deferred compensation, stock options, fringe benefits—there is a large array of methods to reward people for performance. These many different forms of rewarding people all boil down, however, to essentially three basic forms of compensation:

- The entrepreneur earns an undetermined amount of money by taking risk. For society to raise its standard of living, risk is vital—without someone taking risk, there would be no innovation, there would be no progress, and the standard of living would stagnate. The entrepreneur's motive is profit.
- Members of the professions receive a predetermined reward for the pursuit of professionalism and the exercise of expertise.
- And finally, an employee or wage earner receives a monetary reward negotiated between employer and employee or wage earner.

An eloquent defense of the profit motive can be found in Ayn Rand's classic *Atlas Shrugged,* a novel well known for advocating "the virtue of selfishness." Ayn Rand's moral defense of the pursuit of self-interest and her critique of self-sacrifice as a moral standard is at the heart of her book. The pursuit of self-interest, according to Rand, is not a vice—to the contrary, the pursuit of self-interest creates benefits for all and lifts the standard of living for all.

At the same time, however, Rand provides a scathing portrait of what she calls "the aristocracy of pull"—businessmen who scheme, lie, and bribe to win favors. History is resplendent with tales of monopolies, cartels, deceptive business practices, or useless or harmful products businessmen have produced to enrich themselves illegally—businessmen who scheme, lie, and bribe to earn a financial reward. That's why market-oriented democracies have developed rules, regulations, and oversight to protect consumers from excessive greed on the part of business.

Conversely, it is universally accepted that, unlike the businessperson, who receives an undetermined reward for taking risk, members of the professions receive a predetermined reward for the pursuit of professionalism and the exercise of expertise. Doctors, lawyers, accountants, professors, or advisors all earn what I call an ethical reward for the exercise of their expertise. When a doctor applies remedies that are inappropriate for a patient's illness in order to inflate the reward, the doctor has taken self-interest into the realm of criminality.

In the United States, the principle of ethical remuneration does not apply to many members of the legal profession. A large number of American tort attorneys have ceased to be officers of the court and counselors and have become businessmen who, at the expense of or together with their plaintiff partners, scheme, lie, and bribe to further their profitable legal blackmail business. They are not lawyers; they are businessmen who have taken their self-interest into the realm of criminality.

Many of these so-called lawyers refuse plaintiffs unless the plaintiff is willing to share a large portion of the damages with the attorney; others recruit thousands of plaintiffs who receive miniscule settlements for their alleged grievances while the lawyers earn millions and millions of dollars in fees for themselves. There is no relationship between the fee earned and the professional effort made by the attorney. In order to stave off bankruptcy, companies that are the targets of these legal assaults are literally blackmailed out of huge settlements.

Are these tort lawyers the exception? Unfortunately, tort lawyers who are solely motivated by the amount of money they stand to earn are rapidly becoming the norm and not the exception.

A large number of purely American legal practices not found anywhere else in the world, designed by lawyers and pushed through the various American state and federal legislatures as the law of the land, have contributed to this dismal state of legal affairs.

The legal practices I am talking about include, among other things,

- the absence of the loser pays rule,
- the use of juries in civil cases,
- pretrial discovery,
- the contingency fee,
- class action (including both the strike suit and the shareholder derivative suit),
- medical malpractice,
- punitive damages,
- proportional liability,
- forum shopping, and
- settlement mills.

These legal practices have contributed to an American legal system that has become frivolous, full of ambulance chasers and lawyers who earn pennies for their class-action plaintiffs but millions of dollars for themselves. These legal practices have created a legal environment in which the law is being applied arbitrarily and a system that produces damage verdicts not based on proportional culpability but rather on how much a defendant is able to pay. It is a system that employs sympathetic juries who prefer the poor, hapless plaintiffs to the rich and powerful insurance company, bank, tobacco manufacturer, pharmaceutical company, or fast food industry to dispense arbitrary, unequal, and unfair justice. The result is that every citizen, every consumer—except the tort lawyer—is the loser.

The costs to society of these legal practices are enormous. Insurance premiums are driven sky high, health care to protect against malpractice lawsuits becomes vastly more expensive, otherwise beneficial products never come to market, and companies that are under assault frequently go bankrupt, resulting in large numbers of workers losing their jobs.

As early as 1987, the insurance industry in the United States concluded that tort litigation cost the United States approximately 2.4 percent of GDP. The Pacific Research Institute estimates that the American tort system costs the US economy approximately $7,000 for every family in America each year. No surprise then that, according to the American Bar Association, there were 1,143,358 lawyers in the United States in 2007 (in 1970, there were 350,000). As a percentage of the population, the United States has three times as many lawyers as Great Britain, four times as many as Germany, and twenty-one times as many as Japan.

What this is all about is not the often-maligned greed of the businessperson, which is kept in check by numerous regulatory rules and regulations, but the greed of a self-regulated and enormously influential profession scheming, lying, and bribing its way into earning an undetermined financial reward out of proportion to the benefit rendered. The tort lawyer has become not what a lawyer is supposed to be—namely, an officer of the court—but has assumed the role of a risk-taking businessperson plaintiff. Today, the plaintiff lawyer in America has a financial stake in the outcome of the case he brings to court. He or she consequently faces an immoral conflict of interest.

To give an example of what lawyers do to win more business through legislation, let me describe some legislation presently before the US Congress that, if passed, would be one more triumph of the bar at the expense of the common good.

Because of the burden and cost of litigation, a thriving practice of arbitration has developed. In a recent poll, when asked how they would prefer to settle a dispute with a company, 82 percent of Americans chose arbitration; only 15 percent preferred litigation. Consequently many companies enter into contracts that contain a clause specifying that, in case of a dispute, the matter shall be submitted to arbitration. This of course reduces litigation and comes at the expense of attorneys who would participate in such litigation.

That's why the bar is asking the US Congress to prohibit Americans from agreeing at the start of a business relationship to submit disputes to arbitration. Not only do the sponsors of the bill—Representative Hank Johnson, a former attorney in Georgia, and Senator Russ Feingold, a former attorney in Wisconsin—propose forbidding a United States citizen from choosing arbitration if he or she so desires, they have the gall to include in the legislation a clause that requires that all arbitration contracts entered into during the last ten years become null and void. To add insult to injury, Johnson and Feingold have cynically called their legislative proposal the Arbitration Fairness Act.[37]

---

37 The bill has been introduced in the House as HR 1020 by Representative Henry Johnson and in the Senate as S931 by Senator Russell Feingold. I should mention that eliminating arbitration has its defenders. A number of arbitration companies in the US have been unduly influenced by credit card companies and the like, thereby compromising their independence. The solution to this problem, however, is not to throw the baby out with the bathwater and outlaw arbitration, but to enact proper legislation introducing oversight to assure independence of arbitrators.

2.

The Election of Judges

Much of what has been said in Part I about the election of prosecutors applies to the election of judges. Federal judges are appointed (more about the federal judiciary later), but in many states judges, even the ones who serve on state supreme courts, are elected.

I earlier discussed the great influence the trial bar has over these elections. Candidates for a judgeship are proposed and vetted by various bar associations. The result is that judges are beholden to their fellow attorneys and hate to overrule them. As I said before, many simply chair the proceedings, provide the maximum amount of leeway to prosecutor and defense attorney, and make sure the participants do not get too far out of line.

In the majority of states, the people elect some or all of the judges. The problem with electing judges is not only that elected judges tend to make decisions with an eye toward their careers and the chance to get reelected but also that their election campaigns are financed by people who have pending cases before their courts.

On June 8, 2006, the *Los Angeles Times* reported that in Nevada, even judges running unopposed collected hundreds of thousands of dollars in contributions to their reelection campaigns from litigants who had pending cases before their courts. The report revealed that donations were frequently dated within days of when a judge took action in the contributor's case.

According to the National Institute on Money in State Politics, business donors contributed the largest amount of money to state supreme court candidates. Despite the fact that the American Bar Association code of ethics requires judges to recuse themselves whenever their impartiality might be questioned, here are some examples of gross violations of that rule taken from an article in the *Wall Street Journal*.[38]

In the first case, Lloyd Karmeier, the winner of a $9.3 million campaign for the Illinois Supreme Court in 2004 (that's how much two opposing justices spent to get elected), was supported by $350,000 in direct contributions from employees, lawyers, and others directly involved with the insurer State Farm or its then-pending appeal and by an additional $1 million from larger groups of which State Farm was a member or to which it contributed. Almost immediately upon taking the bench, Lloyd Karmeier cast a vote on ending proceedings on a $456 million claim against State Farm.

In December of 2007, Wisconsin Supreme Court Justice Annette Ziegler declined to recuse herself from a case involving Wisconsin Manufacturers & Commerce, which spent $2 million supporting her 2007 election win. Following that decision as well as additional revelations that Judge Ziegler had ruled on eleven cases involving a company for which her husband was a director, editorials around the state called for her resignation.

The third example Sample cites took place in November 2007. West Virginia Chief Justice Elliot Maynard voted in a 3–2 majority to overturn a $76 million judgment against the companies of coal executive Don Blankenship. In January of 2007, photos surfaced depicting Maynard and Blankenship vacationing together in the French Riviera while the appeal was before the court. Another member of the West Virginia Supreme Court, Judge Benjamin, who was also involved in the decision, received a total of $4 million in campaign contributions from the same Mr. Blankenship.

When a citizen offers a police officer five dollars to squash a parking ticket, that citizen goes to jail for attempting to bribe an officer of the peace. In contrast, when Mr. Blankenship vacations with a supreme court justice and pays another member of that same court $4 million to help in

---

38 *Wall Street Journal*, August 16, 2010, in an article by James Sample, an attorney with the Brennan Center for Justice at the New York University School of Law and coauthor of *The New Politics of Judicial Elections 2006* (Justice at Stake, 2007).

his election while his $76 million case is pending before that court, Mr. Blankenship has not broken any laws!

There is, at present, a debate going on in the country over whether judges should be elected or appointed. Some states do appoint their judges. In those states, the governor usually picks one candidate out of three proposed by a judicial commission consisting mostly of lawyers and a few laymen. This system of choosing judges, called the Missouri Plan, is followed by some thirty-nine states. However, at the next election, the appointed judge must stand for a retention election.

The problem with this system is that the governor usually gets to pick one of only three judicial nominees. Since these nominees are preselected by lawyers, the system is incestuous. The system of lawyers selecting one of their colleagues or friends as a potential judge produces judges beholden to lawyers and candidates with suspect judicial philosophies.

When you consider that in the United States most federal judges have excellent reputations—some even dismiss plaintiffs' cases or hold the government in check in criminal cases—you wonder why the states don't follow the federal system and appoint their judges.

Federal judges are appointed for life and can only be dismissed pursuant to an impeachment trial before the United States Senate. Candidates for a federal judgeship are usually proposed by a state's senator, are vetted by the American Bar Association, and are then chosen by the president. The candidate must then win an advice and consent vote in the United States Senate. Presidents usually accept a senator's choice for a district court (lowest level federal court) position. But at the circuit level, presidents tend to make their own choices. The only problem with the selection of federal judges is that politics sometimes keeps a candidate for a judgeship from coming up for a vote by the full senate. When a senator doesn't like a president's choice for a judgeship, he or she can put a hold on the candidate, keeping that candidate from coming up for a vote even if that candidate passed the judiciary committee unanimously.

It should come as no surprise that the bar is against the idea of appointing state judges in the manner federal judges are appointed: it would reduce their clout and leverage over the judges before whom they plead their cases.

When I compare the elements and instruments of American democracy with those in other developed countries, it always strikes me that Americans are obsessed with elections. Don't get me wrong; elections are obviously an essential aspect of any democracy. The question is which office holder should be elected and which office holder should be appointed. In that respect, Americans stand out as the only nation in the world that elects holders of more offices than any other democracy.

The founding fathers, desirous to provide the nation with every possible check on the abuse of office and power, introduced a system of electing office holders in the legislative and executive branches of government that gave the citizenry a chance to regularly change office holders if they so desired. On the federal level, they ordained that the members of the House of Representatives should face the voters every two years. No western democracy holds elections for the lower house of parliament every two years except for the United States—the six-year term of senators is more in line with other democracies.

Our president, however, is allowed to appoint his own secretary of state, his own attorney general—as a matter of fact, his own entire cabinet—as well as all federal judges and all federal prosecutors. Advice and consent is required from the senate, but such consent is rarely denied. Assuming that what is good for the goose is good for the gander, I do not understand why what is good on the federal level is not good on the state level. In other words, why are judges at the federal level, subject to advice and consent, appointed, whereas at the local level judges need to be elected? Why are the attorneys general of the United States, all federal judges, and all federal prosecutors appointed by the nation's chief executive, whereas at the state level the attorneys general, judges, and prosecutors are mostly elected?

It should be noted that in the United States the election of prosecutors and judges has its defenders. The Supreme Court recently ruled that since, under common law, judges' decisions become the law, citizens should have a voice in deciding who should be a judge. Fine, but why does the Constitution make an exception for the Supreme Court and all federal judges and prosecutors? If that exception has merit, it should have equal merit at the state level.

Judges should be independent. Judges should not be beholden to their reelection chances. Election campaigns of judges should not be financed by people who have cases before the courts to which these judges are elected. Members of the legal profession have an undue influence over candidates for judgeships and their election. Judges should not be beholden to the lawyers who argue cases before the courts to which these judges are elected. The reason so many judges on the state level are excessively lenient with attorneys that argue cases before their courts is that judges in America are not independent, do not have tenure, face continuous conflicts of interest, and cannot pursue the basic calling of a good judge, which is the pursuit of fairness.

One more argument against the election of judges: compared to the days of the founding fathers or even one hundred years ago, life has become immeasurably more complicated. Whereas contracts in the old days of rural America were sealed by a handshake, today the use of a credit card requires a contract of multiple pages of small print. Whereas most commerce used to be local, today it is mostly national or international. Whereas the task of doctors once consisted of blood-letting and administering potions, today it consists of MRIs, chemotherapy, and noninvasive laser surgery. Issues that these days come before our judges are exceedingly complicated, which is one more reason an uninformed public should not be charged with choosing these judges.

Many legal scholars who are in favor of the election of judges argue that if you trust a so-called uninformed public with the election of the legislature and the executive, you should equally trust them with the election of judges. I—and our constitution, which provides for the appointment of federal judges—disagree. Citizens know instinctively how they want to be governed—debate about the manner in which we are governed is every citizen's daily nourishment. Knowledge of what goes on in a courtroom, however, is to the average citizen completely foreign.

Finally, whereas in years past every citizen in every local community knew their judge and knew the cases he or she was deciding, today hardly anybody knows who is their local judge or who serves on the state's supreme court. Using a highly nonscientific research method, I have regularly asked my neighbors and friends whether they know who serves on the local court or on the state supreme court. Except for my lawyer friends, nobody ever knows the names of these judges; nor are they familiar with their judicial philosophies. A recent nationwide poll asked people to name a member of the United States Supreme Court. One out of three Americans could not come up with even one name.

Judges cannot be compared to members of the legislature or members of the executive branch of government. Those who write the laws of our land and shape our society and decide how we live should be subject to elections, as should those in the executive who carry out the instructions of the legislature. But judges are like generals—you don't ask soldiers to vote for who should command them. The responsibility of military commanders is one the average citizen or soldier is not familiar with. And so it is with the responsibility and the task of judges.

There is no reason judges on the state level cannot be appointed in the same manner as federal judges. The governor should nominate candidates selected by a panel consisting of an equal number prominent legal scholars and laymen, although the governor should be able to nominate anybody not selected by the panel if the governor so desires. The candidate should then go through the process of advice and consent in the state legislature as is the case with the appointment of judges on the federal level. Judges should serve for life with removal possible only pursuant to an impeachment process in the state legislature.

3.

Loser Pays

When a plaintiff files a lawsuit in practically any jurisdiction in the world and that plaintiff loses the case, that plaintiff pays his or her own legal fees as well as the legal fees of the prevailing party. This so-called English rule is not only followed by common law countries like Britain, Canada, Australia, India, Singapore, Hong Kong, Malaysia, and others, it is the rule followed by all judicial systems in Europe. You might indeed say that the English rule is actually the universal rule. The exception, however, is the United States of America, where the so-called American rule is in effect. In America, even if you are a defendant and you prevail in a case against you, you have to pay for your own legal expenses.[39]

Consequently, in America the prevailing party as well as the losing party pay their own legal fees. Even when a suit is clearly outrageous or frivolous, the as ever accommodating judges will let the case go to trial, and the winner will be obligated to pay the legal fees, which, as we will see later, can be astronomical.

If losers had to pay the legal fees of the prevailing party, people might think twice before filing suit, which is why the idea of the loser paying the legal fees of both parties is fiercely opposed by the trial bar.

---

39 There are some exceptions to this rule. Under federal law, judges may elect to order the loser to pay the attorney fees of the prevailing party. This rarely happens, however. The state of Alaska follows the English rule, and some states allow some exceptions to the American rule.

A few years ago, Roy Pearson took his pants to the dry cleaner in Washington DC and paid $10.50 to have them altered. The shop was owned by the Chung family, Korean immigrants who had labored for twelve years to get the business going. When Pearson came to collect his pants, he was dissatisfied with the job and demanded $1,150 to buy a new suit. The Chungs refused, so Pearson filed suit against the cleaner in the District of Columbia's Superior Court. Not for $10.50, the sum he had paid; not for $1,150, the amount he claimed would pay for a new suit—no, Mr. Pearson, who knew the law, sued the Chungs for $67 million for inconvenience, mental anguish, and attorney's fees (later adjusted to $54 million).

Although this sounds incredible, Mr. Pearson simply applied the various anomalous consumer laws that routinely allow plaintiffs to multiply the stated penalty for a single mistake to astronomical amounts without having to prove actual injury. Mr. Pearson's calculations for why he was entitled to tens of millions of dollars came straight out of the law books. Mr. Pearson demanded half a million dollars for emotional distress; he wanted ten years' worth of week-end car rentals to go to a different dry cleaner; he demanded $542,000 in legal fees; he claimed that the signs on display in the cleaner's office, which read Satisfaction Guaranteed and Same Day Service, were fraudulent and that Washington DC consumer laws entitled him to $1,500 in damages per day. Multiplying twelve violations of the consumer laws by three (the number of Chung family members) and then by twelve hundred, the twelve hundred days the Chungs had allegedly broken the law, he reached the astronomical total of $67 million. There was no need for Mr. Pearson to prove he had been damaged by that amount; all he was doing was applying the law.

The Chungs made a final offer of $12,000 before the case went to trial. What would any sane judge do, what would happen in any other common law or any codified law jurisdiction in the world? Mr. Pearson was clearly abusing the law and afflicting the Chungs with irreparable damage (legal fees to the tune of $108,000 were driving them out of business). Consequently, a judge would be expected to dismiss the claim for any of a host of reasons, such as malicious or frivolous prosecution or abuse of the law.

Instead, the judge handled the matter as a routine business dispute, and the case went to trial. The no-jury bench trial lasted two weeks. Sometime later, the judge, in a twenty-three page opinion ruled that Mr. Pearson's claim was unreasonable. And, before I forget, Roy Pearson, the gentleman who brought the malicious lawsuit, was himself an administrative law judge in Washington DC!

Cases like Mr. Pearson versus the Chung family make American jurisprudence the laughingstock of lawyers around the world. It not only illustrates how unethical and unprofessional a judge like Mr. Pearson can be but it makes a mockery of the manner in which American judges handle cases. For the judge in the Pearson case not to throw out the case is, to a non-American lawyer, simply farcical. Obviously, had the English rule been in effect and had Mr. Pearson been liable to pay the Chungs' $108,000 in legal fees, he never would have filed the suit in the first place.

I mentioned earlier that if losers had to pay the legal fees of the prevailing party, people might think twice before filing suit, meaning fewer lawsuits and fewer fees for attorneys. This is of course vehemently disputed by the majority of American lawyers. They argue that the major reason for the American rule is that having to pay the legal fees of the prevailing party would discourage people from seeking legal redress for perceived wrongs. Society, they argue, would suffer if people were hesitant to pursue meritorious claims merely because they would have to pay the defendant's expenses if they lost.

Cynics respond that this would sound indeed wonderfully idealistic and even romantic if it weren't so self serving. By giving society the right to sue without any consequences, the result is of course many more lawsuits and consequently many more opportunities for lawyers to earn fees.

If the American defenders of the American rule are so parsimoniously concerned about the rights of society to sue, how come the English rule (which, by the way, although in effect in England, has nothing to do with England) has been followed by jurisdictions around the world since the days of the Roman Empire? Why has it worked so well in all modern societies, even societies like Scandinavia, where the concerns of society trump most other concerns? If it works so well all over the world, why wouldn't it work in America? Besides, if the bar is so concerned about society's welfare, why doesn't it balance that concern against the cost to society of the thousands and thousands of nuisance, frivolous, or meritless suits that are the result of the American rule? A loser-pays system obviously reduces litigation cost, discourages meritless lawsuits, and puts tort law in the service of deterring socially harmful conduct.

The Manhattan Institute for Policy Research reports that the direct costs of tort litigation in the United States reached $247 billion in 2006, or $825 per person. Moreover, according to the *US Tort Liability Index: 2010,* tort costs in the United States as a percentage of gross domestic product are far higher than those in the rest of the developed world.[40] In the United States tort costs as a percentage of GDP in 2003 were 2.2 percent, while they were 1.7 percent in Italy, 1.1 percent in Germany, 0.8 percent, in Japan and France, and 0.7 percent in Great Britain.[41] Our tort costs as a percentage of GDP are consequently double the costs in Germany and three times the costs in France or the United Kingdom.

The fact that the legal community is against the idea of loser pays shows that the tort bar is more concerned about its own earnings than creating a fair and equitable society.

Finally a tale of personal experience. In the fall of 1991, I flew on a DC-10 belonging to JAT, then still the Yugoslav national airline, from Belgrade to Chicago, where I was to connect to a flight to my hometown of San Francisco. There were three passengers in first class: a couple sitting on the right side of the aircraft and me, in a window seat on the left.

After cocktails had been served, the chief purser—with, as is customary in former communist countries, a very large number of gold bars on his epaulettes—appeared carrying a tray of canapés. He served the couple first and then offered me some. As I was munching the delicacies, he engaged in small talk and then slipped into the seat next to me, the tray of canapés now on his lap. He proceeded to tell me in a somewhat conspiratorial tone that he was excited to get to Chicago. When I asked him why, he told me he was going to collect a very large amount of money. He then whispered to me that he had been in Chicago some time ago when, crossing the street,

---

40 *US Tort Liability Index: 2010 Report* by Lawrence J. McQuillan and Hovannes Abramyan prepared for the Pacific Research Institute (June 2010),

41 These statistics were published in 2005 by Tillinghast-Towers Perrin in a study entitled *U.S. Tort Costs and Cross-Border Perspectives.* Tillinghast-Towers Perrin is a global reinsurance firm specializing in corporate risk management and insurance actuarial consulting.

he had been hit by a taxi. The taxi had barely nipped him, and he had lost his footing only momentarily, but otherwise no harm was done.

The taxi driver apologized for the inconvenience, and everybody had gone on their merry way when somebody tapped him on his shoulder and asked him whether he had been hurt. He told the gentleman he had not been hurt, whereupon the gentleman told him that he was an attorney and that it was immaterial whether he had been hurt or not. He only had to sign an affidavit that his shoulder and neck hurt, and the attorney could get him quite a lot of money. "So I followed the attorney to his office," the purser told me, "and now I am on my way to Chicago to collect $15,000, more money than I earn in an entire year."

As the purser was telling me the story about his sudden financial windfall, he looked at me with a triumphant gleam in his eyes as if to say, "What do you think about that?" So I told him he was involved in a criminal conspiracy to defraud an insurance company. He stuttered for a moment and then managed to say, "What?" I repeated that he was participating in a criminal conspiracy to steal money from an insurance company. With a rather bewildered look on his face, he jumped out of the seat while struggling to balance the canapés on the silver plate in front of him. As he was standing in the aisle, he turned to me and mumbled, "Who are you anyhow ... FBI or something?" and then disappeared into the pantry. He never returned. Meals were served by another member of the flight crew.

Filing a lawsuit just to blackmail a person or company into settling out of court has become routine in America. People complain about it, yet everybody accepts it. "That's just the way it is," is the prevailing mood; it's the price you pay for a supposedly fair and equitable legal system. The fact that it isn't so in many other developed countries is never mentioned—the average American simply doesn't know that. When moves are afoot in state legislatures or Congress to rein in excesses in the litigation world, the bar, which is rich and powerful, lobbies such moves out of existence.

4.

The Use of Juries in Civil Cases

The use of a jury to decide guilt or innocence in a criminal trial is a centuries-old tradition in both common law and many codified law systems. This is not the case in civil trials, where the use of judges has become the more traditional approach in settling disputes. However, the use of juries in both criminal and civil cases remains the bedrock of the American justice system.

The right to a jury in civil cases was introduced in the Bill of Rights and more particularly through the Seventh Amendment to the Constitution. The authors of that amendment were apparently fearful that future US governments might adopt some of the dictatorial tendencies of British kings or that factions in society might acquire some of the authority of the British landed gentry, which had undue influence on the choice and the appointment of judges. The authors were thus desirous to provide citizens with the protection of a jury against the potential abuse of the powerful.

In most of continental Europe, such as Germany and the Netherlands, juries are not used in either criminal or civil trials; in Belgium and France, they are used in only rare and very serious criminal cases. Except for libel cases, even Great Britain, the source of American common law, has dispensed with the use of juries in civil disputes—only criminals are entitled to a jury trial.

Most modern democracies, even the common law countries, have substituted juries with courts consisting of learned judges—the number of judges sitting in judgment depending on the severity of the case—combined with a system of appeals. Not so in the United States, where the use of juries in civil trials remains the true and tried manner in which to settle disputes.

Consequently, the United States is the only nation in the developed world where highly complex cases—those involving concepts, theories, and terminology that average citizens, even jurors with college degrees, have difficulty in understanding, concepts about which even experts with lifelong experience on the subject may disagree—are still decided by juries.

Not, as we will see later, by juries of one's peers, but by juries consisting mostly of citizens who often do not have high school diplomas and in many cases lack college degrees.

Since the American jury system had its origins in British common law, and despite the fact that the Brits have dispensed with the use of juries in civil cases, it is worthwhile to look at how the British common law system selects its jurors. First a jury pool is established of citizens who are registered inhabitants of the town or municipality where the court is located and trials take place. Jurors are then called in the order they appear on the municipal roles. There are virtually no excuses for service on a jury: everybody who is called has to serve.[42] Before being empanelled, a potential juror has to answer one and only one question: "Can you give a fair hearing to both the Crown and to the defense?" If the answer is no, the potential juror has to give a satisfactory answer why he or she cannot give a fair hearing before being dismissed. If the answer is yes, the juror is seated.

In the United States, the list of potential jurors is prepared in more or less the same manner as in Great Britain and other common law jurisdictions, although in a large number of the states only registered voters and licensed drivers appear on the rolls.

After a potential juror has been called, however, and before that juror is seated, the American jury selection system is totally and entirely different from that used in other countries. There is, of course, nothing wrong with the American legal system selecting jurors differently from how that is done in other countries—that is to say, if the American jury selection process was just as good or better than any other system. Viewed from abroad, however, the selection process called voir dire does not guarantee a plaintiff or defendant a jury of their peers as required by the Constitution

---

42 Trials in Great Britain are considerably shorter than in the United States, reducing the hardship caused by serving as a juror.

and the Bill of Rights. Jurors in America are not one's peers as described in the literature written by the framers of the Constitution. The framers describe peers in various ways but most often use language like "peers are your neighbors and your equals."

In America a jury does not consist of your peers or your neighbors or your equals. In America a jury consists of people the lawyers for the plaintiff or the defendant believe will find for their client. In America jury selection has deteriorated into a knockout fight between lawyers who, irrespective of what is being argued during trial, wish to assure in advance of the trial that the outcome will be in their favor. If this means that the jury should consist of anybody but the plaintiff's or the defendant's peers, so be it.

In important cases, a considerable amount of money is spent by lawyers to discover the psychological profile of the juror most likely to find for their party. Not only does this give the financially well-off, who can spend a lot of money in the selection of sympathetic jurors, a great advantage over the financially inferior party, the system makes a mockery of being judged by one's peers.

Even before the process of voir dire begins, scores of potential jurors are excused from jury duty on grounds of hardship or because they are indispensable to the community. For example, store owners, doctors, politicians, firefighters, or mothers with young children are usually automatically excused. Because policemen and lawyers are involved with the law, they are supposed to be partial and are therefore excused. Businessmen claiming they are irreplaceable are excused. Pharmacists who claim they do not have a substitute are excused. Professors or teachers claim they cannot interrupt class and are excused. To make a long story short, anybody who does not want to serve on a jury is excused.

Payment for jury duty is usually a pittance, hardly enough to pay for a parking fee, another reason so few wish to serve. Finally, the potential juror who cannot find a decent reason for an excuse simply makes one up by claiming bias or claims an association with somebody in law enforcement or by using some other phony excuse.

By the time the process of voir dire begins, the remaining jury pool from which the judge and the lawyers will ultimately select the jurors has been reduced to a collection devoid of professionals or people from the world of business. The remaining people in the jury pool are decidedly not a cross section of the citizenry, decidedly not the defendant's peers, but a collection of people who society can spare for jury duty because they do not have essential jobs. There is nothing wrong with postal clerks or gas station attendants serving on juries. As a matter of fact, they should. They are as much part of our society as everybody else. But so are pharmacists or professors or businessmen or doctors.

The last phase of jury selection, the actual voir dire, consists of oral questions asked of prospective jurors by the judge and the attorneys. This oral questioning, usually supplemented by a written questionnaire, is used to determine whether a potential juror is biased or should otherwise be excluded from jury duty. A number of prospective jurors are called to the jury box, given an oath, and then questioned as a group by the lawyers or the judge. Depending on the jurisdiction, lawyers on both sides have the right to challenge a number of potential jurors for cause or sometimes for an undeclared reason. Supposedly, the purpose of voir dire is to enable the parties to select an impartial panel.

Unless the defendant lives on the fringe of society, the jury that is finally selected most often consists of people who are not a cross section of society and therefore not the defendant's peers, neighbors, or equals.[43]

As mentioned above, in most developed countries the use of juries in civil cases has been dispensed with because jury trials have been increasingly regarded as expensive, unreliable, anachronistic, and utterly time-consuming not only for the courts but especially for the members of the jury and their alternates. Furthermore, to a non-American, it is incomprehensible that educated men and women will allow highly complex civil cases to be decided by a number of people who, in many instances, do not understand the subject matter of the issues they are being asked to judge.

It is often argued that learned judges are in the same position as juries, that judges have as little knowledge of the subject matter of a complex case as do juries. There is a big difference, however, between a judge's ability to learn the intricacies of a complex civil case and the members of a jury. Undergraduate and graduate education teaches a student to think logically, to balance the value of arguments, to attempt to suppress prejudice, and to place logic above emotion. When using juries to settle disputes, prejudice

---

43 See the chapter entitled "The Use of Juries in Criminal Cases" in Part I for a detailed description of the makeup of the jury in the O. J. Simpson criminal trial.

and emotion rather than logic often play the larger role. Moreover, when we use expert courts or judges (for example, bankruptcy courts) to handle specific cases, judges in those specialized courts become experts in the subjects they are called upon to judge.

The result of using juries instead of specialized courts is that it is frequently not the scientific or economic evidence that sways a jury but the theatrics and personality of the attorney. Particularly in medical malpractice cases or product liability cases when a person has been physically hurt, juries will often assign responsibility and award damages not because the scientific evidence points toward guilt or innocence on the part of the defending party but out of a sense of sympathy and a desire to alleviate the plight of a plaintiff's often heartbreaking condition. Redistributing a small piece of the often assumed enormous wealth of the defendant to the hapless victim of misfortune is, for many juries, more attractive than objectively deciding liability. Too often this approach to justice leaves the defendant at a severe disadvantage.

It is exactly because juries consist of people who are not the defendant's peers that large and wealthy companies are found guilty much more frequently than would be the case if learned judges had adjudicated the case. It is exactly because juries do not consist of the defendant's peers that outrageous amounts of money are being awarded, particularly in medical malpractice and product liability cases. America should abolish the use of juries in civil cases just like all other countries in the western world have done. Learned (appointed) judges, such as the ones currently used in bankruptcy courts, would provide more consistency and less emotion in adjudicating civil disputes.

5.

Discovery

In American civil procedure, the process called discovery takes place mostly prior to trial. Pretrial discovery is a phase in a lawsuit in which each party can request documents and other evidence from opposing parties or compel the production of evidence by using a subpoena or a request for production or a deposition, all with minimal judicial oversight. Discovery is wide ranging and, with few exceptions, involves any information or material that is remotely relevant to the case.

Pretrial discovery is a uniquely American civil procedure. Talk to the average European or Asian attorney, and you will often find that he or she is not familiar with the intricacies of American legal procedure during the discovery phase of a dispute. Pretrial discovery as practiced in the United States does not exist anywhere else.

The American procedure of pretrial discovery can be useful to the system of justice. Both parties will know in very great detail the strengths and weaknesses of the opposing party's case prior to trial. It impels both parties to negotiate and hopefully settle without a trial, saving all parties the financial burden of a trial, unclogging the courts, and saving society and juries from unnecessary trials.

As is the case with so many aspects of American legal procedure, it is easy to make the case in favor of the American discovery system. Unfortunately it is just as easy to come up with scores of examples of lawyers abusing the system of pretrial discovery by draining the other party's financial resources until that party folds and settles.

When I was a member of the litigation committee of Transamerica Corporation in the seventies, I learned that when a lawsuit concerned Occidental, at the time one of the largest insurance companies in the United States,[44] the rule was that if the case could be settled for less than $4,000, then one should settle. Every now and then, Occidental would fight a case that could be settled for less than $4,000 all the way through discovery and if necessary all the way through trial just to prove to the litigation attorneys that Occidental was no pushover.

Insurance companies are constrained in many ways. Since they have a contractual obligation to their clients, and the manner in which they deal with that obligation affects their reputations, and since insurance companies are highly regulated and overseen by state insurance commissioners, insurers normally strive to settle claims quickly and fairly. Refusing to negotiate or settle a case in good faith can create a regulatory problem. Attorneys are aware that insurance companies are hamstrung by reputational issues and state and federal regulations and take advantage of that unique situation when filing frivolous lawsuits

Consequently, the merits of the cases that were filed against Occidental and that were quickly settled were often of no importance; the objective was to simply minimize the cost of litigating such cases. (An example of this is the JAT Airline purser collecting $15,000 from an insurance company although, by his own admission, he had not been injured.)

In the late seventies, when I founded my own company, I employed a fairly senior executive of the Reader's Digest in New York. The Digest, fearful that other executives might also leave the company, filed suit against the executive to punish him for breaking his employment contract. My company offered to pay the executive's legal fees. The Digest filed suit in California state court, and their attorneys, San Francisco's most famous and most expensive law firm, commenced the discovery process. They insisted on a large number of depositions both in California and New York, which resulted in spiraling attorneys' fees and travel expenses as our attorneys had to be present at all these depositions.

After three months of very expensive discovery, the Digest attorneys petitioned the court to transfer the case from state court to federal court. The judge agreed, and the process of pretrial discovery started anew. After three months in federal court, the Digest attorneys petitioned the court to transfer the case back to state court. As usual, the judge agreed.

---

44 Occidental is today a US subsidiary of Dutch insurer Aegon.

I was incredulous and tried to convince my attorneys that this was exceedingly unfair and that they should fight the petition on the grounds that the Digest was abusing legal procedure and was simply trying to harm my company and blackmail us into a settlement. My attorneys smiled at me and told me that wasn't the way things were done in American courts. The judge, my attorneys told me, was probably happy to lose a case from his docket and would anyhow not overrule the Digest attorneys, and they educated me in the way American attorneys routinely used legal procedure for nefarious purposes.

After nearly a year of document production and depositions, information requests that were expensive and time consuming, and the production of numerous documents that had hardly any relevance to the case, Reader's Digest, having run out of ways to abuse legal procedure, finally accepted a settlement in the case for a modest amount of money.

I earlier talked about the culture of many practitioners of the American legal system. In the area of discovery, this culture is best described by Cameron Stracher, one of the great legal ethicists in America. Stracher graduated from Amherst College magna cum laude and then graduated from Harvard Law. After practicing law in Washington, he founded the Writing Resource Center at the University of Iowa College of Law and worked as litigation counsel at CBS. In his book *Double Billing* Stracher writes about the discovery process and pretrial discovery, "With the noble sentiment of leveling the playing field so that no party has undue information advantage, the writers of the discovery rules created a multi level playing field where the information-rich can kick the information-poor in the head and escape unscathed ... Hundreds of thousands of dollars to maintain the status quo, to preserve the information-rich at the expense of the information-poor. Thousands of lawyer hours to keep the discovery process as unrevealing as possible. The best minds of a generation thinking of new ways to manipulate, distort, and conceal."[45]

As we will see in subsequent chapters, discovery has become one of the most valuable tools in a litigation attorney's arsenal to terrorize and blackmail the opponent. Particularly in class-action suits, strike suits, or shareholder derivative suits, suits that will put fear in a defendant exactly

---

45   Cameron Stracher. *Double Billing: A Young Lawyer's Tale of Greed, Sex. Lies, and the Pursuit of a Swivel Chair.* New York: William Morrow, October, 1998.

because discovery is so devastating and debilitating, discovery is possibly one of the most abused aspects of American legal rules and procedures.

6.

The Contingency Fee

If there is one aspect of the American legal system that is at the root of many of its anomalies and deficiencies, it is the so-called contingency fee. The contingency fee is a form of lawyer remuneration that has turned the litigation lawyer into a businessperson who has a conflict of interest with his or her client. The contingency fee represents a form of remuneration that thoroughly corrupts the American legal system and its practitioners.

A contingency fee is a fee paid to an attorney with the proviso that the fee is paid only if dispute negotiation or litigation is successful. It is often called the "no win, no fee" or the "no fee unless successful" system, and the fee is usually a percentage of the amount recovered. The fee is frequently 33 percent of the amount if there is a negotiated settlement, 40 percent if the case goes to trial, and 50 percent if the case results in a verdict. In other words, when an attorney handles a case on a contingency fee basis and wins an award of $1 million for the plaintiff, the attorney walks away with between $333,000 and $500,000, and the plaintiff receives the rest.

Although a contingency fee, at first glance, does not give the appearance of a conflict of interest, it represents the most poisonous and destructive aspect of the American litigation system. The contingency fee creates a lawyer remuneration system that does not promote fairness and equity; rather, it creates a perverse incentive for an attorney to serve his or her self interest while appearing to act in the client's interest. One might claim that those interests are aligned, but as we will see, more often than not they are not aligned at all. Case after case will show that this conflict of interest is the reason the contingency fee is not only unethical but intolerable. Nowhere in the world of advanced democracies, and for very good reason, is the contingency fee allowed—except in America.

History

It is difficult to find the historic origins of the contingency fee. When I asked Dr. Jan Lokin, professor of Roman Law at the University of Groningen in the Netherlands, about the origin of the contingency fee, he referred me to an article he wrote in the periodical *Themis* in which he states that Emperor Septimius Severus (193–211) allowed a palmarium, or a success premium, for the lawyer as long as the palmarium consisted of a previously negotiated sum and not a percentage of the amount of money (*pactum de quota litis*) recovered. According to Septimius Severus, a pacta de quota litis would make the client's case the lawyer's case, resulting in the lawyer losing his objectivity and integrity. Emperors Valentinianus and his brother Valens (364–375) decreed that lawyers who were driven by the profit motive had to be regarded as "degenerate and despicable."

The contingency fee is often seen as a substitute for champerty, the practice of an attorney buying a stake in his or her client's litigation. Throughout the history of common law in England, champerty was prohibited. It was deemed unethical for a person to engage in a suit he or she had purchased from the plaintiff.

In the United States we find the first mention of a contingency fee in the early nineteenth century in a case in Ohio.[46] In this case destitute landowners had lost their land to swindlers claiming title, and they could not afford the legal fees to reclaim their land.

As is the case with so many aspects of American legal procedure, the contingency fee was born out of a great societal need, namely, to assure access to the legal system for both rich and poor. As such, the contingency fee has done wonders for fairness and equity in American jurisprudence. Ever since the early nineteenth century, the contingency fee has provided compensation for thousands of Americans who were either physically or materially injured through the negligence or fault of others, people who otherwise would not have been able to afford attorneys' fees.

As with all other unique aspects of the American legal system, it is not the salutary aspects of the contingency fee that create the problem; it is its abuse. Contingency fees, although for a long time controversial and

---

46 Key v. Vattier, 1 OH 123, 136 (1823)

prohibited in many American jurisdictions, were, as mentioned above, originally allowed to provide poor persons access to the courts. The original purpose of this manner of lawyer compensation has, however, completely disappeared.

Most businesses, home owners, automobile owners, doctors, and other professionals carry insurance. This means that when people are sued it is, more often than not, the insurance company that is defending the insured. Ask any insurance company whether its plaintiffs' attorneys are being remunerated on the basis of a contingency fee and the answer is likely to be, "Practically always."

Conflict of Interest

A conflict of interest occurs when a person has multiple interests—interests that are not aligned and one of which could conflict with the motivation to act properly in dealing with the other. Conflicts of interest lead to corruption, which is why they are banned from the world of business, the professions, and (supposedly) from the world of our elected politicians.

A simple example: a doctor is promised payment by a drug company each time that doctor writes a prescription for a drug made by that company. Although the doctor knows that a different drug is better for a particular situation, he nevertheless prescribes the drug made by the company that has promised him a payment. The payment by the drug company has corrupted the doctor's medical decision, because the doctor faces a conflict of interest: the health of the patient versus the doctor's desire for monetary gain.

I am always surprised to learn how few people are concerned about conflicts of interest. It may well be that most people, when faced with a conflict of interest—and we face such conflicts daily—usually resolve their conflicts in an ethical manner. It may also be that they have become so used to conflicts of interest in public life—such as a politician receiving campaign donations from a person or a company with an interest in that politician's legislation—that they have become inured to a conflict of interest's often insidious corrupt influence.

However, just tell the average person an imaginary story of a doctor treating a self-employed person and then asking for 33 percent of that person's income after the patient has recovered. There is no need to pay for the medical treatment if the person does not recover, but 33 percent of the patient's earnings go to the doctor if the patient does recover. People shrink back in horror at the thought of such unethical behavior on the part of a doctor. That, however, is exactly what happens when an attorney asks for a contingency fee in taking on a client's case.

In every legal system in the advanced world an attorney's sole duty is to the interest of the client. When the amount of money an attorney stands to gain is a function of success or failure in the outcome of a case, that attorney faces an immoral conflict of interest.

For example, say an attorney has accepted a number of personal injury cases on a contingency fee basis and is offered a quick $1 million settlement by an insurance company in one of the cases. That attorney has to decide whether to advise the client to accept the settlement offer or not. Although an extra couple of months of work might get the client a much larger settlement, possibly $2 million, settling the case allows the attorney a quick $300,000 to $400,000 fee and will give him time to pursue the other cases. It is clearly in the attorney's interest to settle such a case, but it may well not be in the plaintiff's interest to do so, hence an impermissible conflict of interest.

What makes the attorney's conflict of interest worse is that the attorney's conflict affects the manner in which an insurance company deals with a claim. An insurance company that has concluded that a claim may well end up in a $2 million payment has an incentive to offer the attorney a quick $1 million, because the insurance company knows that a quick $1 million offer, resulting in an immediate $300,000 to $400,000 fee for the attorney, is so attractive to the attorney that the attorney may well accept the offer. The result is that the insured, not knowing the intricacies of insurance litigation, accepts the advice to settle for $1 million, in spite of the fact that the insured may well have a case that ought to settle for $2 million.

The forever returning conflict of interest found in so many aspects of American legal procedure is one of the most important deficiencies of the American legal system. The attorney who accepts a case on the basis of a contingency fee has an economic interest in the case. This economic interest destroys that attorney's ability to act independently and to give independent advice to the plaintiff.

Ironically, Rule 2.1 of the Model Rules of Professional Conduct of the American Bar Association requires that lawyers shall exercise independent professional judgment. How is independent professional judgment possible when the attorney's personal fortunes are dependent on the outcome of the case? How is independent professional judgment possible when an attorney has to advise a client whether to accept a settlement when that attorney's own financial well being depends on the advice he or she gives the client?

Americans are so used to the use of the contingency fee that they no longer pay attention to its insidious consequences. Yet the contingency fee corrupts the entire system. As we will see in the coming paragraphs, the only reason for the explosion of class-action suits in which the plaintiffs earn pennies and the attorneys millions or even hundreds of millions of dollars is the contingency fee. The only reason for the strike suits, the shareholder derivative suits, the asbestos suits, the tobacco suits, the malpractice suits is the contingency fee. The contingency fee has corrupted the American legal system to the point where fairness and equity has been forgotten and lawyering has deteriorated into a dirty, fee-driven business rather than a noble profession.

Extortionary Fees

The following is an e-mail dated June 22, 2003, from a claimant and addressed to Lester Brickman, a law professor at the Benjamin N. Cardozo School of Law:

> On March 2nd this year (2003) my family was hit head on by a snow plow pickup truck that crossed into our lane. My daughter and I were injured but my wife is paralyzed from the waist down and is still in rehabilitation at [a New Jersey hospital]. There is no issue of the other driver's culpability, there was a witness and he pleaded guilty to the summons for the failure to keep to the right. He is well insured with a commercial policy. How do I find an attorney who will work for time and expenses? I have resources to pay. All attorneys that I have contacted to date will only work on a contingency fee basis.

The above is a case in which the claimant can expect a very large amount of money as a result of a negotiated settlement. In more than 85 percent of cases like the one mentioned above, the claim will result in a negotiated settlement, meaning the case will never go to trial or end in a jury verdict. Moreover, because of the exceedingly high medical cost and life-changing injuries, cases similar to the one mentioned above will routinely result in settlements well in excess of $1 million and in many instances well over $10 million.

Why should an attorney in a case like this earn a minimum of $333,000 and possibly much more for merely negotiating a settlement when the facts are not in dispute? Attorneys who, in cases like the one mentioned above, insist on a contingency fee rather than charging hourly rates clearly engage in extortion. Despite wonderful sounding ethics codes that admonish lawyers to charge reasonable fees, the bar associations never discipline attorneys who charge plaintiffs extortionary fees, yet many contingency fees, if not most, are extortionary.

In 1995 the Senate Judiciary Committee held a hearing on "Contingency Fee Abuses." The committee received a letter from Dr. Antonio Falcon, a Texas physician, which is part of the record of the hearing. Dr. Falcon wrote on behalf of his friends, Gilberto and Rosario Alvarez, who did not speak or write English very well and whose daughter was involved in a medical malpractice action, which the defendant doctor did not contest. Dr. Falcon wrote, "Negligence was never an issue in the case and therefore there was no risk or contingency on behalf of the plaintiff lawyer—but the lawyer nevertheless treated it on a contingency fee basis and reaped a huge award." Dr. Falcon further wrote that the attorney handling the case "did virtually no work, yet still managed to receive 40 percent of the Alvarez damage award of $400,000. For writing three letters, [the attorney] was paid a lump sum of $160,846.07."

The case of the daughter of Gilberto and Rosario Alvarez is not unique. To the contrary, the record of such cases is replete with attorneys earning huge fees for hardly any work.

The Corrosive and Corrupting Influence of the Contingency Fee

Finally, as the remaining chapters will illustrate, in high-profile cases, such as asbestos or tobacco litigation or class-action suits, contingency fees do not merely amount to millions of dollars—in many cases they amount to billions of dollars. No surprise then that some of the top trial lawyers in the country are in jail because of fraud, not only because they did not represent their clients properly, but also because they fell for the temptation to use illegal and dishonest legal practices to achieve fraudulent victories and thereby earn their obscenely large contingency fees.

Access to the Courts

Sadly contingency fees do not guarantee access to the courts for plaintiffs who cannot afford attorneys' fees—the original intent and the very reason for the existence of the contingency fee—because attorneys charging a contingency fee routinely select only cases that are most likely to succeed. Poor plaintiffs who have no choice but to proceed on the basis of a contingency fee but have cases that are cumbersome and costly because they require extensive investigation are routinely turned away.

Today, whether the client is rich or poor, many attorneys will accept cases only on the basis of a contingency fee. The result is that the client will frequently recover much less than he or she would have recovered by paying the attorney the standard hourly fee. Moreover, the plaintiff who has an actionable but complicated and cumbersome case but doesn't have the resources to litigate the matter is turned away, whereas the plaintiff who has the resources to pay can only find an attorney who wants an exorbitant amount of money out of proportion to the legal work performed.

Since times immemorial—under old Roman law, under continental Napoleonic law and under British common law—an attorney is and has always been regarded a professional. He or she is an officer of the court, and remuneration has always been a function of the amount of time involved in handling the case.

Studies of earnings by contingency fee lawyers show that such earnings have increased exponentially in the last few decades. For many contingency fee attorneys, earnings today reach thousands of dollars per hour, clearly violating rules of ethical behavior with regard to reasonable fees.

Moreover, the range of acts that are considered tortuous has been greatly enlarged in the last twenty-five years. A good example can be found in asbestos cases. Use of asbestos in the 1950s and 1960s was not tortuous. At the time, nobody knew of the harmful effects of asbestos. Yet most asbestos manufacturers are today held liable for failure to warn users of the dangers of asbestos. How is a manufacturer to warn a user of a danger when the manufacturer is not aware of any danger? Not only has the range of acts that are considered tortuous greatly increased in the last twenty-five years, the amounts recovered—not only in the aggregate but in individual cases—have considerably increased as well.

Contingency fee proponents argue that, when an attorney takes a case on a contingency fee basis, the attorney is entitled to a higher fee to compensate for the risk of no recovery or low recovery. This flies in the face of the fact that few contingency fee cases ever go to trial—according to the US Department of Justice, more than 95 percent are settled out of court. In small claim liability cases, close to 100 percent of claims handled by attorneys on the basis of a contingency fee are settled out of court (see the chapter entitled "Settlement Mills"). Consequently, attorneys bear no meaningful risk of low or no recovery.

In many cases, attorneys even receive cash awards in excess of what the plaintiff receives. In personal injury cases, the plaintiff frequently receives a cash settlement plus a yearly amount of money to compensate for the effects of the injury. To illustrate how this can happen, in one such case, a paraplegic plaintiff received a $2.4 million settlement. The plaintiff received $80,000 in cash and a future yearly payment of $35,000 for life. However, the plaintiff's attorney received $800,000 in cash.

To illustrate how much more contingency fee attorneys earn when compared to non-contingency fee attorneys, a study by the Joint Economic Committee of Congress done in 2001 is informative. The study concluded that in 2001, combined attorneys' fees of plaintiff and defense attorneys in automobile accident cases totaled $16.74 billion. Plaintiff attorneys, nearly all working on a contingency fee basis, earned $11.93 billion, while defense attorneys, working on the basis of regular hourly fees, earned $4.82 billion.

The following chapters will show that the contingency fee is a major vice permeating and perverting significant elements of the American legal system. It is the most important problem in the abuse of class-action, strike, and shareholder derivative suits as well as malpractice litigation. Reining in the contingency fee practice will do wonders for fairness and equity in the American legal system and will go far in building respect for the system around the world. The contingency fee is so deeply ingrained in the American legal system, however, that I doubt its use is reversible.

State Attorneys General (AGs) and the Contingency Fee

As is usual when a novel procedure like the practice of contingency fees is introduced into the American legal system, there is the tendency for the bar to exploit the procedure and use it for purposes different from the original intent. And so it is with the contingency fee.

In the early 1980s, a number of creative lawyers in Massachusetts and Georgia approached their respective state attorneys general with the proposition to do legal work for the state on a contingency fee basis.

The practice is obviously suspect, because when attorneys are given a financial stake in the outcome of the government's business, there is an irreconcilable conflict of interest. As a *Wall Street Journal* editorial stated on April 16, 2009, "When outside lawyers are hired to do the government's business ... the state delegates key decisions—about whether and whom to sue, what legal theory to pursue, whether to settle and what remedy to propose—to private lawyers motivated by profit rather than the public interest."

Furthermore, the practice is "antithetical to the standard of neutrality that an attorney representing the government must meet" (words used by the California Supreme Court in a case in 1985).

The practice of state attorneys general hiring private law firms to do legal work for the state on a contingency fee basis originally met with great resistance. Not anymore—the tort bar has seen to that.

The trial bar swiftly got a good number of states to pass laws legalizing contingency fees for work on behalf of the state. Since the mideighties, contingency work by private law firms on behalf of various states, counties, municipalities, and various state agencies has exploded. As a matter of fact, representing state attorneys general on a contingency fee basis has turned into a racket. This incestuous relationship between attorneys general and private law firms, the sole purpose of which is to extract money from private enterprise to line the coffers of the law firms and the campaign funds of the politicians involved in the relationship, is another example of the tort bar pushing its tentacles into the highest levels of American state governments. All this goes on in the open, yet newspapers, except for the *Wall Street Journal*, rarely report on it. Consequently the public simply doesn't know this type of clearly unethical and despicable relationship between attorneys general and private lawyers even exists.

In 2006 Mr. Bailey, a partner in the Houston law firm of Bailey, Perrin & Bailey, came up with a brilliant and novel idea. Janssen Pharmaceuticals sells an antipsychotic drug called Risperdal. The Food and Drug Administration (FDA) believed that Janssen may have improperly marketed the drug for use not approved by the FDA.

Mr. Bailey heard about the FDA's suspicion and decided to sue. However, he did not want to go the cumbersome route of a class-action suit, in which case he would have had to assemble a class of plaintiffs who had used the drug. No, there was a much simpler way to earn the same gigantic fee a class-action suit might produce. Mr. Bailey went to the attorney general of the State of Pennsylvania and suggested that the State of Pennsylvania sue Janssen Pharmaceuticals and hire Bailey, Perrin & Bailey to bring the action against Janssen on behalf of the state. And Bailey, Perrin & Bailey was to be remunerated on the basis of a contingency fee.

When Mr. Bailey was successful in getting a contract with Pennsylvania (more about that later), he came up with another novel idea. If Janssen was sued not in one state but in a large number of states, the liability exposure of Janssen would be so great the company would certainly keel over and settle in a hurry. So Mr. Bailey went to the attorneys general of Louisiana, South Carolina, Arkansas, Mississippi, and New Mexico with the same proposition. Indeed, all the states' AGs Mr. Bailey approached agreed to hire Bailey, Perrin & Bailey. A brilliant strategy, you would say, but wait until you hear the rest of the story.

As I explained in Part I, every state attorney general is on a career path. Most are on their way, or attempting to be on their way, to becoming state governors, from which position they may jump to the United States Senate or even the presidency. But such a career objective takes money, lots of money.

When Mr. Bailey first approached the Pennsylvania attorney general (a Republican), he was turned down. Mr. Bailey then made considerable campaign contributions to Pennsylvania Governor Ed Rendell's (a Democrat) campaign. In a highly unusual procedure, Governor Rendell then decided to overrule the Pennsylvania attorney general and make the decision himself whether to appoint Bailey, Perrin & Bailey to bring the Janssen suit. After receiving $91,000 in campaign contributions from Bailey, Perrin & Bailey, Governor Rendell appointed Bailey, Perrin & Bailey to bring the suit.

Mr. Bailey then contributed $75,000 to the election campaign of Mississippi Attorney General Jim Hood, a Democrat, and received a contingency fee contract from Mississippi to sue Janssen; he contributed $50,000 to the election campaign of New Mexico Attorney General Gary King, a Democrat, and received a contingency fee contract from New Mexico to sue Janssen; he contributed 20,000 to the election campaign of Louisiana Attorney General Buddy Caldwell, a Democrat, and received a contingency fee contract from Louisiana to sue Janssen; and, finally, he contributed $60,000 to the party of Arkansas Attorney General Dustin

McDaniel, a Democrat, and received a contingency fee contract from Arkansas to sue Janssen.

Mr. Bailey also contributed $85,000 to the Attorneys General Association and contributed $100,000 to the Democratic Governors Association. These political contributions were all paid just weeks before or just weeks after the contingency fee contracts to sue Janssen were awarded to Bailey, Perrin & Bailey.

In violation of every state's rule that contracts with the state are awarded after open bidding, all the contracts to sue Janssen Pharmaceuticals were no-bid contracts—other law firms were not asked to bid for these contracts. The attorneys general conveniently claim that the no-bid rules do not apply to legal services!

The attorneys general involved vehemently deny any relationship between the donations of Bailey, Perrin & Bailey and the awarding of the no-bid contracts, contracts that stand Bailey, Perrin & Bailey to earn millions and millions of dollars in contingency fees.

Janssen is petitioning the Pennsylvania Supreme Court to annul the appointment of Bailey, Perrin & Bailey on the basis of the same arguments used in the California Supreme Court in a case in 1985: conduct "antithetical to the standard of neutrality that an attorney representing the government must meet." The Pennsylvania Supreme Court has agreed to hear the case.

Let us remind ourselves that, when the reader gives a policeman a ten-dollar bill to squash a traffic ticket, it is called a bribe, and the reader may go to jail. If the reader gives an attorney general, the top policeman in the state, $50,000, it's a political donation—a cynic would call it pay-to-play—and the reader doesn't go to jail; the reader receives a multimillion dollar state contract instead.

Just in case the reader might think the Bailey pay-to-sue business is an exception, the law firm Motley Rice of South Carolina did exactly the same in a case they brought on behalf of the attorney general in Rhode Island to whom they had given campaign contributions. Motley Rice filed and won a multibillion dollar suit against three out-of-state paint manufacturers. The verdict was, however, reversed by the Rhode Island Supreme Court.

The issue of state attorneys general subcontracting the state's legal work to private law firms on a contingency basis without the normal bid process points again to the extraordinary lack of ethics and the dismal culture among even the highest lawyers, the highest law enforcement officers in our states. The fact that an attorney general simply rules that the law requiring open bidding for state contracts does not apply to legal work, thereby placing him or herself above the law, is simply perplexing. And the fact that all attorneys general who have subcontracted legal work and have received campaign contributions from law firms just before or just after appointing these firms have strenuously denied that such contributions have anything to do with the attorneys general granting the legal work is obviously a blatant mischaracterization of the facts. Any serious person will agree that such statements are complete and total falsehoods.

It is obvious there is never an explicit quid pro quo. Of all people, lawyers know how to avoid a quid pro quo because a real quid pro quo constitutes a felony. Yet everybody knows there was, or is, at least an understanding. When attorneys general, in televised press conferences, flatly deny, with a straight face, any impropriety in both the awarding of the contracts and the campaign contributions, when the attorneys general themselves so flauntingly show contempt for the law, how can we expect others lower down the line to have respect for the law? Here again we find that attorneys general, in their quests for political careers, will do anything unethical to advance their careers, even if bending the law—the very law they are sworn to uphold—is what is necessary.

Some hopeful news on the contingency front came recently in a California case, *County of Santa Clara v. Atlantic Richfield*, in which the county was represented by private contingency fee attorneys. Defendants cited the California State Supreme Court opinion mentioned above. Judge Komar agreed and disqualified the private attorneys. The matter is on appeal. Furthermore, President Bush, prior to leaving office, signed an executive order barring the federal government from entering into contingency fee agreements with trial lawyers.

7.

Class Action

Class action is a form of litigation to determine a remedy for an injury on behalf of a large number of people whose complaints are similar in law or in fact. Many authors and legal commentators claim that this form of litigation landed on the shores of America with the Pilgrims—they find its foundation in British common law. I have found no evidence that class action has ever been a form of litigation in Great Britain. Furthermore, in the United States, class action was never part of case law until 1820, when it was mentioned in a US court of appeals decision. In 1833, Equity Rule 48, the real precursor of today's class-action procedure, was promulgated, which allowed for representative suits in cases where there were too many plaintiffs

In the average civil dispute, an injured person files suit with the help of an attorney who is an officer of the court. On paper, a class action looks as if a group of injured persons have banded together and have collectively hired an attorney to help them litigate their grievance. That appearance, however, creates the wrong impression.

In a class action, it usually is the attorney who is the plaintiff. It is the attorney who takes the initiative for the lawsuit. It is the attorney who files the suit with the help of the allegedly injured persons. In many cases it is the attorney who tells the people they have been injured, followed by the proposition that they should hire him or her to obtain relief. The injured persons are told the attorney will not charge anything since the attorney will simply take a percentage of the monies paid in remedy (i.e., a contingency fee).

Being in essence both the plaintiff and the plaintiff's attorney is of course an impermissible conflict of interest in practically every legal system in the world. Not so in America, where in the practice of law, conflicts of interest are de rigueur.

Class action in America is an illness. It is an explosive cancer, slowly and gradually invading every aspect of American society. It eats away at the body politic. Moreover, financial rewards for attorneys in class-action lawsuits are so outrageously large that they corrupt even the most successful and the most powerful attorneys. No surprise then that the number of class actions being filed in state and federal courts is growing every year.

Class action, originally meant to determine a remedy for an injury on behalf of a large number of people whose complaints were similar, has grown into a legal procedure against companies that engage in actions causing minor harm to a lot of individuals. The action is supposedly needed because, without the class action, such companies might not be held accountable for that harm. If a harmed individual can only expect a small recovery, the small recovery does not provide sufficient incentive for that individual to bring action against the company. Consequently, the company would not face any consequences for the harm it caused. By combining all the parties with similar complaints against the company into one lawsuit, the company can be held accountable for the harm caused. In most other legal systems, however, that company is held accountable through government oversight, through criminal proceedings or fines, or by other remedies, not by lawyers assembling a large number of claimants with potentially small recoveries.

In the United States, where attorneys write the laws, it is only too logical that trial attorneys prefer a system whereby the offending party is forced to reimburse individuals for their injuries, even if the injured person receives pennies for his or her injury. By being able to combine the claims of thousands of injured persons, the aggregate of the pennies each individual is entitled to add up to millions of dollars, allowing the attorneys a massive amount of compensation in the form of a contingency fee if the case is successful.

Regarding the power of class-action attorneys, the asbestos class-action cases that have wound their way through the American courts are illustrative. By far the largest number of class-action cases involving one single issue are about asbestos.

For many years, asbestos was used as a cheap insulating agent against heat and electricity. Scores of companies, large and small, either manufactured products using the material or used it in construction projects. When it became clear that airborne carcinogenic asbestos fibers were being inhaled and that they were too large for the lungs to eject, resulting in lung cancer, the class-action tort bar feasted on an orgy of lawsuits. The vast majority of large companies that had been involved in asbestos manufacturing or its use had no choice but to file for bankruptcy.

In the United States, there are various forms of bankruptcy. In a Chapter 11 bankruptcy, a company's debts are frozen while the company is allowed to reorganize in an attempt to regain its viability. Nearly all asbestos-related bankruptcies are Chapter 11 cases.

In a Chapter 11 situation, a bankruptcy judge becomes more or less the chairman of the board of the company, and the creditors form a committee that can be compared to a board of directors. The bankruptcy judge cannot approve any reorganization or any plan for the company to reemerge from Chapter 11 without the approval of 75 percent of the creditors.

Since the asbestos claims frequently amount to more than 75 percent of the company's debts, the class-action attorneys, allegedly representing the majority of creditors and therefore the de facto board of directors of the company, have complete control over the company's actions. The company has become hostage to anything the class-action attorneys want. Consequently—and as we have seen above, in class-action suits the attorney is in effect not only the plaintiff but also the attorney for the plaintiff—he or she is frequently also in complete control of the opposing party. When all is said and done, it is the class-action attorney who walks away with an exorbitant share of the money paid in remedy.

Finally, very few class-action suits go to trial. Trying such cases is exceedingly expensive for both plaintiffs' attorneys as well as the defendant. Moreover, the defendant's risk of an outrageous jury verdict is a constant incentive to settle the case. Since most class-action cases do not go to trial, the settlement value of the cases often has little or no relationship to the settlement value a trial might produce. Consequently, class-action cases tend to settle for what Janet Cooper Alexander, the Frederick I. Richman Professor of Law at Stanford University, calls the "going rate," an amount divorced from the class-action claim's underlying merit.

Attorney Richard Scruggs, the king of all tort lawyers, not only revolutionized but also corrupted American tort law during the 1980s and 1990s. He did so not only by representing one client at a time but, with the assistance of a few attorneys around the country, assembled thousands and thousands of plaintiffs, combined them into a so-called class of plaintiffs, and went after big companies, such as construction companies over asbestos use, pharmaceuticals over ill-performing drugs, and tobacco companies over health costs.

In the largest case ever settled in the United States, in 1998 Scruggs, on behalf of forty-six states, forced the tobacco companies into a $206 billion settlement to reimburse the states for health expenditures as a result of tobacco use, earning him a cool $1 billion in the process.

As well as paying other attorneys and law firms money to assist him in setting up classes of plaintiffs, Mr. Scruggs paid scores of intermediaries to help him with legislative, political, or legal arrangements. In addition to his well-paid intermediaries, Mr. Scruggs had top-notch political connections. Trent Lott, the former majority leader in the United States Senate, is his brother-in-law.

Members of the US Senate nominate candidates for federal judgeships. At one point during Mr. Scruggs's career he suggested through an intermediary to a circuit county judge by the name of Bobby DeLaughter, who was adjudicating a fee dispute Scruggs had with other attorneys, that he could arrange for such a federal judgeship. Shortly thereafter, Mr. Lott's office called Judge DeLaughter to discuss the position.

Soon after the phone call, an outside expert hired by Judge DeLaughter to assist him in adjudicating the fee dispute recommended that Scruggs owed his associate $15 million. Instead of following the advice of the outside expert, Judge De Laughter ruled in favor of Scruggs and awarded Scruggs's associate only $1.5 million.

Scruggs's career as the king of class-action lawsuits began when Scruggs's law school classmate became the attorney general in Mississippi. The attorney general hired Scruggs to sue users of asbestos on behalf of the state of Mississippi, arguing that asbestos users should pay to remove the material from state buildings. Mr. Scruggs took the case on the basis of a contingency fee and earned his first $5 million.

Mr. Scruggs, however, was accused of receiving preferential treatment from the attorney general in return for generous campaign contributions by Scruggs to that attorney general. To solve this problem, Mr. Scruggs hired Pete Johnson, a former state auditor, to push through legislation authorizing the attorney general to hire private firms on a contingency fee basis. Mr. Johnson, court documents show, was promised a handsome reward if the legislation was successful. It indeed was.

As a result of the astronomical amounts of money Mr. Scruggs earned in fees, fee disputes with Mr. Scruggs's associates became the order of the day. Time and again, associates had to sue Scruggs for their share of the fees. It finally caught up with him.

After hurricane Katrina, Scruggs assembled thousands of plaintiffs to sue insurance companies to pay for damage to or destruction of homes caused by water. Although water damage was specifically excluded in hurricane insurance policies, Scruggs argued that the damage was the result of wind, not water. In early 2007 State Farm Insurance settled out of court, and Scruggs and his associates earned $26.5 million in fees. Scruggs paid his associates $1.6 million, whereupon the associates sued Scruggs for a larger share of the bounty. Scruggs, his son, and three other partners, attempting to devise a way to beat the associates, decided to bribe the judge to whom the case had been assigned. During the negotiations over the bribe, the judge went to the FBI, which proceeded to wiretap all further communications between the judge and the Scruggs group. Total payments to the judge, all wiretapped, amounted to $50,000.

Recently Richard "Dickie" Scruggs, the king of torts and the CEO of the Scruggs Class Action Criminal Enterprise, pleaded guilty to bribing a judge. He lost his law license and was sentenced to five years in jail.

Since his sentencing, other cases are falling into place. One involves Judge Bobby DeLaughter, the judge who ruled for Scruggs in awarding his opponent $1.5 million instead of $15 million as the expert consultant had recommended. On July 30, 2009, Judge DeLaughter pleaded guilty to obstruction of justice charges and lying to the FBI in various bribery cases.

To get some idea of how high up corruption in class-action cases has reached, Judge DeLaughter is a former prosecutor, a past president of the Mississippi Prosecutors' Association, and a former member of the board of directors of the National District Attorneys Association. Judge DeLaughter has been honored as one of *Mississippi Magazine's* fifteen great Mississippians and was a lawyer-in-residence at Pepperdine Law School.

Class Action Goes Abroad

If jackpot class-action cases in the United States can earn an attorney millions and millions of dollars, why stop at the borders of the United States of America? After all, especially since the second world war, scores of large American companies have operated all over the world.

Forget about Europe. US attorneys launching class-action cases wouldn't be welcome in European courts. Forget about southeast Asia. Jurisdictions like Singapore, Malaysia, Thailand, South Korea, or Japan abhor legal corruption and simply dismiss the judicial attempts to destroy large corporations by nefarious means commonly employed by American attorneys.

The obvious place to take class-action suits was Central America and a few countries in South America. Countries like Nicaragua, Honduras, Guatemala, and Ecuador, poor countries with corrupt civil and judicial authorities, countries with large numbers of poor, uneducated peasants, countries where bribes are a way of life, are places where large US mining companies, oil companies, and food service companies (fruit and vegetables) have been active for years. Those countries are like paradise; low-hanging, juicy class-action apples are there for the picking.

During the second half of the last century, Texaco operated an oil field called Shushufindi 61 in the Ecuadorian jungle. In 1977 Petroecuador, the Ecuadorian national oil company, bought a 62.5 percent stake in the operation while Texaco continued to operate the field. In 1992 Petroecuador took over the entire operation and Texaco left Ecuador.

In 1993 a class-action suit was filed against Texaco on behalf of no fewer than thirty thousand Ecuadorians. The suit alleged that Texaco had dumped billions of gallons of waste that needed to be cleaned up and that compensation was due to the indigenous Indian people who had been displaced because of the oil company's operations. Time and again, American courts ruled they had no jurisdiction.

However, Texaco did enter into negotiations with the Ecuadorian government to clean up the dumps. The parties agreed Texaco would clean up 161 sites at a cost of $40 million. In 1998 the work was completed, and the Ecuadorian government signed an agreement with Texaco releasing Texaco from any and all further liability.

In 2003 the original plaintiffs filed a $6 billion claim against Chevron (which had acquired Texaco in 2001) in Ecuador under a new Ecuadorian environmental law that is very specifically not a retroactive law. The Ecuadorian court appointed an "expert" by the name of Ricardo Cabrera, whose four thousand-page report argued that Texaco was not liable for $6 billion but $27.3 billion: $9.5 billion in compensation for 1400 deaths from cancer, $8.4 billion for unjust enrichment by Texaco, and the remainder for further environmental cleanup.

As for the claim for $9.5 billion in compensation for 1400 deaths, in 2007 US federal judge William Alsup ruled that there was no scientific evidence supporting claims that the pollution caused cancer. The judge went as far as imposing sanctions, including a $45,000 fine, against three attorneys who were part of the lawsuit against Texaco and Chevron. The plaintiffs' attorneys had cited three cases of cancer as proof for their claim. Chevron's attorneys produced evidence that the first one had never been diagnosed with breast cancer, that the second one, a woman, had falsely claimed her son had leukemia, and that the third one had admitted he had no injuries whatsoever. All evidence had been fabricated.

In its ruling, the court wrote, "This is not the first evidence of possible misconduct by plaintiffs' counsel in this case. It is clear to the court that this case was manufactured by plaintiffs' counsel for reasons other than to seek a recovery on plaintiffs' behalf. This litigation is likely a smaller piece of some larger scheme against defendants."

As for the claim of $8.4 billion for unjust enrichment by Texaco, Texaco's total profits from operating the Shushufindi 61 field amounted to $497 million. The Ecuadorian government, however, received $25.3 billion in royalties and taxes.

The Ecuadorian judge who is expected to rule later has clearly indicated that he is sympathetic to the plaintiffs. If the court grants the claim, the US attorneys will file suit in a US court to collect on the verdict—more often than not, US courts respect verdicts from courts in other countries. If the attorneys win this case, they will receive some $5 billion in compensation!

Since the writing of this chapter, Chevron issued the following press releases:

September 7, 2009: Chevron Provides Ecuador Authorities Evidence in Bribe Plot

September 23, 2009: Chevron Files International Arbitration Against the Government of Ecuador over Violations

February 9, 2010: Court Appointee in Chevron Ecuador Lawsuit Tied to Ecuador State-Owned Oil Company

March 30, 2010: Chevron Wins Arbitration Claim Against the Government of Ecuador

April 5, 2010: Plaintiff's Expert Reveals Fraud by Lawyers in Ecuador Lawsuit

May 24, 2010: Proceedings Reveal New Evidence of Fraud and Plaintiff's Undisclosed Links to Ecuadorian Court Expert Richard Cabrera

August 6, 2010: Chevron Files Petition in Ecuador Seeking Dismissal of Lawsuit

Dole, the largest fruit and vegetable company in the world, has operations all over Central America. As is the case with all agricultural companies, Dole used the pesticide DBCP in its banana fields. It discontinued the use of the pesticide when it became clear it might be harmful to human health.

Nicaragua passed a law in 2001 tailor made for alleged victims of DBCP. Shortly thereafter American attorneys, with the help of Nicaraguan attorneys, won a $490 million suit in a Nicaraguan court against Dole as well as Dow Chemical and Shell, makers of the pesticide. The attorneys then sued in US court to collect on the Nicaraguan judgment.

I have spent a lot of time going over the records of this case—many posted on the Internet—and can write a book about it. But the reader wouldn't believe me, thinking that I was writing a movie script for a fictional case about a mafia-inspired criminal conspiracy. Consequently, let me just quote sections of the Californian court's verdict in dismissing the case on behalf of Nicaraguan plaintiffs who had falsely claimed they were sterile as a result of exposure to DBCP on Dole's banana farms thirty years ago:

"[There is] clear and convincing evidence that the plaintiffs and certain of their attorneys [Nicaraguan *and* American] fabricated their claims, engaged in a long running conspiracy to commit fraud on the court, used threats of violence to frighten witnesses and suppress the truth, and conspired with corrupt Nicaraguan judges to use a targeted Nicaraguan statute to deprive Dole and other companies of due process."

The findings go on to state that "the court was presented with detailed, undisputed testimony … [that Los Angeles–based trial attorneys and Nicaraguan counsel] … conspired and colluded with other DBCP plaintiffs' lawyers & Nicaraguan laboratories and corrupt Nicaraguan judges in position to influence the outcome of DPCP cases. The purpose of this conspiracy was to manufacture evidence and improperly influence DBCP cases pending in Nicaragua and the United States to obtain millions of dollars in judgments that would then be enforced in the US and possibly elsewhere."

And as if this isn't enough, the court goes on to describe the conspiracy of the lawyers in further detail:

> They ... and others ... conspired to (a) recruit fraudulent plaintiffs, (b) use scripts, videos and brochures to educate plaintiffs about life and work on banana farms—teaching them to lie about life and work on banana farms that they never did, (c) conduct 'field trips' to see the physical layout of the farms, (d) falsify employment documents, (e) falsify medical records related to sterility testing, (f) suppress evidence of children born to plaintiffs claiming sterility, (g) making payments to persons in exchange for falsified documents, (h) conduct meetings with a Nicaraguan judge to manufacture evidence, to 'Jinx' the outcomes of court cases in Nicaragua, resulting in hundreds of millions of dollars in judgments, (i) threaten violence against witnesses and their families and investigators, and (j) air radio broadcasts telling listeners not to cooperate with investigators.

Before the California court ruling, a number of companies with operations in Nicaragua had already succumbed to lawsuits and settled out of court for millions of dollars!

I have argued before that the amount of money attorneys earn in class-action cases has no relationship to the legal work performed. In the Texaco/Chevron litigation, because of the many hearings and appeals involved, the contingency fee would normally be 50 percent of the amount recovered. Since the claim against Chevron is for close to $30 billion, if successful, the payout to attorneys would be $15 billion. Even if the amount were reduced on appeal, as often happens in such high-damage cases, the amounts involved are so astronomical as to guarantee that criminal elements in society would conspire to enter the class-action contingency fee racket. And since the self-regulating bar is essentially unregulated (particularly when attorneys operate outside our borders in the corrupt environment of Central America), criminal elements in the bar find their way into class-action lawyering.

Criminal enterprises like extortion rackets, drug trafficking, or prostitution attract the fringes of society who prefer the thrill and excitement of a criminal career and its potential riches over the hard work and sometimes drab aspects of private enterprise or a profession.

In class action, however, it is a *lawyer* who, attracted by the prospect of unimaginable riches, succumbs to the temptation to pervert the legal process to assure victory—the lawyer who, as an officer of the court, should be in the vanguard of those whose task it is to protect the foundations of our legal system.

8.

Class Action and the Contingency Fee

Class-action lawsuits combined with the practice of contingency fees make for a toxic brew. It is the contingency fee, however, that is the most poisonous ingredient in this unhealthy potion.

Take the class-action suit involving the more than nine thousand 9/11 World Trade Center rescue workers who filed suit against ninety government and private entities alleging that contaminants at the site made them ill. Plaintiffs include firefighters, police officers, and construction workers. Most of these men and women are members of firefighters, police, or other labor unions.

When, after 9/11, evidence surfaced that many of the firefighters, police officers, and construction workers who had been involved in the rescue and cleanup operations were becoming ill, a large number of class-action lawsuits were filed that were later combined into one action.

A settlement in that action was announced in June of 2010. The settlement provided for approximately $712 million to be paid out to the more than nine thousand claimants and approximately $178 million (or 25 percent of the award) to be paid as a contingency fee to the attorneys.

The suit was originally filed in September of 2004. Assuming the lawsuit was one full year in preparation, the attorneys will receive $178 million for six years of work. Imagine for a moment that the fire fighters union, together with the police officer unions and construction unions, had initiated the suit on behalf of their members and paid attorneys a normal hourly fee rather than a contingency fee. What amount of legal assistance could they have bought for $178 million? How many hours of work by the very best lawyers in the country would have been available to them for even half of the $178 million contingency fee?[47]

Assuming an hourly attorney fee of $400,[48] the $178 million legal fee the attorneys will earn in the 9/11 workers class-action case will buy 445,000 hours of work from some of the very best lawyers in the country. Assuming a lawyer works 1,920 hours a year, $178 million will buy you the services of forty of the very best lawyers in the nation working full time on nothing else but the 9/11 workers case for a full six years.

Consequently, had the unions been allowed to represent their members in the 9/11 health case by using their in-house lawyers or outside lawyers on the basis of an hourly fee, these unions could have hired twenty of the best lawyers in the nation to work full time on this case for a full six years and would have saved $89 million dollars that would have been available to the 9/11 workers, who need the money more than the lawyers. But the unions are not allowed to represent their members in this matter.

The question arises why the class-action attorneys have to earn $178 million. Why should it be this way? The issues are not in dispute. Way back in 2004, Congress had already set up a federally financed insurance fund, called the WTC Captive Insurance Company, with a one billion dollar FEMA grant.

Why then do injured firemen, police officers, and construction workers at the 9/11 site have to give up so many millions of dollars that could pay for the cost of health care associated with their work to millionaire lawyers whose task it is to negotiate a fair way to distribute the one billion dollars congress has set aside for the injured 9/11 workers? Doctors who are treating the 9/11 workers get paid an hourly fee. Why shouldn't the

---

47 An earlier settlement agreement rejected by Judge Hellerstein of the United States District Court in Manhattan awarded the lawyers a $220 million contingency fee, 33 percent of the award.

48 Attorneys' fees vary widely from state to state to state and from large to small law firms. However, $400 an hour is the average fee charged by the larger law firms for an attorney with fifteen years of experience.

lawyers helping the 9/11 workers get paid an hourly fee? The answer is the contingency fee.

To give the reader an idea of the world of contingency fee law firms, let's examine the law firm that negotiated the $712 million award and the $178 million lawyers' fee in the case of the 9/11 workers. That law firm is Worby Groner Edelman LLP of White Plains New York. [49] Worby Groner Edelman, according to their website, which touts their legal services, is a ten-attorney law firm. The firm won't earn the entire $178 million fee all for themselves, as they will have to share a good chunk of the fee with other lawyers in the syndicate that represented the nine thousand workers. However, on their website Worby Groner Edelman announces other settlements they have recently won for their clients, mostly awards they do not have to share with other law firms, as Worby Groner Edelman was the only firm representing the client.

According to their website, Worby Groner Edelman recently won the following rewards for their clients:

Motor Vehicle Accidents
- $2,581,741 awarded for reckless trooper causing fatal crash
- $14,596,343* to a boy hit by a van[50]
- $2,451,033* in a truck crossover accident
- $2,435,967* for negligence by school bus and truck drivers
- $3,000,000 in a car and truck collision
- $72,500 for a fractured wrist injury resulting from an auto accident
- $20,000 for a pinky finger injury sustained in a car accident

Medical Malpractice Lawsuits
- $43,000,000* for the negligent delivery of a baby
- $9,262,794* for OB/GYN negligence
- $8,778,911* for hospital negligence in treating an auto accident fracture
- $1,675,000 for failure to treat a spinal infection

49 Worby Groner Edelman formed a joint venture company, Worby Groner Edelman & Napoli Bern, to handle the 9/11 case.
50 Awards with a * represent expected lifetime payouts

- $2,450,000* for improper catheter placement
- $7,181,700* for negligent treatment of a blood disorder

Construction Accidents / Premises Liability
- $7,900,000 to a laborer injured on a rooftop
- $4,675,000 in a scaffold accident
- $2,400,000 to a carpenter injured at a construction site
- $4,176,676* to a worker who fell off a roof
- $66,000 for an ankle sprain due to an uneven elevator
- $85,000 for an elbow fracture caused by a slip on ice

Miscellaneous Personal Injury Cases
- $10,316,058* for improper roadway repair
- $7,172,017* for negligent daycare supervision
- $5,050,000 for unsafe design by an auto manufacturer
- $2,175,000 for defective design of salt spreader truck resulting in worker's death
- $85,000 for a scar resulting from a dog bite
- $60,000 for poor supervision of children at a school

In addition, the Worby Groner Edelman website claims that the law firm achieved, or is working on, the following verdicts or settlements:

- $18 million negligence award believed to be county's largest
- $30 million suit in school bus death
- $1 million award for bad diagnosis by a doctor

The total amount of published awards Worby Groner Edelman recently earned for their clients in addition to the fee earned in the World Trade Center case amounts to $141,666,740. If Worby Groner Edelman received a pretty standard 35 percent of the awards as a contingency fee, Worby Groner Edelman recently earned, in addition to the World Trade Center fee, $49,583,359 in contingency fees, or close to $5 million per attorney in the ten-attorney firm.

The amount of money contingency fee lawyers extract from the US economy is simply astronomical. Law websites announcing contingency fee victories read like advertisements for the Football Hall of Fame. Law firm after law firm boasts about the millions and millions of dollars they have won either in settlements or by persuading a jury that playing Robin Hood is the highest calling in the land. State attorney associations elect the attorney of the year not by touting brilliant legal work but by touting the amount of money earned in settlements or awards. Some even elect the young attorney of the year, the freshman lawyer who has won the largest amount of money.

Money and the contingency fee are driving the American legal system. Money and the contingency fee are the cancer invading and destroying the system. Neither fairness and equity, nor equal justice under the law, nor professionalism is what motivates the tort lawyer—rather, he or she is motivated by an unadulterated, unregulated thirst for the contingency fee.

9.

The Strike Suit

In a strike suit, plaintiffs allege fraud on the part of senior executives of a company that has caused the company's share price to go down, resulting in a loss for the shareholders. The class-action attorneys then file a class-action suit against the officers of the company on behalf of the shareholders. After the company has been sued, the attorneys negotiate a settlement and extract huge amounts of money (an average of close to $200 million per case) from these companies, in the process earning millions of dollars by taking 33 percent or more of the amount paid in settlement.

The law firm Milberg, Weiss, Bershad, Hynes & Lerach, commonly called Milberg Weiss, was for years the premier law firm in what is called the strike suit. Mel Weiss presided over the firm's office in New York and Bill Lerach over the office in San Diego.

Milberg Weiss always presented itself as the defender of the little guy, the poor shareholder who was duped by the shenanigans of the criminal corporate executives. During the thirty-odd years leading up to 2008, Milberg Weiss extracted $45 billion from its prey, most of it after 1985, earning the firm and its fellow attorneys approximately $15 billion in the process. By the early 1990s, the number of class-action security cases filed by Milberg Weiss was greater than the total number of strike suit cases filed by all other securities law firms in the United States.

The irony of the shareholder lawsuits is that these lawsuits are definitely not in the shareholders' interest. They are ostensibly filed to defend the shareholders against corporate mismanagement. The payment extracted from the company, however, is at the shareholders' expense—the shareholders in effect sue themselves and then pay themselves. However, in the process they lose the cost of litigation and the outsized contingency fees. In a strike suit, the shareholders are always worse off after the case is settled than before the lawsuit was filed.

Why then do these shareholders file these suits? The answer is that, in reality, they do not file these suits. It is the class-action lawyers who in effect drum up a few shareholders in a particular company, promise these shareholders a nice amount of money when all is said and done, and then use these shareholders' names to file the suit. They only need a few shareholders to commit who then, supposedly, sue on behalf of all shareholders.

These so-called named shareholders often own only ten or fifteen shares in the company, amounting in some cases to less than a hundred dollars. After the case has been filed, the attorneys own the suit; they manage the suit, they finance the suit, and they make all the decisions how to proceed.

Like the Cosa Nostra, law firms in many class-action cases form syndicates with other law firms and negotiate prior to forming the syndicate how the proceeds will be divided among the participating firms (see the Toyota and BP class-action suits mentioned later). Time and again, the law firms in question feel cheated by their partners in the syndicate and go to court to sue for a larger share of the loot.

In 2007 the Milberg Weiss law firm was lead counsel in seventeen strike suits. Corporations coughed up a total of $3.8 billion in these seventeen suits, an average of $190 million per case, and all cases settled out of court. The fees paid to the lawyers in these cases were in excess of $1 billion. As we will see later, each case was the result of pure fraud, not on the part of the defendants, as you might expect, but on the part of Melvyn Weiss.

In 2003 a few named members of the classes of plaintiffs Milberg Weiss had put together to go after various companies started to talk. When the US attorney's office in Los Angeles investigated, it became clear that most of the lawsuits filed by Milberg Weiss over the years were fraudulent.

Lead counsel status in a class-action lawsuit is of paramount importance. When alleged wrongdoing on the part of a company is ripe for a class-action lawsuit, the law firm that recruits the largest number of members of the class and is first in filing the case in court usually becomes lead counsel.

A law firm that is lead counsel in a class-action lawsuit is entitled to the largest share of the fee when the case is finished.

In an investigation that took more than five years, Los Angeles prosecutors revealed that class members in most of Milberg Weiss's cases were never harmed. They consequently had no standing in the cases the firm had filed. As a matter of fact, a number of members of the classes of plaintiffs in Milberg Weiss's lawsuits were on Milberg Weiss's payroll— they were in the employ of Milberg Weiss. They simply served as people who, on Milberg Weiss's behalf, bought a small amount of shares in every new IPO, primarily IPOs of Silicon Valley's 1980s and 1990s exploding technology companies, or they served as standbys ready to immediately buy shares in companies whose stock was expected to drop. The persons in Milberg Weiss's employ who owned shares in IPOs or had bought shares in other companies on the instructions of Milberg Weiss were ready at all times to sign up as named plaintiffs to represent absent class members when the stock in any of those companies dropped.

Milberg Weiss paid these phony plaintiffs millions of dollars in kickback money to perform their roles. Melvyn Weiss, the senior partner in the firm, personally netted $210 million from these fraudulent lawsuits. Kickbacks to the fraudulent plaintiffs amounted to $11.3 million.

In 2008 William Lerach and Melvyn Weiss pleaded guilty to the kickback scheme. Lerach was sentenced to a fine of $8 million and two years in jail, Weiss to 2 1/2 years in jail and a $10 million fine.

The saga of Milberg Weiss and in particular the two partners Melvyn Weiss and William Lerach, which began in the late 1970s and ended with their convictions in 2008, illustrates vividly what is wrong with the American legal system. It clearly shows the deficient culture of certain aspects of American justice.

First and foremost, class-action strike suits are perfectly legal under American law and civil procedure. Yet they are most often a smoke screen for blackmail in its purest form. Defending a strike suit is so expensive, and the threat of a trial that may take months is so utterly disruptive to a company that even if that company is completely innocent of the charges alleged in the suit, it has little choice but to settle. The inconvenience to management and company directors who must spend days and weeks on end defending themselves is so threatening that a company willing to fight a strike suit would risk not being able to attract competent directors. Furthermore, losing a strike suit in court means the cost of the company's directors' and officers' insurance (liability insurance that covers losses as a result of alleged wrongful acts while acting on behalf of a company) would skyrocket, which is another reason why a company hit by a strike suit would normally prefer to settle the case by attempting to buy off the opposing attorneys.

Defense attorneys usually advise the management and directors of a company hit by a strike suit to settle. That's why the entire process is nothing more than blackmail or extortion.

A clear illustration of strike suits being tantamount to blackmail is a suit Lerach filed in 1992 against Alliance Pharmaceutical Company. The young company was in the process of developing a blood substitute called Oxygent. At one point, the Food and Drug Administration asked some questions about the company's testing procedures. As a result of the inquiry, the company temporarily delayed the clinical trials, an event that caused the company's stock to drop. The company's management was stunned by Lerach's suit, as nothing out of the ordinary had happened.

Ted Roth, one of the company's directors, knew Lerach. Roth's daughter and Lerach's daughter were friends and sometimes spent the night at each other's homes. Roth went to see Lerach to explain that nothing was amiss, that the company would fully cooperate with Lerach, and that the clinical trials would soon resume. Lerach's answer, according to Patrick Dillon and Carl Cannon in their book *Circle of Greed* was, "I don't give a fuck about the merits. We've already calculated the damages—and it's $10 million to $15 million. If you want to talk about a settlement, we can negotiate."

Roth replied, "Bill, look who you are talking to."

Lerach cut him off. "As I told you, this is not personal. It is business."[51]

In just one simple sentence, Lerach described the essence of shareholder class-action lawsuits. "I don't give a fuck about the merits ... It is business." Merits are not important, Lerach seems to be saying; fairness and equity is what the law is all about, but this isn't about the law. This is about business.

---

51 Patrick Dillon and Carl Cannon. *Circle of Greed, The Spectacular Rise and Fall of the Lawyer Who Brought Corporate America to Its Knees*. New York: Broadway Books, 2010

The huge amount of money a company that is the target of a strike suit has to spend to defend itself and the operational disruptions the company has to endure are in large part the result of pretrial discovery. In the pretrial discovery phase of a strike suit (which, as a I mentioned before, is a perfectly legal process under American law), the target company might as well close down and make its entire files, often covering years and years of operation, available to the class-action attorneys. Not only its files but most of its management and senior employees will have to be available for depositions. And each time the strike suit attorneys take a deposition or look at the company's files, the company's defense lawyers have to be present. This process is so expensive and so disruptive to the target company, the damage the process does to the target company's operations is so great, that it is always preferable to settle the case, always preferable to buy off the opposing attorneys, always preferable to give in to the blackmail.

The contingency fees that strike suit attorneys earn are so obscenely large that, as the guilty pleas of Weiss and Lerach (and other examples described below) show, they corrupt some of the most prominent members of the tort bar. Furthermore, the business of strike suits takes place almost entirely without judicial oversight, almost entirely outside the court system. In the case Lerach filed against Alliance Pharmaceutical Company, the conversation between Lerach and Ted Roth about a settlement took place even before the case had been assigned to a judge, before there even had been any hearing in a court of law.

In a strike suit attorneys file a case, a judge certifies the class, and from that moment on the fight is between plaintiff attorneys using the tools of pretrial discovery and the management of the targeted company assisted by the defense attorneys. The judge assigned to the case is hardly ever involved. As this process goes on, there are constant negotiations to settle the case. When the plaintiff attorneys reach an agreement with the defense attorneys about a settlement, the agreement is presented to the judge for his approval. Rarely does a judge disapprove—after all, both parties have accepted the agreement.

A further reason why a strike suit is tantamount to blackmail is the threat of a confused jury in a highly complex case awarding plaintiffs an outrageous amount of money. That threat is so great that a company defending against a strike suit all the way through to a jury trial would be seen as gambling with its financial viability. Ask any attorney defending companies against strike suits why they advise not to go to trial, and you will hear that strike suits are highly complicated legal battles. Like Wall Street and some of its arcane products, such as collateralized debt obligations or derivatives—financial instruments few outside Wall Street understand—strike suits involve the intricacies of finance, accounting rules, the workings of the stock market, a company's business plan, management decisions that may position the company for the long term rather than the next quarter's results—issues normally way above the head of the average member of a jury. Management simply cannot take the chance that a jury, not understanding such complex issues, will reach a verdict that costs the company not millions but often hundreds of millions of dollars.

As in all other tort cases, in strike suits there is no oversight from the bar—the bar is self regulating. Debra Yang, the federal prosecutor in Los Angeles who indicted Milberg Weiss and four of its partners, charged the law firm with multiple felonies, including obstruction of justice, perjury, bribery, and fraud. In a press conference on November 3, 2006, she said, "This case is about protecting the integrity of the justice system in America." But lack of oversight allowed Weiss and Lerach to continue their illegal strike suit business for more than two decades. Newspapers were full of stories about the harmful effects of these suits, yet the number of strike suits increased every year. Lerach's suits were so frequent and formidable that a phrase was coined by corporate leaders—"getting Lerached."

Rumors about Weiss and Lerach paying named shareholder plaintiffs to function as stooges began nearly eight years before their conviction. Nothing happened until federal prosecutors in Los Angeles finally had an ironclad case ready to be filed in 2008. Most attorneys who break the law get away with it—disbarment is a rare occurrence—and criminal penalties for those who get caught are lenient when compared to penalties meted out to other persons convicted of white-collar crimes.

Take the sentences of Melvyn Weiss and Bill Lerach. Just in 2007, the year before Weiss and Lerach were sent to jail, the Milberg Weiss law firm, as mentioned above, was lead counsel in seventeen strike suits resulting in settlements amounting to $3.8 billion. Not one of these cases went to trial; every case settled out of court. The fees paid to the lawyers in these seventeen cases were in excess of $1 billion. Yet in 2008, only one year later (and, as might be expected, as the result of a plea agreement), Lerach was sentenced to a mere twenty-four months in Lompoc—a minimum security prison outside Los Angeles that is often referred to as the country club of jails—and a fine of $ 7.5 million in addition to probation and community service.[52] Weiss was sentenced to a fine of $9.5 million and thirty months in jail. For those gentlemen, fines of $7.5 million and $9.5 million respectively amount to mere luncheon money. When their jail sentences are complete, these two gentlemen will remain among the richest lawyers in the United States despite the fact that their wealth is the fruit of legalized blackmail. Compared to sentences other white-collar criminals normally receive, the short time Lerach and Weiss spent in jail flies in the face of equal justice for all.

The Milberg Weiss case, moreover, shows the corrosive and suffocating influence the trial bar has over legislation not only on the state level or even the national level but all the way into the White House.

In the late 1980s and the early 1990s, the clamor about class-action suits and the furor on the part of companies that had been victim of such suits increased dramatically. Pressure on members of the House and the Senate in Washington DC from company CEOs, the US Chamber of Commerce, and consumer protection organizations to do something about it and rein in the attorneys and the trial bar finally reached a climax.

However, as long as the Democrats were in power in Washington, legislation to reform the tort system had little chance. American lawyers are the single largest contributors to the Democratic Party, and with the Democratic Party in control of both houses of Congress during the eighties and early nineties, tort reform legislation was not on the legislative radar.

Before the 1994 election trial attorneys, in order to make sure Democrats would retain control of congress, donated $49.5 million to members of Congress's election campaigns. Hardly a penny went to Republicans. Milberg Weiss donated $587,000 (Lerach himself $255,000)—all of it to Democratic members of congress.

Everything changed, however, when the Republican party and Newt Gingrich, touting his Contract with America, which included litigation reform, won control of both houses of Congress in 1994. Although Bill

---

52 During sentencing of Lerach, the judge indicated that "without the plea agreement I would have been considering a sentence considerably in excess of the agreed-upon two-year sentence." This shows that, in plea agreements between prosecutors and criminals who are their fellow attorneys, very light sentences are likely.

Clinton was in the White House, the Republicans were now in control of the legislative agenda.

The Republicans quickly introduced the Common Sense Legal Reform Act. The legislation included a loser-pays provision and various other measures, some specifically targeted at regulating strike suits. Fierce battles in committee hearings eliminated many of the more salutary provisions contained in the proposed legislation, such as the loser-pays provision (except in case of fraud on the part of a plaintiff's attorney). A watered down version of the bill, now called the Private Securities Litigation Act, passed the House by a vote of 325 to 99 and the Senate by a vote of 70 to 29. Despite the trial lawyers' hold over the Democratic party, the legislation passed both houses of Congress with substantial Democratic support.

At this point, the only obstacle to the legislation becoming law was a veto by President Clinton. With so many of Clinton's Democratic colleagues in the House and the Senate voting in favor of the legislation, however, Clinton would surely not stand up to his own party.

Those who thought so didn't count on the trial bar's influence. They put solid pressure on the president to use his veto power to kill the bill. Lerach, attending a Democratic fundraiser at the Hay Adams hotel in Washington DC just days before the veto deadline, even approached Bill Clinton personally and pleaded for the president to veto the bill.

On December 19, less than two weeks after Clinton had been approached by Lerach, Clinton, the lawyer and former attorney general of Arkansas and recipient of trial lawyers' financial largesse in his campaigns for office, did veto the bill.[53]

The bar's influence is not restricted to politicians. A large segment of the media see these billionaire class-action lawyers as modern Robin Hoods who rob the rich and give to the poor, in this case the defenseless shareholders.

A few pages back, I mentioned the book *Circle of Greed* by Patrick Dillon and Carl M. Cannon. It is indeed the most authoritative and well researched book about Lerach, and it describes Lerach's crimes in minute detail. Carl Cannon is no slouch. He is the Digest's Washington Bureau Chief and a contributing editor for the *National Journal*. Before joining Reader's Digest, he covered the White House for fifteen years.

Yet in an interview on August 1, 2010, on the Public Broadcasting Service (PBS) about his book, Cannon mentioned that when fighting monsters, one has to be careful not to become a monster. The supposed

---

53 Congress subsequently voted to override Clinton's veto.

monsters Lerach was fighting were the corrupt, lying, and scheming CEOs of public companies. In fighting these villains, Lerach had sadly become infected by these CEOs' corrupt shenanigans. Cannon mentioned in his closing remarks that he couldn't wait for Lerach to leave jail and reenter the public limelight. "This man has obviously something to say," he proclaimed.

I am mentioning this to explain why, despite Lerach's despicable behavior as an attorney, so many ordinary citizens are either unaware of such felonious behavior or do not seem particularly bothered by it.

In Cannon's PBS interview, it became abundantly clear that, as is so stereotypical of many journalists who have never had an opportunity to work on the executive floor of a publicly traded company or meet CEOs at conferences or work sessions, he regards CEOs of publicly listed companies as crooks, whereas the Lerachs of this world are the good guys, albeit sometimes succumbing to improper means to reach their goals. So many journalists, as good as they are in many aspects of their trade, simply refuse to accept that the majority of CEOs believe that honesty, openness, and integrity; quality products; superb human resources management; and the best possible customer relations are good for profits. The mortgage crisis teaches us that there are dishonest characters among CEOs. To paint all CEOs with the same brush, however, is exceedingly naïve, yet among journalists it is sadly commonplace.

Finally, in any civic community, the Lerachs of this world would be outcasts. Particularly in the legal world of attorneys, prosecutors, judges, and academics who study law, one would expect Lerach to be persona non grata. A convicted felon, a guy who spent a couple of years in jail, is not your average cocktail party guest, let alone a celebrated player in the legal community.

During sentencing, this is what Judge Walter said of Lerach:

> In the court's view, Mr. Lerach's criminal conduct is by far one of the most serious crimes that comes before this court. The scope and duration of this conspiracy was breathtaking. It was a nationwide conspiracy that began in the early seventies and continued for decades ... The scheme to conceal these secret payments [to the named shareholder plaintiffs that were in fact stooges on Milberg Weiss's payroll] also extended to the many judges who presided over these class actions and the fraud perpetrated on those judges is, in my view, what makes this crime so very serious and deserving of a substantial prison

sentence. What Mr. Lerach and others did goes to the core of our judicial system. The most egregious wrong that a lawyer can commit is to first commit a fraud on his clients; the second is to commit a fraud on the court.

Many white-collar criminals are repentant and frequently spend their years after jail doing social work. Think of Profumo in Britain and Michael Milken in the Drexel Burnham Lambert investment scandal in the States, both well-known examples of disgrace followed by shame, humility, civic service, and redemption.

Not so for Lerach. In March of 2010, Lerach finished his piddling sentence unrepentant, accusing his prosecutorial tormentors of having picked on the wrong guy and claiming that, if he had to do it over again, he wouldn't change a thing. What happened after his release goes to the heart of the lack of legal ethics and the bankrupt culture of so many legal practitioners in the United States, even in academia.

In the days after Lerach finished serving his sentence, he announced that he might be teaching an upper level course at the University of California Irvine School of Law. He furthermore claimed he was in discussion with various law school deans to lecture at other law schools.

Here we have a member of the legal community who is a convicted felon. Here we have a lawyer who has been disbarred. Here we have a man who, during his sentencing hearing, apologized to his family, his former law firm, and "to the legal system I have abused." Is this a man we want to stand up as an example of wisdom, fairness, integrity, and ethics in front of the future lawyers of America? What does a law school professorship for Lerach say about the deans and the faculties of our hallowed law schools? Is there no respect for the law, is there no respect for ethics, is there no support for fairness and equity, is there no shame in our legal community?

Prominent members of America's law academia and many others see in Lerach a titan of justice and fairness, a Joan of Arc on a crusade to protect the little guy shareholder against the abusers of the business world, a brilliant legal trailblazer who unfortunately used a few wrong tactics in pursuing the right cause, whereas in fact Lerach is nothing more than a conman using methods borrowed from the mafia and the venture capital industry to enrich himself while using the law as a convenient veneer to claim legitimacy.

Professor Lerach ... a modern day Al Capone with a law degree.

After the downfall of Lerach and after Congress passed the Private Securities Litigation Act of 1995, which requires that investors must have facts in hand that strongly suggest a deliberate fraud before being able to proceed with a case in federal court, one would expect that frivolous strike suits would diminish. Not so—the number of strike suits in federal court went down, but the number of such suits is increasing every year in state courts. If federal laws provide a roadblock for attorneys to earn fees, they simply circumvent federal laws and file an action in state courts, where such roadblocks often do not exist.

Particularly in the Mergers & Acquisitions (M&A) area, strike suits are not just common—they essentially are filed in every merger or acquisition of a publicly traded company of a significant size. In 2006 twenty-seven strike suits were filed in publicly traded company takeovers. In 2007 the number was 20; in 2008 36; in 2009 191, and in 2010, just through the month of September, 195.

The value of a publicly traded company is not the simple result of a mathematical calculation. Data used to make a fair estimate of the value of a company will always produce an estimate with a range of values. The buyer of a company will insist on the lowest possible value in that range, whereas the seller believes the value of his company is higher. Consequently, in a merger of companies there will always be a shareholder of the company being acquired who claims management accepted too low a price and a shareholder in the acquiring company who claims management paid too much. Moreover, when two companies strike a deal in a merger or acquisition, the companies want that deal to close as soon as possible. Time is always of the essence. The result is an automatic strike suit.

Attorneys filing these suits know companies involved in a merger or acquisition want to close the transaction rapidly and know the companies want to settle a suit quickly. As I mentioned above, in 2007, the year before Weiss and Lerach were sent to jail, the Milberg Weiss law firm was lead counsel in seventeen strike suits resulting in settlements amounting to $3.8 billion. Not one of these cases went to trial; every case settled out of court. Consequently, nearly 100 percent of strike suits settle out of court and settle quickly, and the attorneys walk away with a considerable fee. Filing such suits is so profitable for attorneys that they fall over each other to be first in filing a complaint, hoping to become lead counsel in the class action. Filings of strike suits in mergers or acquisitions often take place the very same day the companies file their prospectus with the Securities and Exchange Commission (SEC)—some have even been filed prior to the SEC filing.

Companies involved in mergers and acquisitions know they will be sued whatever they do. They consequently budget the cost of the suit and the cost of settlement in advance of announcing a merger or acquisition. Paying attorneys to go away and leave a company alone is part of doing business in America—it is so routine it has become something *you budget for*.

The longest running and best known asbestos class-action case involves W. R. Grace, an old American specialty chemicals company. Many years ago, W. R. Grace used asbestos in its manufacturing processes and was subsequently sued by a class of plaintiffs who claimed their health had been seriously impaired. In 2001 W. R. Grace, faced with mammoth claims from 110,000 allegedly injured individuals totaling more than $6 billion, filed for Chapter 11 bankruptcy.

W. R. Grace is one of the very few companies who took on the class-action attorneys in what amounts to seven years of nonstop litigation. As we have seen before, because of the immense power of class-action attorneys, companies that are the target of a class action are usually only too eager to cooperate with the plaintiff's attorneys in the hope of a speedy and favorable settlement. Litigating these cases is so costly and so time consuming for the target company that an overgenerous settlement in favor of the plaintiffs is preferable to protracted litigation.

Here again we are faced with a terrible conflict of interest. The target company will endeavor to sweeten the pot for the class-action attorneys to the maximum possible extent at the expense of the injured parties in order to induce the attorneys to settle the case.

In a class-action suit against General Motors a number of years ago, the class-action attorneys alleged that a wrongly placed fuel tank in pickup trucks resulted in aggravated human injury during crashes. GM was so desirous to get rid of the suit that it settled with the class-action attorneys after only a few weeks of negotiations. The agreement provided injured plaintiffs with a $750 voucher redeemable when buying a new GM pickup truck (useless for about 80 percent of the plaintiffs, who were not interested in buying new cars) whereas it proposed to pay the attorneys millions of dollars in cash. Judges routinely approve class-action settlements—after all, they have been accepted by both parties. In the GM case, the public outcry was so severe that the judge in the case ordered both parties to negotiate a better settlement for the plaintiffs.

In the W. R. Grace case, notwithstanding the excessive injury protracted litigation would cause for the chances of the company to reemerge from Chapter 11 bankruptcy, the company went after the class-action attorneys to show that tens of thousands of the plaintiffs' claims were completely bogus. W. R. Grace argued that most of the plaintiffs had never been exposed to asbestos;[54] that a large number of the plaintiffs were the same as the plaintiffs in many other asbestos class-action cases; that the experts the class-action attorneys had called to testify to the veracity of the claims were paid exceedingly high fees for their testimony and therefore in effect in the employ of the class-action attorneys; and that the calculation of damages covered potential plaintiffs that might or might not get sick ten, twenty, and even thirty years hence.

W. R. Grace went as far as requesting medical evidence from each of the over 110,000 plaintiffs in the class. In early 2008, W. R. Grace wore down the class-action attorneys to the point where instead of the $6 billion the attorneys had sued for, they accepted a settlement of between $600 million and $900 million.

Sadly, W. R. Grace's stubbornness is rare. Class-action attorneys usually crush their target companies to the point where settlements look more like the fruits of blackmail than the results of a judicious process that is fair and equitable.[55]

---

54 Professor George Priest of Yale Law School likes to tell the story of the plaintiff who was exposed for one day when his church was renovated. He never became sick but won a $4.5 million settlement.

55 According to the Rand Corporation, a highly respected think tank, the legal bill for resolving more than 700,000 asbestos claims in the United States has topped $70 billion. A large number of those cases, according to Rand, were filed by persons who received rewards although no malignant cancer was ever found. Nearly $21 billion of the settlements (about 30 percent) was paid out to class action attorneys. Even after all these years of asbestos litigation, law firm advertisements on TV soliciting people who think they may have been exposed to asbestos are a daily occurrence.

I mentioned above that time and again, class-action suits are filed in cases where members of the class, the so-called plaintiffs, stand to receives pennies for their injuries.

Some time ago, I received a notice from the US district court in Philadelphia advising me that I was a member of a class-action suit against Visa and Master Card, that the case had been settled, and that I was entitled to damages. As usual in a class action, I had no idea that I was a plaintiff in the case. If you do not want to participate in a class-action case, you have to take the initiative to opt out as a plaintiff. Since hardly anybody ever knows he or she is a member of a particular class of plaintiffs, hardly anybody ever opts out. If you do not opt out, the court conveniently assumes you want to be in as a plaintiff.

Apparently Visa and Master Card had charged card members who used their cards outside the United States a very small fee to convert their foreign currency charges into dollars. This fee had not been disclosed, and card members were entitled to a refund. The Securities and Exchange Commission (SEC), which guards against this kind of fraud, had already fined the two companies. Using the information gathered by the SEC, a number of attorneys filed a class-action suit against the two companies to reimburse the poor and hapless victims of the Visa and Master Card fraud.

I should mention that during the last forty years, I have traveled abroad (to Central and South America, North Africa, Europe, the Middle East, and East Asia) an average of five times per year, each trip lasting an average of two weeks. At all times, I used a credit card to pay for air travel, taxies, hotels, meals, and so on. I consequently assumed that I would be among the most severely injured persons in the class.

I was advised that I could expect to receive about twenty-five dollars. As I mentioned above, Visa and MasterCard had already been punished by the SEC for their allegedly unlawful behavior, and when you consider that in the class action most cardholders got less than twenty-five dollars, you may wonder what purpose would be served by filing this suit. The answer is that the class-action attorneys received in excess of $125 million (about 30 percent of the total award) for their effort to defend me and the other hapless and poor plaintiffs who on average were damaged to the tune of a few dollars.

As a footnote, I should mention that when I received notice of the class-action suit against Visa and Master Card, I wondered why American Express had not been the target of our creative class-action attorneys.

Although American Express might not have charged an extra penny in converting foreign currency charges, a company like American Express, which has tens of millions of high-end card holders, must have made a minor mistake somewhere and would therefore be a very juicy morsel for a class-action attorney.

Sure enough, a couple of months later I was advised that I was a member of a class-action suit against American Express and was entitled to damages. The credit card company had overcharged a few pennies in its charges for travel insurance.

By far the greatest bonanzas for America's class-action attorneys in 2010 are the Toyota's acceleration problem and the BP Gulf Coast oil well leak. Toyota and BP's troubles are manna from heaven. Like spring flowers, lawsuits against Toyota and BP are sprouting all around the country.

Approximately 150 lawsuits have been filed in federal courts against Toyota, hundreds more in state courts. In federal cases, the US Judicial Panel on Multidistrict Legislation will combine these class-action cases into one or a few class-action lawsuits and will decide where the case or cases will be heard. For Toyota and BP, billions of dollars are at stake not only as a result of expected verdicts or out-of-court negotiated settlements but also because of the huge cost in defending the suits. For the class-action attorneys, the contingency fee stakes are just as high.

On March 25, 2010, the Judicial Panel on Multidistrict Legislation convened in San Diego to hear the Toyota plaintiffs' attorneys' pleas as to why the lawsuits should be heard in their jurisdictions—there are nineteen US judicial jurisdictions in total. With home-court advantage, the lawyers stand a good chance to reap huge awards, because they are in the best position to become the lead attorney(s) in the case(s).

The day before the hearing, the one hundred or so attorneys who had descended on San Diego like wasps on a honey pot met at a local hotel for a Toyota Recall Litigation Conference. Being first to file a case is often an argument for being chosen lead counsel. Consequently, one attorney who introduced himself started off by telling the audience he was first in filing suit in Rhode Island and North Carolina. The *Wall Street Journal* reported the words of attorney Mark Lanier from Houston, Texas, who won a $253 million dollar award against pharmaceutical Merck in the famous Vioxx case, as follows: "In a booming speech that seemed straight off a campaign trail, Mr. Lanier noted to a rapt audience how he can tailor his courtroom demeanor from judge to judge, ranging from ballet to World Wrestling

Federation depending on the judge's tastes." In other words, if you want somebody who can manipulate judges, I am the one. Attorney Mark Geragos, whose clients included Michael Jackson, thundered, "Everyone in this room is on the precipice of the opportunity to expose the greatest corporate malfeasance." Really?

According to some who attended the hearing before the Judicial Panel on Multidistrict Legislation the next day, the hearing was a zoo. With so many attorneys vying for home-court advantage, each attorney was allowed two minutes to plead with the panel why their jurisdiction should be chosen. With so many attorneys present, they had to decide among themselves who would get the privilege of the two minutes. Some attorneys used what appeared to be exceedingly naïve and laughable arguments to stand out in the crowd and get the panel's attention.

This circus of jockeying attorneys illustrates how deep American jurisprudence has sunk. Lawyers attending hearings of the Judicial Panel on Multidistrict Legislation were not arguing the law, they were not arguing fairness or equity, they were not debating legal theories of liability. They were there totally and entirely divorced from their clients' issues. They attended these hearings exclusively on behalf of themselves. They were out to promote themselves, not the cases of their clients—just themselves. The law should be about accuser and accused, and as officers of the court, attorneys should assist the accuser or the accused. But in American jurisprudence, the issue isn't the fair resolution of conflict. It has become a question of which lawyer will earn the most. It is not what is good for justice, it is purely an issue of what is good for the lawyer. Lawyering as a profession has turned into lawyering as a business, a greedy business. Without the contingency fee, this never would have happened.

As I mentioned in the opening paragraphs of this chapter, class actions are a purely American form of litigation. In some European countries (Austria, France, Germany, and Spain), consumer organizations are in certain instances allowed to file a suit on behalf of their members. In the Netherlands, the law only allows collective actions brought by associations on behalf of injured parties seeking a judicial declaration that the company is liable for the damage it has caused. In Switzerland, the law does not permit any sort of class-action suit. In Britain the Office of Fair Trading is proposing the possibility of class-action lawsuits with severe restrictions, such as a prohibition against contingency fees, strong powers for judges to avoid frivolous lawsuits, and meaningful supervision over funding and settlement arrangements.

The European Commission is drafting new Europe-wide rules for class actions and is wisely staying away from American-style litigation. Neelie Kroes, the former European Commissioner for competition policy, who drafted new legislation in competition law, said in a speech before the European Consumer Association in Strasbourg on April 22, 2008:

> But let me be crystal clear on this: we are not proposing an American-style opt-out class action, where basically anyone can bring a claim on behalf of a group of unidentified victims, who are in the boat unless they explicitly decide to be out. What [we] propose is an opt-in collective action, where victims have to actively decide whether or not they want to be part of the action. Besides, much of the US class-action litigation excesses in competition cases is due to other factors such as treble damages, jury trials, contingency fees and overly broad and burdensome pre-trial discovery. None of this is part of what [we] propose.

Those lucky Europeans!

One anecdotal item: in countries like Germany, the Netherlands, or Great Britain, the titans in the financial services industries or the CEOs of some of the largest publicly traded companies are often among the wealthiest few. Only in the United States are some of the class-action and contingency fee lawyers members of the same elite club.

10.

The Shareholder Derivative Suit

My American lawyer friends defend the many anomalies of the American legal system, such as the loser in a dispute not having to pay the legal fees of the prevailing party, the abuse of discovery, the contingency fee, and class actions, to mention a few, as the means by which the American legal system is out to protect the little guy, the small shareholder, the consumer, the employee who has been the subject of discrimination—in other words, the person without means who has been wronged. They claim that European legal systems are rooted in Roman law and the codified Napoleonic laws that were created when societal structures were feudal, when the rich and powerful ruled the realm and laborers and peasants had no rights.

Equal justice under law, the phrase inscribed on the front of the United States Supreme Court building in Washington DC, American lawyers claim, represents the bedrock of the American legal system, which requires lawyers to make sure every member of our society, whether rich or poor, has access to the courts in order to be able to redress a grievance. What critics of the American legal system call anomalies, defenders of the system describe as the tools of a more just society. This would all be greatly uplifting and laudatory if only it were true.

First, the term *equal justice* isn't an American invention; it dates back to well before the birth of Christ. As a matter of fact, it appears in 430 BC in the magnificent funeral oration of Pericles, the Athenian politician and general, honoring the dead of war. In ancient Greek history, Pericles's oration takes the same solemn place as Lincoln's Gettysburg address does in American history.

Pericles, proud of his city state and the level of democracy it had achieved, could well have been talking about the United States, another proud democracy that would grace the face of the earth two-and-a-half thousand years later, when he said:

> Our form of government does not enter into rivalry with the institutions of others. We do not copy our neighbors, but are an example to them. It is true that we are called a democracy, for the administration is in the hands of the many and not of the few. But while the law secures *equal justice to all* alike in their private disputes, the claim of excellence is also recognized; and when a citizen is in any way distinguished, he is preferred to the public service, not as a matter of privilege, but as the reward of merit. Neither is poverty a bar, but a man may benefit his country whatever be the obscurity of his condition." [emphasis added][56]

Furthermore, throughout much of the twentieth century, Europe has more often than not been governed by left-of-center governments. These left-of-center governments have seen to it that the leftovers of medieval feudal laws are expunged from society. When it comes to equality under the law, western Europe, especially the Scandinavian countries and countries like the United Kingdom, Holland, or France boast today equality under law that rivals or betters American justice (see "The Quality of the American Legal System as Compared to Systems in Other Countries" in

---

56 The speech was delivered by Pericles, an eminent Athenian politician, at the end of the first year of the Peloponnesian War (431–404 BC) as a part of the annual public funeral for the war dead. Pericles. *Funeral Oration*, 431 BC Translation: Benjamin Jowett, Master of Balliol College, Regius Professor of Greek in the University of Oxford and Doctor In Theology of the University of Leyden, in his book Thucydides' *History*, published in London by Spottiswoode and Co. in 1881

Part III). European equality under the law has been achieved through laws and regulations promulgated by elected legislatures providing oversight and enforcement, not through the interference of unelected, unregulated lawyers who claim to have a monopoly on being able to right the wrongs of society and who strive to reach their goal by extracting millions and millions of dollars in payment for themselves.

A new type of lawsuit that has developed and has become increasingly popular in the last ten years is called the shareholder derivative suit. This type of lawsuit is clearly an example of tort lawyers trying to generate earnings rather than working for the betterment of American business or in the defense of the American shareholder.

A derivative suit is a lawsuit filed by one or more shareholders not on behalf of themselves but on behalf of the company. A plaintiff in a derivative suit isn't after monetary damages but seeks to protect the investment in the company by forcing changes in corporate governance and management. If the lawsuit results in a monetary reward, the reward goes to the company, not to the plaintiff.

A derivative suit develops very much the way a strike suit develops. The great advantage of the derivative suit, however, is that in a strike suit the attorneys need a number of shareholders who are suing the company who then become a class. Consequently, attorneys need to find and then solicit a number of shareholders—an often difficult and cumbersome task.

In a derivative suit, no such recruitment of shareholders is needed—one shareholder suffices. When a company's stock goes down, all an attorney needs to do is call one shareholder, usually a pension fund, hedge fund, or a college endowment with an investment in the company or an individual shareholder. If that shareholder agrees, the attorney files the case, and the attorney is in charge of the case—in fact, for all intents and purposes, the suit is then the attorney's suit. The plaintiff won't receive a monetary reward, which absolves the attorney from having to consult the plaintiff with regard to damages.

Derivative suits are nearly always settled. However, they have the same debilitating effect on companies as strike suits. Since the suit is against the company, its corporate governance and management, management and the directors are directly involved in the defense of the suit, more so than in a strike suit. Consequently, derivative suits are not only very expensive to defend; they are exceedingly time consuming for management and the board of directors. Furthermore, as is the case in a strike suit, the cost of a company's directors' and officers' insurance policy is at stake.

Attorneys involved in a derivative suit know they have tremendous leverage. They have the upper hand to the point where the pressure on the company to settle without going to trial is so great it is tantamount to blackmail. When all is said and done and the suit is settled, the company usually doesn't have to pay a penny in damages—all the company has to do is adopt some additional rules with regard to the company's corporate governance and pay the suing attorneys a small fortune to go away and leave the company in peace.

Consequently, the greater the pressure on the company, its management, and the board of directors—in other words, the greater the blackmail—the more eager the company is to settle and the larger the amount of money the company is willing to pay the attorneys to leave the company alone.

HP (the old Hewlett Packard) is a very successful, highly respected, and well-managed Silicon Valley technology company. The company is a world leader in information technology and in the manufacture of computers and printers. In the last five years, since Mark Hurd became its CEO, the company's stock has doubled.

Some time ago, Mark Hurd became involved with a female outside contractor of the company. Both parties agree it was a nonsexual relationship. However, the contractor complained about the relationship, and the matter was settled.

When HP's directors were informed, they immediately ordered an investigation. Although Mr. Hurd's violation of company policy (mostly involving the accuracy of his expense accounts) had a monetary value of less than $20,000 and he had reimbursed the company, the directors, holding the chief executive to the same standards as the company's lowliest employee, fired Mr. Hurd (allowed him to resign) on Friday, August 6, 2010.

On Tuesday, August 10, 2010, exactly four days after Mr. Hurd's dismissal became known to the outside world, a shareholder derivative suit was filed against HP's board in Santa Clara County Superior Court in California. The suit alleges that directors violated their fiduciary duties in connection with the events surrounding the resignation of the company's CEO, Mark Hurd. The suit furthermore alleges that the board is guilty of gross mismanagement, has wasted corporate assets, has violated the California corporation code, has misappropriated information, and has unjustly enriched itself. The suit is seeking not only restitution and other injunctive relief but changes to HP's corporate governance policies. It additionally seeks not just damages but treble damages.

Within ninety-six hours of Mr. Hurd's dismissal becoming known, Brockton Contributory Retirement System of Connecticut, the plaintiff, and Scott & Scott LLP, the attorneys for the plaintiff, had obviously seriously consulted with each other on the suit and had, as one would expect, done their due diligence in order to make sure that the board was indeed guilty of gross mismanagement, had wasted corporate assets, had violated the California corporation code, had misappropriated information, and had unjustly enriched itself.

This means that we are supposed to believe that the Brockton Contributory Retirement System and in particular Arthur Shingler and Mary K. Blasy of the law firm Scott & Scott LLP, within only ninety-six hours, were able to obtain sufficient information that, in firing Mark Hurd, HP's directors were clearly guilty of gross mismanagement and more specifically that they were able to conclude that some officers or directors had unjustly enriched themselves.

Add to this the fact that Brockton Contributory Retirement System, the so-called plaintiff in this suit, is located in Connecticut, whereas the attorneys are located a continent away in California; add to this the fact that the ninety-six hours mentioned above included a Saturday and a Sunday, and one can only conclude that the plaintiff's masterful legal research in such a short period of time simply strains all credulity. The filing of this derivative suit resembles the kid who, walking into a room full of manure, immediately grabs a shovel and starts digging with the words, "Where there is so much shit, there must be a pony."

Immediately after HP fired Mark Hurd, HP's stock dropped 10 percent. Any company losing a CEO with the track record of Mark Hurd would see its stock take a tumble. Had Mark Hurd dropped dead, the same thing would have happened. To a derivative suit attorney, however, a drop in the value of HP's stock automatically means mismanagement.

The suit also alleges that Mark Hurd sold millions in HP stock before HP announced the outside contractor's harassment claim against him. Furthermore, Catherine Lesjak, HP's chief financial officer prior to Hurd's resignation, sold more than $265,000 in company shares a week before the problem with Mark Hurd became public.

What the general public may not know, however, is that a company executive with stock options faces many hurdles in selling the company's stock. First, options expire, which means that an executive often has no choice but to exercise options. Second, executives may be overweight in company stock, requiring a sale of company stock to balance an investment portfolio. Third, in order to avoid even the appearance of a conflict of interest, company executives frequently put their company stock holdings in a blind trust and do not know whether or when that stock is sold. Fourth, executives face numerous SEC restrictions as to when they are allowed to sell stock. Windows when an executive can sell stock are often short and few and far between. Consequently, executives often plan and order the sale of stock in their companies well in advance of the actual selling date. Many have standing sell orders, meaning the broker has to sell a certain number of shares at certain times, such as twice a year or quarterly.

The derivative suit against HP's management and board simply assumes that Hurd and Lesjak benefited from insider knowledge when they sold their stock prior to Hurd's resignation. Anybody who has professional knowledge of the rules and regulations regarding executives selling their companies' stock and the rules and regulations with regard to insider trading knows that the sale of such stock has to be immediately reported to the SEC and is therefore public knowledge. To assume in a lawsuit that a person like Ms. Lesjak, HP's chief financial officer, would make such an obvious and utterly dumb mistake and sell stock in HP while knowing the stock would take a plunge after Hurd's resignation shows that the plaintiff's attorneys in the HP suit are on a fishing expedition and are simply out to harass HP's management.

We will probably never know. The HP suit will most likely not go to trial and will be settled. Company officers will not admit any wrongdoing, some nice language will be added to HP's governance policies, and Scott & Scott LLP, the plaintiff's attorneys, will walk away with a huge amount of money to remunerate them for their effort to make HP a better company.

The Brockton Contributory Retirement System and Scott & Scott LLP's case against HP could never be filed in the average western European court of law or in a jurisdiction like Singapore, South Korea, or Japan. In any other jurisdiction in the developed world, the lawsuit filed against HP would not be a real lawsuit.

The action Scott & Scott LLP took on behalf of its client is not the filing of a lawsuit in which the claimant is citing reason and fact for the allegation that the Brockton Contributory Retirement System has been damaged. In reality the lawyers are telling the court that Brockton might have suffered damage. They are not quite sure, but they would like to find out. And, because Brockton might have been damaged, attorneys for Brockton are petitioning the court to let them start discovery, take depositions of HP's senior management and HP's board of directors, and start rummaging through HP's files so they can find our whether Brockton has been damaged or not. And everybody knows—Brockton, Scott & Scott LLP, and the judge—that discovery in this case is so disruptive to HP's board and management that HP will pay Scott & Scott LLP a good deal of money for Scott and Scott LLP and Brockton to go away and leave HP alone.

What is happening here is not the unfolding of an orderly judicial process but simply a request by a number of lawyers to the court to let the lawyers become such a nuisance to HP that the lawyers, with the sanction of the court, can wring some money out of the company. In judicial systems where the integrity of the judicial process is paramount, Brockton and Scott & Scott LLP's actions would be called blackmail. In the United States, Brockton and Scott & Scott LLP's actions are called a shareholder derivative suit.

The question the American legal system needs to answer is why we need the shareholder derivative suit. The accusations against HP and most other companies facing a shareholder derivative suit are clearly the jurisdiction of the SEC, a regulatory agency created by a democratically elected Congress to guard against abuses like insider trading. As a matter of fact, in pursuing insider trading cases or unjust enrichment—insider trading is a major element of the complaint against HP—the SEC has a very good track record. If Hurd and Lesjak have violated insider trading rules, everybody knows the SEC will handle that matter admirably—America does not need Scott & Scott LLP for that.

Furthermore, the complaint against HP alleges that HP's board wasted corporate assets. Because Hurd was allowed to resign, he received a contractual $30 million plus severance package. By allowing Hurd to resign, HP supposedly wasted $30 million of the company's assets.

Whether it was wise for HP to let Hurd resign rather than fire him is clearly for the board of directors to decide. That's why shareholders elect a board: to make decisions, such as whether it is better to let Hurd resign at a cost of $30 million or fire him and face a lawsuit from Hurd that may cost HP more than $30 million. Why should we let Scott & Scott LLP, or a jury for that matter, substitute their judgment for the judgment of HP's board of directors, a board that includes such captains of industry as Netscape founder and eBay and Facebook director Mark Andreessen?

It is clear that most derivative litigation is brought by entrepreneurial attorneys who notice that a company's stock has dropped or, as in the case of HP, can reasonably anticipate the stock will drop and quickly find a shareholder who agrees to sue the company for mismanagement. The attorney then negotiates with the company to settle in exchange for a generous payment to that attorney. Ergo: the payment to the attorney is not the result of the settlement, but the settlement is a function of the payment to the attorney.

A derivative suit is a wholly unnecessary form of litigation. This kind of suit merely illustrates that a good number of American tort attorneys are out for a buck rather than serving justice under the law.

11.

Winner Pays the Loser's Attorney Fees
(The new approach by the tort bar)

I mentioned earlier that contingency fees in class-action suits are usually one third of the settlement plus payment of the plaintiff's attorneys' out-of-pocket expenses. Consequently, in a $100 million settlement, plaintiff attorneys will receive $33 million plus expenses that, just by themselves, routinely add up to millions of dollars.

What about attorneys who, in filing a class-action suit, miscalculated? What about cases in which plaintiff attorneys find out during discovery that they have a very weak case and won't be able to obtain a large settlement and rake in the millions and millions of dollars they hoped for? The answer to this question came in a class-action suit against Volkswagen of America of which I was recently told I was a member. In this case, the class-action attorneys were the clear losers. They consequently came up with a novel idea: Why not ask the judge to declare that the prevailing party should pay the losers' legal fees? Not just reimbursement for hourly fees—that wouldn't do. The prevailing party should pay the losers' legal fees as if the losers had won the case.

Car companies are every class-action attorney's dream. Cars get old—because of old-fashioned wear and tear, they develop problems. For the class-action attorney, however, wear and tear is a synonym for negligence in designing the car resulting in harm and financial loss to the car buyer.

Consequently, it will not come as a surprise that car companies are routinely the subject of product liability class-action lawsuits.

The complaint against Volkswagen of America in the class-action suit of which I was recently told I was a member is so trivial and so obviously phony it is laughable. Sadly, however, the case also perfectly illustrates to what level of absurdity American litigation has sunk. The suit means that in manufacturing in America, whatever you do, no matter how well you design your products or how well you manufacture them, you will find yourself the subject of a class-action suit accusing you of negligence. It means that, if you want to sell a manufactured product in America, you have to factor the cost of future litigation and class-action settlements into the cost of your product.

In the case of the class action against Volkswagen I mentioned above, the plaintiff attorneys alleged that after years and years of use, particularly if a Volkswagen had been constantly parked outside, dirt would creep into the rails guiding the sunroof. Consequently, if the rails were not cleaned, the sunroof wouldn't close properly, resulting in water entering the car through the not entirely closed sunroof. Volkswagen was thus liable for all the poor Volkswagen owners whose car upholstery had been damaged by water dripping from the sunroof. How many car owners had had their upholstery damaged because they had forgotten to close the sunroof wasn't mentioned. Nor was it mentioned that car owners could have avoided the problem by now and then using a brush to clean out the dirt and grit that had gotten onto the rails of the sunroof.

In this case, however, the attorneys had clearly miscalculated. After discovery and negotiations to settle the case, all the plaintiff attorneys could get out of Volkswagen was a mere $8 million settlement to reimburse expenses for damage to the upholstery of VW car owners who had supposedly leaky sunroofs. All the plaintiff lawyers would receive was an amount somewhere in the $2.5 to $3 million range.

For class-action attorneys, an award of $2.5 to $3 million means not only that they have lost the case but that their reputation will be damaged.

We should remember that, according to the tort bar, the main reason for large contingency fees is the fact that lawyers need these fees to compensate for the expenses incurred in cases in which they do not prevail. So in the Volkswagen case mentioned above, one would say, "Tough luck for the plaintiffs' attorneys, Mazie Slater Katz & Freeman LLC and Schoengold & Sporn PC."

In this case, however, the plaintiffs' attorneys introduced a novel procedure that, if it works, will undoubtedly become the standard in class-action cases. Not satisfied with the $2.5 to $3 million contingency fee, they have asked the court to award them $30 million for attorneys' fees and $1.5 million reimbursement of costs and expenses incurred in the prosecution and settlement of the case.

This is not a typo. Volkswagen agreed to pay $8 million to the supposedly injured car owners who had leaking sunroofs. Yet the court is asked to award $30 million to the plaintiffs' attorneys, 375 percent of the amount paid by Volkswagen in settlement. Whereas 33 percent in such cases is more or less standard, Mazie Slater Katz & Freeman and Schoengold & Sporn believe they should be paid not 33 percent of the settlement but a whopping 375 percent, or more than ten times the usual fee.

Mazie Slater Katz & Freeman and Schoengold & Sporn claim that Volkswagen's agreement to pay $8 million combined with their agreement to warn car owners about the problem and to add a notice to the car owners' manuals is worth $125 million which justifies the fee of $30 million plus $1.5 million in expenses.

How dare lawyers ask for such extortionate amounts in fees? And how dare they ask for such fees not from the defendants with whom they negotiated the settlement but from the court itself. "Your Honor, you will agree we are the good guys—after all, we are the lawyers. We have worked very hard on this Volkswagen case, and we respectfully request that we be paid a fee of $31.5 million to compensate us for our utter stupidity in suing Volkswagen."

The request for the $30 million fee and the $1.5 million in expense reimbursement was filed before Judge Patty Shwartz, United States magistrate judge for the District of New Jersey. In august of 2010 Judge Shwartz awarded Mazie Slater Katz & Freeman and Schoengold & Sporn $9.2 million in fees and $675,000 in costs.

12.

Medical Malpractice

Medical malpractice is defined as an act or omission by a health care provider or care provided that does not meet accepted standards of medical practice and causes injury or death to a patient. Health care providers who are accused of medical malpractice, be they doctors, nurses, hospitals, pharmaceutical companies, or medical equipment companies, are usually accused of negligence.

Needless to say, doctors or nurses or hospitals who are negligent in carrying out their duties and cause harm to a patient should be held accountable for their acts. Particularly where such negligence has caused the patient injury, the health care provider should be liable for the damage caused.

The problem with medical malpractice litigation is that over the years, juries have awarded astronomical amounts of money to plaintiffs because of pain and suffering or as a result of punitive damages. I could fill the pages of this entire book with medical malpractice cases in which plaintiffs are routinely awarded tens of millions of dollars for pain and suffering or for punitive damages. Outrageous awards are often reduced on appeal, yet even on appeal they frequently end up in the tens of millions of dollars.

The reader may well ask what is wrong with the plaintiff receiving damages. There is of course nothing wrong with the plaintiff receiving damages.

- What is wrong is the amount. One in twelve obstetricians report they have stopped delivering babies as a result of the risk or fear of professional liability claims. According to the American Medical Association, defensive medicine increases health costs by between $84 billion and $151 billion each year. Studies place the direct and indirect costs of malpractice between 5 percent and 10 percent of total US medical costs.
- What is wrong is that the plaintiff's award has no relationship to the plaintiff's damages.
- What is wrong is the astronomical amount of money the plaintiff's attorney earns in many of these medical malpractice cases.
- What is wrong is the total absence of consistency, the total arbitrariness of awards for near total similarity in damage to the plaintiff.[57]
- What is wrong is that juries, unfamiliar with the highly complicated aspects of medical practice, are the ones that decide awards in medical malpractice cases.
- What is wrong is that these outrageous jury awards have nothing to do with fairness or equity. The awards depend to a large extent on the quality of the theatrical performance of the plaintiff's lawyer and how impressionable the jury is. When a jury observes a plaintiff who is disfigured or is wasting away with a horrible disease, it is normal and human for the jury to feel sympathy for the plaintiff. When such an out-of-luck plaintiff is up against a rich doctor and all-powerful insurance company, it is only too logical that the jury tends to want to help the victim even when the doctor is not

---

57 John Edwards, our unsuccessful vice presidential and presidential candidate, when he was a medical malpractice attorney, won a number of fairly similar malpractice cases with very dissimilar results: in *Griffin v. Teague,* delay in performing a c-section resulted in brain damage to a child; the award was $23.25 million. In *Campbell v. Pitt County Memorial Hosp.,* breech birth rather than c-section resulted in brain damage to a child. The award was $5.75 million.

at fault. Moreover, in modern medicine one doctor will propose one treatment when another doctor will propose another. There is not just one solution in medical science, and often doctors face situations for which there is no medical solution. The size of the awards are a function of a jury's heightened emotion and whipped up passion and prejudices rather than rational legal reasoning.[58]

- What is wrong is that as a result of these outrageous monetary awards in medical malpractice cases, in order to make sure they can never be accused of malpractice, doctors have been forced to change from normal medical practice to defensive medical practice. In a defensive medical practice, doctors use many more tests than is necessary; they prefer to deliver babies with c-section rather than using the normal vaginal method, or they leave the medical practice altogether in states where medical malpractice jury awards are like pay-outs at a casino's craps table.

- What is wrong is the enormous cost to society of these outrageous malpractice awards not only as a result of premiums for malpractice insurance for doctors skyrocketing to as much as $450,000 per year but also because of the cost of defensive medicine. A 2003 study by the US Department of Health and Human Services estimated that limits on malpractice could save over $100 billion (that is more than one thousand million dollars) per year.

- What is wrong is that in the states and counties where juries are prone to outrageous malpractice awards, there are no obstetrics and gynecology or emergency room doctors. When, in 2003, medical liability reform was introduced in Texas, physicians from all over the country moved to Texas. According to the Texas Medical Board, medical license applications jumped from 2,561 in 2003 to 4,041 in 2004, an increase of 58 percent. Between May of 2003 and May of 2008, Texas saw a 7.2 percent growth in the number of ob-

---

58 In the closing argument of *Lakey v. Sta Rite Industries*, John Edwards spoke to the jury for an hour and a half, during which he mentioned his own son Wade, who had been killed in a car accident at the beginning of the trial. The jury awarded the family of a five-year-old child killed in a swimming pool accident $25 million, the largest personal injury award in North Carolina history.

gyns. Similar increases were found in other specialties. Finally, according to the Texas Insurance Department, malpractice insurance rates dropped 25 percent after the law had been adopted by the Texas legislature.

- What is wrong is that the American legal system allows a medical malpractice tort system that, by comparison to the tort systems of any other developed country in the world, is simply a charade. The American tort bar has taken hold of medical malpractice litigation and is getting drunk on a gusher of contingency fees.

Defenders of the system argue that 60 percent of liability claims against doctors are dropped, withdrawn, or dismissed without payment. But even in cases where the claim was dropped, doctors had to hire lawyers to defend themselves. In 2007 the average cost for a doctor to defend against malpractice claims that were dropped or dismissed was $18,000. In 2008 the cost had risen to $22,000.

Class-action lawsuits, product liability cases, medical malpractice—taken together, they clearly illustrate what is wrong with tort in America. All these legal actions have little to do with fairness or equity but everything to do with unsupervised and unregulated greed.

If equal justice under the law is indeed the promise of our legal system, why does one stillborn baby merit $5 million in damages and another $25 million? The answer is that there is no equal justice in tort. It's capricious, it depends on whipping up the emotion of juries, it depends on the theatrics of the plaintiff attorney, it depends on the locale where the action is brought—it has nothing to do with the law, nothing with fairness or equity. Why do we let these attorneys do so much damage to our society?

"They don't do damage to our society," the defenders of the system claim. "They allow citizens who are harmed to seek justice and receive compensation." If that's the case, what about the mothers who cannot find an ob-gyn to help with the birth of their babies because all the ob-gyns have fled the area to avoid outrageous malpractice awards? Are these women not damaged? Are they not entitled to compensation?

And what about the monetary awards for pain and suffering? How do you measure pain and suffering? Is the loss of a child worth one million, two million, or twenty-five million dollars?

And why is our country alone in all this? Why is there no legal system on the face of the earth that has a damage regime like the one we find in the United States of America?

The answer to these questions is the contingency fee, the cancer that completely distorts our tort system and permeates every aspect of our otherwise fair and equitable society.

13.

Liability and Damages

If there is one element the various judicial systems in the developed world have in common, it is that justice and the law strive for fairness. The law should, where possible, strive to eliminate inequity when or wherever it occurs. This rule does not seem to apply to our laws about liability and damages.

American laws and jurisprudence with respect to liability and damages are unjust, they are unfair, they have no basis in any recognized standard of equity, and they are different and often completely contradictory from state to state.

Under British common law and European Roman or Napoleonic codified law, liability requires a violation of accepted standards of behavior resulting in injury. Not so in the United States.

Under British common law and European Roman or Napoleonic codified law, damages should compensate the injured party for tangible and sometimes intangible loss but should never be used to punish the offending party. Punishment is governed by criminal law. Not so in the United States.

Under British common law and European Roman or Napoleonic codified law, damages should not be arbitrary and inconsistent. Not so in the United States of America, where damages are exceedingly arbitrary and completely inconsistent.

In the United States of America, lawyers have pushed legislation through the various state legislatures, legislation that attempts to guarantee every injured party a monetary award. Even if the party causing the injury is incapable of paying the monetary award, the law makes sure the injured party receives the monetary award from another party. Even if that other party has not violated any accepted standards of behavior, in the United States such persons or entities are routinely found guilty of having caused a miniscule element of the harm, which makes them liable for the entire monetary reward.

What could be the reason for such a convoluted, unfair, and arbitrary system? The explanation used by the tort bar for this unjust and unfair liability and damage regime is the common good; the bar claims the system simply assures a harmed person receives payment for damage incurred. There is certainly social value in making sure a harmed person is compensated, but definitely not if the payment the harmed person receives is charged to a totally innocent person or entity, which is exactly what happens all the time in the United States of America.

When you research the laws about liability and damages, however, there can only be one conclusion about why these laws were promulgated: attorneys have riddled the law books with laws that assure the contingency lawyer always gets his or her fee. There can be no other reason, no other logical motivation for the utter unfairness in the laws about liability and damages.

The lawyers' motto is, "Give Paul, the injured party, a reward for damages, and if the defender is insolvent, just steal from Peter—who has nothing to do with the alleged tort—to pay Paul, and the lawyer gets his contingency fee."

- It is clear beyond any reasonable doubt that the legislation and much of the common law with regard to liability and damages is lawyer driven and motivated exclusively by the lawyers' monetary gain.
- It would be unthinkable in any other judicial system that one party is found responsible for 1 percent of the tort yet is ordered to pay 100 percent of the award as routinely happens in our country.
- It would be unthinkable in any other judicial system that the driver of a rented automobile can be found liable for a fatal accident but the rental company, although obligated by law to rent to any person, can then be found liable for the entire monetary award simply because the rental company owns

the car, as has happened to a number of American car rental companies.

- It would be unthinkable in any other judicial system to allow a harmed person to turn civil law into criminal law and receive an astronomical monetary reward not for compensation of the tort but to punish the offending party—only in America.

Moreover, as mentioned above, in every justice system except in America, liability requires a violation of accepted standards of behavior resulting in injury. Harm that is intentional or the result of negligence certainly violates accepted standards of behavior. But in the United States the responsibility for harm caused has been divorced from intentional or negligent behavior. Under American law, any relationship to a person who causes harm, however remote, may make you liable for that person's actions. The employer is liable for the actions of an employee even though the employee's actions have nothing to do with his or her employment; the rental car company is liable for the actions of the renter. Finally, liability is often established for occurrences that in other legal jurisdictions are called acts of God.

A very clear example of the difference in the way the British common law system deals with negligence is harm to a child delivered while in the breech position, a not uncommon problem.

An American couple sued a doctor in the United States for malpractice and damages. Their about-to-be-born child was in the breech position, and the doctor had turned the baby. During the procedure, the pressure of the doctor's thumb had fractured the skull of the baby, and the baby was born with brain damage. The American court ruled that the doctor's pressure on the baby's skull had caused the skull fracture. It held the doctor liable and awarded $10.5 million in damages.

The British High Court, in an identical case, also ruled that the doctor's pressure on the baby's skull had caused the skull fracture. However, the court ruled that the doctor had done his utmost to use his skill and expertise to deliver a healthy baby and was therefore not liable. The court awarded damages in the amount of two pound sterling (in Britain the traditional nominal award).

No wonder birth by Caesarian section has become routine in the United States, even when unnecessary. Doctors will not take the risk of being sued in case a problem develops during a child's delivery.

Joint and Several Liability

Under joint liability, all parties are liable for the full amount of an obligation. When one of the parties satisfies the obligation, the other parties are relieved from the obligation. If one party dies, the other parties become liable for the full amount of the obligation

Under several liability, each party's liability is restricted to a predetermined amount or percentage of an obligation.

Under joint and several liability, each of the parties is responsible for the full amount of the obligation. The parties—not the creditor—have to work out among themselves which party is liable for which part of the obligation.

In practically every jurisdiction in the world except for jurisdictions that use sharia law, parties that have lost a tort case are severally liable for damages. Their obligation is proportionate. Consequently, if a party is held responsible for 1 percent of the tort, that party pays 1 percent of the award in damages. Again this treatment of liability is different in America. As mentioned above, in the United States, if a party is held responsible for 1 percent of the tort, the party is liable for 50 percent and in many jurisdictions for 100 percent of the award in damages.

This rob-Peter-to-pay-Paul principle is patently unfair and unjust. It certainly benefits the prevailing party. That party is practically always guaranteed to be able to collect on an award. However, it also makes a party that is very remotely connected to the tort, and often by every accepted norm of behavior not culpable for the tort, end up as the one that is the most severely damaged. Who cares whether this is just or not! After all, by using several liability in tort cases, attorneys always earn their contingency fees. And in our legal system, that's all that matters.

In establishing liability and in awarding damages, American jurisprudence has, in the last one hundred years, totally and entirely veered away from British common law. In the United States any relationship to an occurrence, however remote or unintended, establishes liability (see also Deep Pockets below). And once liability has been established, the amount awarded in damages frequently reaches the stratosphere. The contingency fee drives the dollar amount awarded in damages up and up and up, whereas the increasing dollar amount of damages encourages the contingency fee practice in an everlasting, vicious circle.

Furthermore, what sets US jurisprudence further apart from other Anglo Saxon jurisdictions and European jurisprudence is that punitive and treble damages are meant to punish the offending party. This punishment is imposed upon the offending party in a civil procedure, not a criminal procedure. What in most other jurisdictions is adjudicated in a criminal law proceeding is, in the US, allowed to be adjudicated in a purely civil procedure. The reason this is important is that, for good reason, the burden of proof in a civil procedure is less stringent than in criminal proceedings.

Add to this situation the fact that in most states there are no binding guidelines as to the dollar amounts of damages, add to this the corrupting influence of the contingency fee and class action, add to this the unpredictability of jury awards, and you find damages awarded in the United States routinely amounting not to millions but billions of dollars.

Many states have attempted to repeal their joint and several liability statutes. They are nearly always frustrated by the trial bar's campaign contributions and lobbying efforts. Most proposals die in committee and never reach a floor vote.

Deep Pockets (Cash-Rich People or Entities)

In most jurisdictions in developed countries, liability is proportionate. Not so in America. To make sure the cash for damages is always available, a defendant who is ruled liable for a small element of the tort can be held liable for fully 50 percent of the damages or, in some jurisdictions, even 100 percent of the damages. Consequently, plaintiff attorneys always make sure that at least one deep-pocketed or cash-rich entity is a defendant.

For instance, in a car accident, even if it was caused by a drunk person going through a red light, plaintiff attorneys always include the city where the accident occurred, claiming insufficient street lights or improper road conditions; or include the car manufacturer, claiming some sort of deficiency in the manufacture of the car, such as the brakes; or any other deep pocketed entity, just in case the drunk person has no insurance or insufficient insurance to pay the verdict.

Even if the city or car company is judged to be responsible for 1 percent of the tort, in case the other defendants are unable to pay the verdict, the city or car company is liable for 50 percent of the damages and, in many jurisdictions, even 100 percent of the damages. Consequently, if the drunken defendant is unable to pay the damages, the plaintiff attorneys are still in a position to collect the total amount of the contingency fee.

Since public entities like cities and counties have deep pockets, they are routinely included as defendants in anything that happens within their geographical boundaries. The same goes for pharmaceutical companies, hospitals, insurance companies, car companies, and banks. Any and all companies with deep pockets are the favorite target of attorneys whose remuneration is in the form of a contingency fee.

In September of 2003, Frederick Nesbitt, age nineteen, walked into a New Jersey bar and joined his friends, who were drinking pitchers of beer. The waitress, who knew Nesbitt and knew he was under age, did not serve him alcohol, only soda water. Nesbitt had, however, been drinking alcohol before he came to the bar.

On the way home, Nesbitt lost control of his car and killed James Hamby. An autopsy showed he was drunk at the time of the accident. Hamby's estate sued Nesbitt for millions of dollars, but Nesbitt had only $50,000 in insurance coverage. Consequently, despite the fact that Nesbitt had not been served any alcohol in the bar, the plaintiffs, looking for deep pockets, sued the bar under New Jersey's dram statute. A dram statute, which exists in thirty-eight states, requires a bar to order a taxi for a patron who appears to be intoxicated.

New Jersey's dram statute explicitly states that a patron who appears to be intoxicated must be offered a taxi only when that person has consumed alcohol in that bar. This is quite logical, as otherwise the bar would have to provide transportation to any intoxicated person walking into the bar simply to use the toilet facilities.

Hamby's estate lost in the lower court but won on appeal. The appellate court ruled that, contrary to its explicit wording, the intent of the statute was to compel bars to provide transportation to anybody who appeared intoxicated.

As a result of the Nesbitt case, insurance premiums for bars are considerably higher in New Jersey than anywhere else in the country, and New Jersey patrons pay the price in more expensive drinks.

Recently a Rhode Island jury found a restaurant 25 percent responsible for a drunk-driving accident. The uninsured culprit, Timothy Beaugirard, was assigned 75 percent culpability. Under Rhode Island's law, which states that each defendant is jointly and severally liable for all of the plaintiff's damages, the restaurant had to pay the full $15.2 million award. The attorney received a contingency fee of $4.2 million.

In the closing paragraphs of the previous chapter, I posed the question of why we do not have equal justice under the law. There are many answers to this question—greed being one of them. But another equally important one is the unholy alliance of lawyers and legislators. Every example in this chapter about the inequity of damages is the result of a law passed by a legislature to provide attorneys with another tool with which to earn a contingency fee. And when you say that I am paranoid, that I see a dollar sign behind every law and every attorney, tell me how it is possible, as we have seen in the case of the person in Washington DC who sued the drycleaner for $54 million, that the DC consumer laws allow plaintiffs to multiply the penalty for a single mistake to astronomical amounts *without having to prove injury*. Who wrote those patently unfair, even laughable, consumer laws? Small shop owners like Mr. Chung, the Korean dry cleaner, or lawyers?

14.

Forum Shopping

Forum shopping is a practice routinely pursued by attorneys to get their cases heard in a court of law most likely to give their clients a favorable verdict. During the early days of our country, you had to sue a person where he lived. The legal profession has changed this time-tested principle.

In common law systems, such as the ones in use in the United States and Canada and Great Britain, the way laws change or new laws are added to old ones is very different from how this happens in jurisdictions that use the continental European codified law. In common law systems, in addition to the laws written by the legislature, court opinions have the force of law.

In the United States, with fifty states and hundreds and hundreds of courts writing decisions every day, the speed with which the law mutates is much greater than in any other country. Of course, decisions by state courts have the force of law only in that state, and only rulings by federal courts have the force of law in all states. Litigators and state courts constantly look over their shoulders, however, to see how courts in other states handle a particular issue. It is only logical, then, that an innovative theory that has made its way into a ruling in a particular state court will be copied very rapidly in the ruling of a court in another state.

When the United States inherited the British common law system, and as the various states developed their own judicial systems, the age-old principle of *actor forum rei sequitor,* which began with Roman law, was universally accepted. Literally translated, this Roman maxim means the party taking the action (or the plaintiff) follows the jurisdiction of the thing involved. Or, in more modern language, "You must be sued in the jurisdiction of the subject of the lawsuit or where the defendant lives." For a very long time, this was the bedrock of American law—the Supreme Court upheld this right on numerous occasions.

And then, in a few cases in the nineteenth century and a few more in the beginning of the twentieth, lawyers began to nibble on this principle. A company selling something by mail into a state other than the one in which the company was domiciled meant the company could be sued in the state where its product had been received. People in car accidents in states other than the ones in which they lived were sued in the state where the accident occurred. And then in the 1950s, one exception after another was introduced so rapidly in court after court and in state after state that, in a very short period of time, the principle of actor forum rei sequitur completely disappeared.

Hallelujah. Attorneys could now cherry-pick the courts in which they filed their cases. And since one jurisdiction was known for juries that awarded huge sums in personal injury cases, and another for juries that awarded huge sums of money in medical malpractice cases, and another for awarding not only huge damage awards but large punitive damages to boot, attorneys now could survey the country for the place where they could expect the largest reward and where they would be able to earn the largest contingency fee.

Needless to say, in our modern world, where much commerce is conducted in cyber space or is interstate or international, the old principle of actor forum rei sequitur in deciding forum is insufficient. As usual, however, in deviating from the principle and in adapting the principle to today's situations, American jurisprudence began to abuse the need for change. Even where the principle still should apply, the principle is simply discarded by plaintiffs' attorneys, because the jury system does not dispense equal justice for all, and the American tort lawyer practices law not to pursue what is fair and equitable but to exploit the failures of the system. As we will see later, dollars and cents are more important than logic, fairness, and equity. Dollars and cents are a sufficient reason to game the system and to set the judicial system on its head.

The state of Mississippi, population 3.5 million, has always been a rural state. Aside from a few cities, such as Jackson (population 210,000), Hattiesburg (population 70,000), and Meridian (population 65,000), and a few small cities on the Gulf coast, only modest sized towns dot the map.

As is the case with all other states in the United States, the state is divided into counties, each county with its own prosecutors and its own courts. Since there are very few large companies that call Mississippi home, there are few large law firms. Law is practiced mostly by single practitioners or very small law firms. Attorneys all know each other; they usually are friends. Attorneys all know the prosecutors, and the judges are nearly all former colleagues of the attorneys that practice before their courts. It is all one big happy family. What these rural attorneys mostly deal with is family law, inheritance law, small business law, and real estate law—much of it consumer-oriented law. This explains why most rural judges, who formerly were small-time attorneys, are consumer-protection oriented judges.

Richard "Dickie" Scruggs, the king of all torts, as he is called, is from Mississippi. We saw earlier how Mr. Scruggs, through his connections with his friend the attorney general and his ability to get legislation passed favorable to the tort bar, became one of the richest men in the state of Mississippi. But it wasn't only Mr. Scruggs who became rich beyond all proportion; his many lawyer friends did likewise by making sure that Mississippi became the venue or forum of choice for contingency fee lawyers seeking outrageous awards for their class-action plaintiffs.

And so it came to pass that in the last thirty years Mississippi, and in particular Jefferson County, a county in the middle of nowhere, became the lawsuit capital of the United States. At one point Jefferson County had more plaintiffs than residents. As the present Mississippi Governor, Haley Barbour, with his typical southern sense of humor and southern drawl recently described the situation, "We were America's number one judicial hellhole for jackpot jury verdicts." To illustrate what a contingency fee lawyer can do with a choice of venue in a consumer-oriented court, a Jefferson County jury awarded one family of a woman who had taken the diet pill Pondimin (part of fen-phen, which later was banned) $1 billion—one thousand million dollars—in damages.

This was possible as a result of a number of court rulings and laws that allowed plaintiffs to establish forum or venue against a nonresident in any Mississippi county where the tort occurred even if the most insignificant elements of the plaintiff's damages had occurred in that county. For instance, a plaintiff had merely to travel to a particular county and claim he or she had suffered pain in that county to be able to sue in that county.

Moreover, only one member of a class in a class-action lawsuit had to have a relationship, however insignificant, with that county to allow all class members to sue in that county. Whereas in most other states class-action members' complaints require near complete similarity in law or in fact, the Mississippi Supreme Court ruled that plaintiffs' lawyers could join hundreds or thousands of plaintiffs in one lawsuit based on the most minimal similarity of their claims.

Without limits on noneconomic damages or punitive damages, Mississippi gradually turned into the largest litigation gambling casino in the world.

On May 21, 2005, Ruth and Richard Singleton and their seven-year-old granddaughter were traveling in their Volkswagen Golf on a freeway in Dallas when their car was rear-ended by Colin Little. The collision sent the Golf spinning across the freeway, resulting in the Gulf plowing into a flatbed truck parked on the shoulder. The Singletons' granddaughter later died of a skull fracture.

The manner in which the attorneys handled this case, the way the case traveled through the courts from one court to another and all the way to the Supreme Court of the United States, vividly illustrates to what extent the legal profession has turned American jurisprudence into a Gordian knot and to what extent legal proceedings have become a travesty of what is logical, what is reasonable, or what is fair.

After losing their granddaughter in this heartbreaking accident, the Singletons needed to decide what to do. Needless to say, they consulted an attorney to see what redress they could expect from Colin Little, who had rear-ended them and who had set in motion the events leading to their granddaughter's death. Anybody would say that consulting an attorney about the relief they might expect from Colin Little sounds reasonable and makes sense. Not to a tort attorney, however.

A contingency fee attorney looks at the dollars and cents, at the cash register. From a financial point of view, suing Colin Little, who might not carry much insurance and who might not be the type to inspire a jury to award the Singletons a huge amount of money, didn't make much sense. Suing Volkswagen, however, a big corporation with deep pockets, a faceless corporation juries just might be inclined to find the culprit in this accident, made imminent sense.

The problem, of course, was that Colin Little was the logical target—he was the one who rear-ended the Golf. How to get Volkswagen involved? The answer was an easy one: just claim a defect in the design of the car, claim the automobile manufacturer knew about this defect all along, and sue the irresponsible and reckless auto company.[59]

Designing a car that will withstand absolutely every type of accident is impossible. No passenger car can withstand a head-on collision with a ten-ton truck traveling sixty miles an hour. Consequently, when a person is killed in a car accident as a result of a collapsing side door or a disintegrating dashboard or an exploding gas tank, at what point does the destroyed side door or dashboard or gas tank become negligence in the design of the car on the part of the car manufacturer?

It is certainly possible to build a side door out of steel that even a ten-ton truck cannot penetrate. A dashboard can be designed that will not collapse or a gas tank that cannot be pierced and will not explode. Designing a car that way—and everybody knows it—is impossible. When designing a car, numerous compromises must be made: time and again, safety and reliability must be balanced against cost. Car companies spend years designing and testing a car. Their engineers spend thousands and thousands of hours making sure that in balancing cost and reliability, they err on the safe side. The tragic part of American jurisprudence is that tort lawyers spend years and years building cases against car companies that will convince a jury—a jury that hasn't the foggiest idea what it takes to build and design a car—that the car company has been recklessly negligent in building the car and owes the victim not just millions but tens of millions of dollars. It's like the craps table. Roll the dice in a sufficient

---

59 In practically all car crashes with bodily injury, the manufacturer of the car is sued. As is the case in the hugely profitable strike suits, yearly thousands of lawsuits are filed against car manufacturers. In practically every case, the plaintiff's attorney has no idea that a defect in the car involved in the crash contributed to the accident. However, after filing the suit, the plaintiff's attorneys use discovery to go on a fact-finding expedition through the manufacturer's records to uncover hints of malfeasance. As in strike suits, suits against car manufacturers are so costly and inconvenient for the car maker that most suits are settled out of court.

number of car crashes by suing the car company, and at some point you will hit the jackpot.

Consequently, the Singletons (or rather their attorneys) decided to sue Volkswagen. Since it was the collapsing front seat of the Golf that had crashed into the Singletons' granddaughter's skull when the car careened into the truck, Volkswagen was sued for negligence in designing the car seat.

Maybe we should not be upset about the Singletons suing Volkswagen. One never knows. Their attorneys may have found that an exceedingly incompetent and negligent engineer in Wolfsburg, Germany, designed a recklessly unsafe front seat in the Golf and that Volkswagen was derelict in its duty not to sell Golfs that might kill a child when catapulted into a parked flatbed truck. Let's forgive them for deciding to sue Volkswagen.

Now consider this: (1) the Volkswagen Golf was purchased in Dallas County, Texas; (2) the accident occurred on a freeway in Dallas; (3) Dallas residents witnessed the accident; (4) Dallas police and paramedics responded and took action; (5) a Dallas doctor performed the autopsy; (6) the third-party defendant, Colin Little, lives in Dallas County.

Consequently, you would expect that the case would be filed in Dallas. If any case screamed for being filed in Dallas rather than anywhere else, it would be this particular case.

Wrong. What is logical or reasonable or judicious in most everybody's opinion is not so in the opinion of an American tort attorney. Although none of the plaintiffs lived in the Marshall Division of the Eastern District of Texas, although no known party or significant non-party witness lived in the Marshall Division of the Eastern District of Texas, and although none of the facts giving rise to the suit against Volkswagen occurred in the Marshall Division of the Eastern District of Texas, the Singletons' attorneys decided to file the case in the Marshall Division of the Eastern District of Texas.

Why? Because Marshall, a town with 25,000 residents near the border with Louisiana, is known for the speed of its proceedings, the large number of cases that go to a jury trial, and the large verdicts awarded by those juries. The Marshall Division of the Eastern District of Texas is known as a plaintiff-friendly venue that produces much higher awards to plaintiffs than does the court in Dallas. Consequently, the Marshall Division of the Eastern District of Texas has a hugely abnormal number of product liability cases—17 percent of all federal automobile product liability lawsuits in the United States are litigated in that venue.

The decision by the Singleton attorneys to defy age-old tradition, a tradition followed in practically all non-American jurisdictions, and to defy all common logic, which dictates that since all the parties involved lived in Dallas the case should be filed in Dallas, shows what is so utterly wrong with American law and procedure and to what extent tort lawyers will abuse the system to chase the almighty dollar. And it's not just the tort lawyers; judges approve these actions, and as we will see later, law professors write amicus briefs for the courts involved to urge on the practice even in cases where the chosen venue doesn't make any legal or equitable sense.

And all this is just the beginning. Volkswagen, obviously, moved to transfer venue to the Dallas Division of the Northern District of Texas. Volkswagen asserted that a transfer was warranted since the Volkswagen Golf was purchased in Dallas, the accident occurred on a freeway in Dallas, Dallas residents witnessed the accident, Dallas police and paramedics responded and took action, a Dallas doctor performed the autopsy; the third-party defendant lived in Dallas, none of the plaintiffs lived in the Marshall Division, no known party or significant non-party witness lived in the Marshall Division, and finally none of the facts giving rise to the suit occurred in the Marshall Division.

Open and shut case, you would think. Wrong. The district court refused to transfer the case to Dallas.

Volkswagen appealed. It went to the Fifth Circuit Court of Appeals and asked the court to order the eastern district to transfer the case to Dallas. The fifth circuit refused to grant Volkswagen's request. US District Judge John Ward wrote, "The plaintiff's choice of forum is a paramount consideration in any determination of a transfer request and that choice should not be lightly distributed." In other words: Volkswagen, your request is denied, because it is up to the plaintiff's attorney in which venue the case should be tried.

Volkswagen then appealed the decision to the entire fifth circuit court. The court upheld the eastern district's decision, stating that it (the eastern district) "did not clearly abuse its discretion."

Volkswagen then decided upon a most unusual procedure, albeit one that, everybody would agree was the only reasonable course of action left in view of the circumstances. It appealed the fifth circuit decision by filing a petition for a rehearing before the very same court.

Surprise, surprise. After three rounds of briefings and two oral arguments, the fifth circuit, in a ten-to-seven, decision finally agreed with Volkswagen that Judge Ward of the eastern district had abused his discretion by applying the wrong legal standard and by not properly weighing interest factors (primarily matters of convenience).

One would assume that justice was finally done and that this would be the end of the case. Not in this case. The Singletons (the Singletons' attorneys, I should say) appealed the decision to the United States Supreme Court.

On February 23, 2009, a full four years after the case started its sorry journey through the labyrinth of hearings, decisions, appeals, rehearings, reconsiderations, and written and oral arguments, after thousands of hours of lawyers wasting their time on the simple question of whether a case should go to trial where all the parties in question resided, the Supreme Court of the United States finally approved of the transfer of the case to Dallas by refusing to hear the appeal. Four years after the accident and after huge amounts of money had been wasted in attorneys' fees as well as the cost to the courts in question, in February of 2009 *Singleton v. Volkswagen* could finally go to trial in Dallas. The proper judicial process to adjudicate the Singleton complaint could finally begin.

One of the anomalies of the American legal system is the use of juries in deciding disputes—an anomaly not only because juries provide uneven, unequal justice but also because the rest of the world has abolished the old-fashioned, outdated, and primitive use of juries in settling disputes. Routine forum shopping by lawyers magnifies the injustice of juries and renders the unfair jury system even worse.

It is not only the attorneys' decision to shop for the most advantageous forum that is, through the eyes of a non-American observer and by the legal standards of most advanced democracies, an abuse of the judicial process. As shown in the constantly changing decisions of the judges of the fifth district in the matter of *Singleton v. Volkswagen* and the court's final ten-to-seven decision, scores of judges also find that a plaintiff's choice of venue is the most important consideration when deciding where to try a case. Consequently, the disease of the appropriateness of forum shopping equally infects judges.

Add to the attorneys and judges a good number of prominent law professors of our venerable law schools. In the Singletons' struggle not to transfer the case to Dallas, the Singletons were aided by an amicus brief written by a number of prominent professors of some well-known law schools. Consequently, forum shopping is not only practiced by many attorneys, it is condoned by many judges and supported by numerous law professors.

It is of course the use of a jury in settling disputes, particularly in product liability cases, and the fact that juries in certain areas of the country will grant outrageous awards, that is at the heart of the problem and leads to forum shopping. Attorneys with whom I discussed this matter often disagreed with me by arguing that if we didn't use a jury system and instead used a system of judges, plaintiff awards would still vary from state to state and within states. They cite the famous or infamous Ninth Circuit Court of Appeals decisions, 76 percent of which were overturned by the Supreme Court in the 2009 term. The *Los Angeles Times* reports that from prisoners' rights to environmental protection, laws set by the west's most powerful appeals court were overturned in fifteen of the sixteen cases reviewed by the Supreme Court in the 2009 term.

Judges' decisions would indeed vary from one state to another or from one federal jurisdiction to another. No system would ever be able to guarantee complete equality in justice. Judges would be much more temperate, however, in passing judgment, particularly since they are always looking over their shoulders to avoid being reversed on appeal. Outrageous awards, often referred to as jackpot justice, would disappear, and the need for forum shopping would disappear with it.

15.

Assembly Line Justice

or

Settlement Mills

Between 1908 and 1915, Henry Ford revolutionized manufacturing by building cars the individual parts of which were added sequentially along a moving assembly line. The logistics of this manufacturing process produced cars in a much shorter time than was usual, it lowered the cost of the finished product, and it significantly increased profit. If this process works in manufacturing, why not in lawyering?

Traditional tort lawyering requires a number of meetings between lawyer and client, an in-depth evaluation of the claim, the filing of a lawsuit, pretrial discovery, and negotiations with the attorneys of the opposing party. Depending on the outcome of the negotiations, the case will be settled or the parties will go to trial. After a verdict is rendered, one of the parties to the dispute may appeal the case. Consequently, it often takes more than a year before the dispute is finally settled and the books are closed. In America, the process of conflict resolution is lawyer intensive, time consuming, and expensive.

Consequently, why not learn from Ford and streamline the process of tort claims by introducing an assembly line for conflict resolution? Why not solicit hundreds of cases (if possible thousands of cases); have clients sign a standard, preprinted agreement that includes a contingency fee for the law firm; have an attorney supervise a cadre of nonlawyer conflict-resolution negotiators who settle cases with insurance adjusters and are

179

paid on the basis of a commission; avoid having to go to trial at all cost; forget about ethics and forget about the interests of the client; and just settle every case that comes through the front door in the shortest period of time?

The problem with this kind of lawyering is of course the need to recruit hundreds of clients—its success depends heavily on the number of clients law firms can induce to come through their front doors.

The Supreme Court of the United States solved that problem in 1977. In *Bates v. State Bar of Arizona*, the Supreme Court held that attorney advertising is protected by the First Amendment (which guarantees the freedom of speech). Consequently, if one spends a sufficient amount of money on advertising—a sufficient amount to guarantee that hundreds of clients (if not more) will take their cases to the law firm—the assembly line of lawyering will work and will make an attorney using this approach rich. Hence the birth of the new kind of law firm sometimes referred to as the settlement mill.

A settlement mill is a law firm that, instead of using reputation or expertise to attract clients, uses advertising almost exclusively to solicit a very large number of personal injury clients whose claims are settled in a very short period of time. Settlement of the claim takes place without interaction between lawyer and client and practically always without filing a lawsuit. The fact that lawsuits are rarely filed means that the settlement process operates without the threat of a trial and takes place entirely outside the normal judicial process. In other words, the settlement mill operates not within the law but in the shadow of the law.

In the last ten years, settlement mills have proliferated. They have avoided scrutiny both in the world of academia and in the media because, as I mentioned above, they largely operate in the shadow of the legal system.

Everybody is familiar and quite used to lawyers' constant and highly intrusive advertising—their advertisements are an annoying staple of everyday television. Of the 532 pages in my local yellow pages telephone book, 39 pages consist of advertisements by attorneys or law firms. More than 7 percent of all advertisements in my local yellow pages solicit clients for lawyers. Although some law firms operate both as traditional law firms and settlement mills, a number of the law firms in my local yellow pages appear to operate solely as settlement mills.

I have mentioned before that the average injured person with a small claim today cannot find a lawyer to handle the case. When the harm is relatively modest and the claim is small, the contingency fee is insufficient to entice a lawyer to take the case. Consequently, for the person with a relatively small claim, the settlement mill appears to be an ideal solution. It affords a claimant with modest means access to a law firm and potential relief. Consequently, the question arises, what's wrong with settlement mils? The answer is "everything."

My interest in settlement mills did not come about as a result of personal experience or articles in newspapers or postings on law blogs on the Internet. Somewhat familiar with the cost of TV and yellow book advertising and realizing how expensive this form of advertising is, I became curious about how it was possible for some law firms to spend such large amounts of money on advertising. It didn't take long to come to the conclusion that, for local law firms seeking mostly personal injury claims, expensive advertising works because it brings in a large number of clients whose cases are relatively easy and cheap to settle. [60]

I was surprised, however, that when I researched the matter I could hardly find any literature on the subject: no stories in the newspapers, no postings on law blogs, no articles in law magazines. There was one exception: an in-depth and learned sixty-page treatise entitled "Run-of-the-Mill Justice" published in 2009 in the *Georgetown Journal of Legal Ethics* by Nora Freeman Engstrom, Assistant Professor of Law at Stanford University. Without the knowledge gained from this impressively well-researched work and the sporadic commentary in a few law blogs, I could not have written this chapter.

By interviewing attorneys who had worked for nine different law firms that might be called settlement mills; by talking to their personnel (in particular employees whose task it was to negotiate with insurance companies and the employees who dealt with the clients); by studying the agreements clients had to sign; and by analyzing the settlements, the lawyer fee structure, and a number of other details, "Run-of-the-Mill Justice" provides a complete and exceedingly detailed picture of how settlement mills work and how they make lawyers rich.

---

60 Auto, motorcycle, or pedestrian accidents; slip and fall injuries; and, although rare, wrongful death or malpractice cases.

How Do Settlement Mills Operate?

When, as a result of a law firm's advertisement, a client consults the firm, the client frequently does not see a lawyer but may be asked to watch a video of how the law firm works.[61] The video obviously emphasizes the laudable record of the firm in reaching favorable settlements for its clients. The video explains the contract between the law firm and the client and explains the tiered contingency fee the law firm earns upon settlement. In many settlement mills, the contract for legal services specifies that the fee is 33 percent of the settlement amount, 40 percent if a lawsuit has to be filed, and 50 percent if a verdict is appealed.

Somebody in the law firm (usually not a lawyer) contacts the insurer and enters into a settlement negotiation guided by a set of negotiating guidelines including a monetary settlement target developed by the law firm.

In "Plaintiffs' Lawyers, Specialization, and Medical Malpractice," Stephen Daniels and Joanne Martin, reporting on data from a 2000 survey of Texas plaintiffs' lawyers, found that conventional personal injury attorneys have approximately seventy open files at one time and serve approximately 110 clients per year.[62] Settlement mill attorneys often have three hundred open files to deal with, serving three hundred to four hundred clients per year. One Georgia settlement mill attorney reported that she personally settled between six hundred and seven hundred claims in a thirteen-month period, and an Arizona settlement mill attorney reported settling between five hundred and six hundred cases in one year.

Personnel in settlement mills, whether they are attorneys, claim negotiators, or front office personnel who sign up clients, are often remunerated on the basis of commissions (often combined with bonuses) tied to the amount of contingency fee income the employee has generated for the firm. Consequently, in settlement mills there is a constant pressure to bring in more and more clients and to settle more and more cases as quickly as possible. Studies show that the average time it takes to settle a personal injury claim when the client is represented by counsel is

---

61 According to Nora Engstrom, clients of law firms she interviewed recovered an average of $4,900 for their clients, representing an amount between two and four times the amount of the client's medical bills.

62 Stephen Daniels and Joanne Martin. *Plaintiffs' Lawyers, Specialization, and Medical Malpractice, Vanderbilt University Law Review* (May 2006).

approximately one year. In settlement mills, settlements take place after as little as two months and seldom take longer than eight months.

As we have seen in the chapter about strike suits and shareholder derivative suits, in settlement mills, the practice of law has changed from a profession into a business. Numbers, efficiency, results, speed, and standardization are what counts, not established legal procedure. Like the check cashing business or payday loans, settlement mills prey on uninformed clients with modest or very little means who do not know or care about the law and are usually in need of cash.

Why Do Insurance Companies Tolerate Settlement Mills?

In answering this question, we will begin to understand why settlement mills are so hideous, perverting fairness and equity. In our extremely litigious society, insurers are constantly defending themselves against frivolous lawsuits as well as meritorious lawsuits that nevertheless pose a great risk to the insurer not just because of the unpredictability of jury verdicts but also because of the potential for multimillion dollar jackpot verdicts and punitive damages

That risk disappears when an insurer deals with a settlement mill. The threat of a trial and an outrageous jury verdict is gone. The financial exposure of the insurer is greatly diminished, which explains why insurers like dealing with settlement mills. Rather than having to work with a law firm that operates in the conventional manner and files a lawsuit, insurers end up saving money when settling a claim with a settlement mill.

"So what?" you might ask. What is wrong with a small claim client, who these days has no access to the judicial process, having access to a settlement process that provides him or her with relief at very little out-of-pocket cost?

The answer is that the settlement process takes place without the lawyer or law firm looking into whether the claim is meritorious or not and, more importantly, without regard to the economic harm done to the client. The amount of the payment a settlement mill negotiates on behalf of its client has no relationship whatsoever to the actual damage to the client. The settlement mill settles for an amount of money the insurer, in the estimation of the settlement mill, will be willing to pay—not the amount the client will accept, as it should be. In other words, the settlement mill does not settle for the amount that approximates the damage done to the client, which is essential to a well-functioning insurance industry, but for an amount the insurer will accept and will accept quickly.

The client is uninformed. When the client receives a check, the client is happy even if the amount is less than what the client had expected. Moreover, when the settlement check is handed over to the client (normally by a lawyer), the client is told how lucky he or she is and what a fabulous job the attorney has been able to do on behalf of the client.

Professor Freeman Engstrom's research has shown unequivocally that clients with small, dubious claims do reasonably well. However, clients with large, meritorious claims suffer tremendously by having their claims settled by a settlement mill. The large, meritorious claim is exactly the kind of claim the insurance company wants to settle quickly. Consequently, the interests of the insurer and the settlement mill overlap—an inadmissible conflict of interest for both the insurer and the law firm. Thus the large, meritorious claim is settled for a much lower amount than the claimant would normally be entitled to. The larger, meritorious claims actually pay for the settlement of the smaller, dubious claims.

The settlement mill does not follow established principles of jurisprudence with regard to the traditional tort system's delivery of compensation. Rather, the settlement mill follows a business plan that produces a steady stream of contingency fee income to the settlement mill lawyer without regard to the law or legal procedure and without regard to the interest of the client—in other words, without regard to legal principles of fairness and equity.

PART III

OVERSIGHT AND REFORM

What is good for Wall Street is good for Law Street

1.

The Quality of the American Legal System as Compared to Legal Systems in Other Countries

Is there a tort system where the loser pays the attorney fees of the prevailing party and where the attorney is paid an hourly, professional fee, a system that does not allow the American form of class action and where civil disputes are settled by learned judges, not by juries? If you think such a judicial system doesn't exist—most Americans I have talked to are convinced such a system isn't possible and, if it did exist, would not be equitable—look at Sweden, Germany, the Netherlands, France, Japan, Australia, South Korea, or Singapore, to name just a few examples—they all have such a legal system.

The price of everything in America includes the cost of a dysfunctional, costly, and often corrupt tort system. Because we have a tort system that is focused on the interests of the attorney rather than the consumer, everything the American consumer buys costs a lot more, most likely 1 percent to 2 percent more and possibly more than that. Medical insurance is much more expensive, thousands of citizens are wasting their time on jury duty (close to 1.5 million Americans serve on juries every year), our television is clogged by attorney advertising chasing mesotheleoma victims, and our recovery from disputed insurance claims is 20 to 25 percent less than it should be. Without class action or the contingency fee, the management of our companies and their directors—entities in our economic system that provide jobs—would be freed from having to spend time to satisfy the greed of class-action attorneys, and doctors would practice the type of medicine that is good for patients rather than preventive medicine—the type of medical practice that is good for a defense attorney in case the doctor is sued.

The question arises, however, whether a legal system without loser pays laws and with contingency fees, class actions, and jury trials in civil cases is indeed such a bad system compared to other legal systems—after all, no system is perfect. In other words, doesn't such a system provide better access to the courts and increased fairness or equity compared to legal systems that lack these controversial aspects of the American legal system?

That question has been answered by an authoritative and in-depth study by the World Justice Project in its *Rule of Law Index*.[63] The World Justice Project (WJP) is a multinational organization that seeks to strengthen the rule of law around the world. The project was launched in 2006 by the American Bar Association and has since become an independent, not-for-profit organization with twenty-one international sponsoring organizations. WJP defines the rule of law on the basis of four principles:

- Governments should be accountable under the law.
- There should be fair and comprehensible laws that protect fundamental rights.
- Legal processes should be fair and efficient.
- People should have access to justice provided by diverse, competent, and independent judges and lawyers.

WJP's *Rule of Law Index* shows that, while the United States is among the top countries in the world when viewed from the perspective of open government (it places third behind Sweden and the Netherlands), it lacks in most other areas of justice:

---

63 The Rule of Law Index of the World Justice Project is a quantitative assessment tool used to offer a detailed and comprehensive picture of the extent to which countries adhere to the rule of law. The 2010 Rule of Law Index was released on October 14, 2010 at the National Press Club in Washington DC.

- In the Absence of Corruption category, the United States ranked tenth, behind Sweden, the Netherlands, Austria, Singapore, Canada, Australia, France, Japan, and Spain.
- Undoubtedly because of the many different state laws and the US common law system, in the category of Clear, Publicized and Stable Laws, the United States ranked ninth, behind Sweden, the Netherlands, Japan, Canada, Australia, Austria, Singapore, and France.
- In the category of Fundamental Rights, the United States again ranked ninth, behind Austria, Sweden, the Netherlands, Canada, Spain, Australia, South Korea, Japan, and France.
- In the Access to Civil Justice category—a very important category because many apologists for the American legal system claim that the contingency fee has made it possible for persons of modest means to have access to civil justice—America ranks eleventh, behind Singapore, Sweden, the Netherlands, Austria, South Korea, Australia, Spain, Canada, France, and Japan.
- In the Effective Criminal Justice category, the United States comes in seventh, behind Austria, Japan, Sweden, the Netherlands, Singapore, and France.
- Taking into consideration all nine categories on which countries were judged, the United States came in at ten.

For such a proud country as the United States, a mature democracy that, most often successfully, strives for excellence in human rights, this is a dismal legal score card. It proves without a doubt that all those legal scholars who constantly sing the praises of the American legal system ought, for once, to look over their shoulders to see whether other countries do a better job in managing their legal systems. The World Justice Project's *Rule of Law Index* clearly illustrates that the American legal system is not as perfect as so many self-serving American attorneys claim.

In the United States, judicial reform seems to be a sisyphean task—impossible to accomplish. Not for want of trying, however. For years the United States has struggled with the issue. It has frequently attempted to reform the system, especially at the state level, but so far little has been accomplished.

2.

Oversight of Prosecutors and Lawyers: The Bar Associations

More so than in any other democracy, the executive and the legislature in the United States are subject to constant voter oversight. Being able to dismiss members of the House of Representatives every two years, Senators every six years, and the president every four years gives the American people more than ample opportunity to use the ballot box to kick the bums out if they so desire.

The American legal system has few checks and balances, however. The framers of the constitution created a federal judiciary that is independent and exemplifies the highest quality and integrity. When federal judges who are appointed are accused of misconduct, they are subject to impeachment in the Senate. In the history of the United States, a total of thirteen federal judges have been impeached. That this has occurred so few times should not be a surprise. With the required advice and consent of the United States Senate, federal judges undergo a rigorous selection process. Consequently, most serve with distinction. The same can be said for our US attorneys (our federal prosecutors).

State judges, however, are usually elected, which means every few years the voters get a chance to get a misbehaving judge off the bench. Because few voters have any idea what goes on in the local courtroom, the fact that voters are able to remove a sitting state judge is relatively meaningless.

Lawyers and prosecutors are a completely different matter. Since they operate with hardly any oversight, they are beyond reproach. When legal scholars argue that local prosecutors are subject to the ballot box, I counter that that is a myth. Prosecutors are sources of news. Consequently, prosecutors have a strong influence over and access to the local media. Their ability to call well-attended press conferences in which they tout their achievements is so complete, and the media's love of prosecutors is so pervasive, that a proper and unbiased review of their conduct by the electorate is simply impossible. Consequently, misconduct by a local prosecutor is rarely if ever the reason the prosecutor loses reelection.

This book has chronicled a large number of instances of misconduct on the part of prosecutors and lawyers in the criminal justice area as well as in tort litigation. As a matter of fact, as the record shows, misconduct is not rare. It happens so often that one can argue that lawyer misconduct in the United States is endemic.

This sounds like an exaggeration. However, the reason both the defenders of the American legal system and I may be right is that what I call lawyer misconduct is often accepted by the legal community as par for the course.

- In my view, an attorney abusing pretrial discovery—and the abuse of pretrial discover is indeed a daily occurrence—constitutes lawyer misconduct. Defenders of the pretrial discovery argue, however, that abuse of pretrial discovery is simply gaming the system, not lawyer misconduct.
- When an attorney refuses a case unless the client accepts a contingency fee, I call that misconduct.
- When a class-action attorney, or a strike suit attorney, or a shareholder derivative suit attorney files suit simply to blackmail the target into a settlement, every attorney will tell you they have not broken the law—it is part of the American system; it is the way the system strives for fairness and equity. I call it legal misconduct.
- When a prosecutor withholds exculpating evidence from the defense, everybody agrees it amounts to prosecutorial misconduct. Yet it happens all the time and not just with small-town prosecutors out in the middle of nowhere. As we have seen in the previous chapters, it happens everywhere, even, as *US v. Senator Stevens* shows, in the highest echelons of the Justice Department.

- When Justice Department lawyers or regulatory agency lawyers threaten company indictments instead of going after individuals in companies who have broken the law (as in the case of Arthur Anderson) or threaten companies with indictments unless they cooperate by throwing their employees under the buss (as in the case of KPMG), or when prosecutors offer leniency to an accused if the lawyer representing the accused refrains from defending another client in the case (like Ms. Martha Coakley, prosecutor in Middlesex County, Massachusetts, in the Fells Acre Day Care Center case), I call that lawyer misconduct.
- When a local judge, even a state supreme court judge, sits in judgment of a case in which one of the litigants has contributed hundreds and thousand of dollars to the judge's reelection, I don't call this lawyer misconduct. I call it fraud.

The Bar Associations

Most Americans are so used to their lawyers' way of lawyering that it has become condoned. It is just the way it is. Everybody has become inured to it and has stopped complaining about it.

Who is supposed to oversee and regulate lawyers, and how are lawyers punished for misconduct? The answer is the state bar associations. It is their duty to monitor the professional conduct of their members and sanction attorneys who break the rules. Herein lies part of the problem with America's dysfunctional and often corrupt legal system. The bar associations' role in overseeing the conduct of lawyers is a farce—I will go as far as to call it a self-serving, cynical joke.

I have read the codes of conduct and the ethics rules of a number of state bar associations. They certainly strive for their members to adhere to very lofty ideals of professional conduct. They use soaring language in proclaiming to the world that theirs is a profession beyond reproach and that those who violate their high standards of professional conduct shall be reprimanded, censured, or in the case of egregious misconduct, disbarred.

Looking at the record of oversight by the bar associations, however, their protestations ring hollow. What they say will happen in case of professional misconduct simply doesn't happen.

In the chapter about the election of prosecutors, a list of twenty-eight child molestation cases detailed prosecutorial misconduct by scores of prosecutors, putting hundreds of innocent people in jail, ruining families, depriving children of being raised by their own parents, and forcing children to live with the debilitating stigma of parents in jail for child molestation, one of the most despised crimes. None of those prosecutors was ever punished by their bar associations.

In nearly every case cited in this book, there is clear evidence of prosecutorial or lawyer misconduct, not just by my definition of misconduct but by the bar associations' own definition. With the exception of lawyers who behaved like common criminals, lawyers like Lerach and Scruggs, I have not been able to find much evidence of the lawyers mentioned in these cases ever being punished.

Lawyers do not seem to punish their colleagues for inappropriate and unprofessional or even corrupt behavior. As the case against Lerach shows, prosecutors won't even treat their felonious colleagues as criminals. The judge who sentenced Lerach was furious about the prosecutor's plea bargain with Lerach, which included a mere two-year sentence. Moreover, since many bar associations do not publish their disciplinary records, to find out if bar associations do censure their erring colleagues is exceedingly difficult. Transparency works like an antiseptic. For the bar associations, however, secrecy is the preferred approach.

Judge Emmet Sullivan, the presiding judge in Alaska Senator Stevens's case, has publicly urged a change in the national judicial rules to establish consequences for prosecutors who do not follow the rules about turning over evidence to defendants. He—himself a federal judge—simply does not trust the bar associations or even the Justice Department to do so.

In the course of the work they do, the various law school innocence projects come across prosecutorial misconduct rather frequently. When action on their part sets an innocent convict free, the innocence projects often look into what caused the miscarriage of justice. They frequently stumble on prosecutorial misconduct.

Recently the Northern California Innocence Project at Santa Clara University School of Law released a study entitled "Preventable Error: A Report on Prosecutorial Misconduct in California 1997–2009."[64] The

---

64 Preventable Error: A Report on Prosecutorial Misconduct in California 1997–2009, by Kathleen M Ridolfi and Maurice Possley. Published October 2010 by the Northern California Innocence Project, Santa Clara University School of Law.

study detailed hundreds of cases in California state and federal courts where prosecutorial misconduct was evident. The study's authors, Kathleen M. Ridolfi, a law professor at Santa Clara University, and Maurice Possley, an acclaimed journalist and investigative reporter, wrote that prosecutorial misconduct "fundamentally perverts the course of justice" and "undermines our trust in the reliability of the justice system."

The study looked at the appellate court records of more than four thousand cases in California between 1997 and the 2009. Of the 3000 cases that were dismissed by the appellate courts, 707, according to the courts' conclusions, showed clear evidence of prosecutorial misconduct. When the authors of the study looked at the state bar's public disciplinary records, they found that, despite the fact that 67 of the 707 prosecutors had been accused of misconduct more than once and 3 had committed misconduct in four cases and 2 had committed misconduct in five, only 6 of the 707 prosecutors had been sanctioned. The California state bar disciplined less than 1 percent of the prosecutors who had been found to break the rules of professional conduct in prosecuting alleged criminals.

The report described Los Angeles County Deputy District Attorney Grace Rai as "a striking example of repeat prosecutorial misconduct that has not been publicly disciplined."

We should ask ourselves why we are—appropriately, I should say—indignant when Iran violates the human rights of three innocent American hikers who have strayed into Iranian territory yet never seem to be indignant about the violation of the human rights of the scores of innocent Americans languishing in American jails because of the misconduct of our own American lawyers. If Ahmadinejad deserves our scorn, why are our fellow American lawyers beyond reproach? America cries out for proper lawyer oversight. What is good for Wall Street is good for Law Street.

3.

Legal Reform

Can our legal system be improved? In 1994 Newt Gingrich's Contract with America included tort reform. The contract proposed loser-pays laws, stricter rules with regard to expert evidence, reasonable limits on punitive damages combined with reform of product liability laws, new rules requiring attorneys to account for the exact hours worked and to produce a detailed description of work performed, and proposed limits on strike suits.

After a veto by President Clinton, in 1995 Congress nevertheless overrode the veto and passed what was called the Private Securities Litigation Reform Act. Prior to enactment of the law, however, loser-pays proposals and many other elements of the proposed tort reform had been stripped out of the legislation and, despite the new law, the anomalies of the American legal system continued unabated.

Although it has been demonstrated by legal systems all around the world and in the state of Alaska that loser pays works and is vital to stemming frivolous lawsuits, the absence of loser pays is not the only or even the major culprit in our dysfunctional and often corrupt legal system.

The major problem is that the tort lawyer is not a professional but a businessperson—a businessperson with a business model crafted over the years through lawyer-driven legislative intervention and the forever exploding mountain of lawyer-produced law.

The tort lawyers' business model creates value through the use of the contingency fee combined with legally sanctioned blackmail. The architecture of the business model uses a strategy that includes fierce protection of a legal monopoly combined with the use of nuisance, discovery, class action, forum shopping, jury manipulation, nationwide TV advertising, and client solicitation.

The tort business model is simple but ingenious: pick a target, blackmail the target with a threat to sue, use the threat to negotiate a settlement, and walk away with 33 percent or more of the money paid in settlement.

This business model has proven exceedingly profitable and beats the business models of some of our most sophisticated and successful companies in its perfection. In the old days, even the mafia's blackmail business model could not extract 33 percent from clients of its company protection rackets—society would simply not tolerate such a degree of extortion—but lawyers can. And because lawyers, through their influence on the state and national legislatures, write the laws of the land, their unethical and confiscatory business model is difficult to beat.

Will tort lawyers ever give up this lucrative racket? America, I am afraid, is stuck with a dysfunctional legal system unless and until its citizens, left or right, Democrat or Republican, finally realize what is happening and unite in an effort to change the system.

Americans complain about losing their competitiveness. Many observers and economists point to causes like an uncompetitive corporate tax system, overly generous salaries, benefits and pensions forced upon the country by labor unions, a secondary school system that is among the worst in the developed world, an aging infrastructure, and an inefficient and costly health care system. Hardly ever mentioned is the country's abysmal legal system, which drives up the cost of our products to the point where they are priced out of the world markets and the jobs that produced those products migrate overseas. Somehow the anomalies of our legal system remain under the radar of the average person.

What we need is the equivalent of the slowly rising popular concern about the dismal state of our public school system. If, twenty-five years ago, when our public primary and secondary schools were just as bad as they are today, someone had suggested charter schools or vouchers to liberate our schools from the suffocating bureaucracy of school boards and teacher unions, that someone would have been told to stop dreaming. And yet charter schools are today popping up all over, and a movie titled *Waiting for Superman* is waking up the nation to a national disgrace. Solutions to a failing school system are beginning to be implemented, and improved results are showing up in many school districts.

This is what we need for our legal system. In the criminal law area, the outcry against miscarriages of justice has, in the last ten years, woken up a number of concerned law professors and hundreds of young, idealistic law students. The resulting innocence projects have led to the release of untold innocent prisoners from jail. As such, the innocence projects have made great progress in alerting the nation that our criminal law system is seriously deficient.

The innocence projects obviously do not solve the deficiencies of our criminal justice system. For every innocent prisoner released from jail, the release comes too late, since the finding of innocence should have come before the guilty verdict was pronounced. But with innocent men and women being released from jail now a daily occurrence, the nation is at least waking up to the problems in our criminal justice system.

Consequently, who knows? Someday we Americans may wake up and begin to rethink our tort system and improve our legal rules and procedures, protect the winner in a lawsuit with loser-pays rules, remunerate our lawyers with a proper hourly fee, demand that our bar associations enforce their ethics laws, appoint our prosecutors and judges pursuant to the advice and consent of our legislatures, rein in the influence of the bar in the state and federal legislatures, and most importantly, change the ethics culture of the law schools that incubate our young lawyers.

Loser-Pays Rules

As is already the case in Alaska, legal reform should begin with rules requiring the loser in a lawsuit to pay the legal fees of the prevailing party. In one fell swoop, the vast majority of frivolous lawsuits and settlement mills would disappear.

I mentioned earlier that the Private Securities Litigation Reform Act of 1995 (the result of Gingrich's Contract with America) originally included a loser-pays rule as part of the legislation. The watered-down version of the act (the one that was finally passed) did not mandate a loser-pays rule but allowed a federal judge to order a loser to pay the legal fees of the prevailing party. The federal loser-pays rule is consequently at the discretion of the judge, not a mandate. Sadly, federal judges rarely order losing parties to pay the legal fees of the prevailing party. But the federal rule on loser pays is a beginning. Loser-pays rules have a better chance at the state level, however.

As an aside, I should mention that tort reform in America is a political issue. Democrats and Republicans are squarely at opposite sides of the issue. For left-of-center Americans, America's tort regime provides an opportunity to level the playing field between the rich and the poor, to promote social justice, and to punish what they see as the sins of the rich and powerful they believe are endemic in our society. Damages and particularly punitive damages redistribute wealth from the powerful to the little guy. This approach of the American left to law and legal procedure provides the underpinning of much in the American tort system. It is an approach the legal profession staunchly defends as ethical and appropriate. Consequently, not only do lawyers, because of their large numbers in the state legislatures, have enormous influence over legislation affecting their profession with which to fight legal reform, states with a Democratic governor or a state legislature where Democrats are in the majority are traditionally inhospitable to legal reform.

In the November 2010 election, an unusually large number of states elected Republican governors or Republican-controlled state legislatures.[65] Many of these Republican governors and many of the new Republican members of the state legislatures came into office on the basis of a platform that includes tort reform. Consequently, loser-pay laws like the one in Alaska have a chance.

Let's not think these newly elected Republican governors or state legislatures are a panacea, however. Many Republican members of the state legislatures are attorneys reluctant to vote for legislation that inhibits the business model of the American legal enterprise.

---

65 As a result of the 2010 elections, there are twenty-nine Republican governors and twenty Democratic governors (one governor is independent). Twelve Democratic governorships went to the Republicans. Republicans, furthermore, picked up twenty state legislatures, giving them control over twenty-six state legislatures.

The Contingency Fee

In the chapter about contingency fees, I mentioned that reining in the contingency fee practice would do wonders for fairness and equity in the American legal system It is so deeply ingrained in the American legal system and the business model of the lawyer entrepreneur, however, that I doubt the system of lawyer compensation based on the contingency fee is reversible.

What is possible, however, is to put limits on the fees—to reduce the standard 33 percent or 40 percent or 50 percent to a more reasonable level. This legislative limiting of the size of contingency fees is beginning to occur.

In the class-action suit of the 9/11 first responders, the contingency fee for the lawyers was reduced from $220 million to $178 million. This was a judge-induced limiting of the fee. When the First Responders Health Care bill came up for a vote in the lame-duck session of Congress in December of 2010, the bill passed with a provision that contingency fees for lawyers representing first responders would be limited to 10 percent. This result came about through pressure from Republican Senator Tom Coburn of Oklahoma whose vote was needed to get other Republican senators on board.

State legislatures should take up the issue and begin to place limits on the contingency fee lawyers may charge their clients.

Class Action

The problem with reforming class action as it exists in the United States is that, in order to adjudicate complaints by a very large number of people that are similar in law or in fact, class action is a very appropriate form of litigation. European legal systems (as well as Singapore and South Korea), understanding the need to unclog the legal system from many complaints that are similar, are on the verge of introducing or have recently introduced class action—however, class action without the possibility of a contingency fee. Consequently, it is not class action by itself that is such a scourge of American jurisprudence; it is the way class actions in America have evolved and are today not plaintiff driven but lawyer and contingency fee driven.

American class action is not a legal procedure anymore; it has become a business—the lawyers' business. It is such a big business and such a hugely profitable business, and the business has so firmly established itself in the fabric of American society, that it will be very difficult if not impossible to reform.

The only way to lance the class-action boil is to regulate the contingency fee. By limiting what attorneys can charge in class-action cases, class action becomes less attractive to lawyers playing roulette with the American legal system.

Damages

Compared to reforming loser-pays rules, the contingency fee, or class action, reforming the system of damages has made much more progress, particularly in the field of medical malpractice.

The reason medical malpractice tort reform has made relatively good progress is that, unlike other aspects of the tort system, the American public became aware of the damage runaway malpractice awards were doing to the delivery of health care. Not only did such awards drive up the cost of health care (doctors had no choice but to pass on the skyrocketing cost of their medical malpractice insurance, and by practicing defense medicine, they performed many unnecessary tests), the spiraling cost of malpractice insurance was driving doctors to leave certain states. Because of the high awards for pain and suffering, some states were losing their obstetrics and gynecology and emergency room doctors in droves.

The resulting public outcry forced state legislatures to act and cap medical malpractice awards for pain and suffering. The cost of lost wages and medical care as a result of medical malpractice, called economic damages, has not been capped and should not be capped. Sadly, a few of our state supreme courts have ruled such caps on malpractice awards to be in violation of the right to trial by jury.

However, many states have adopted laws capping pain and suffering awards to between $250,000 and $500,000, eliminated joint liability, imposed a statute of limitations, and allowed periodic payments of awards instead of payment in one lump sum, laws that have passed muster with state supreme courts. Texas, Colorado, and California, for example, have caps on pain and suffering damages of $250,000.

Until and unless the general population becomes aware of the economic damage uneven and outrageously high damage awards are doing to the general economy and to what extent joint and several liability drives up the cost of local municipalities (which, because of their deep pockets, often pay the price of damage awards), I am afraid further tort reform where damages are concerned is not in the cards.

Appointment of Prosecutors and Judges

In the chapter about the election of prosecutors and state judges, I have given the reasons why prosecutors and judges should be appointed by the governor of the state subject to advice and consent from the state's legislature.

Abolishing Jury Trial in Civil Cases

There is no need to talk about abolishing the jury system in civil cases as other modern legal systems have done. The right to a jury trial is in the Constitution. America is not going to change its Constitution because the Brits or the French or the Dutch have done so. Not even a popular uprising would force Americans to change their Constitution.

Reducing the granting of excuses from jury duty and changing voir dire to assure a defendant is judged by a jury consisting of his or her equals and peers is another matter.

Postscript

Jack Goldstone, an American sociologist and political scientist and a professor at George Mason University, defines revolution as "an effort to transform the political institutions and the justification for political authority in society accompanied by formal or informal mass mobilization … that undermine authorities."[66]

Using Goldstone's definition of revolution, the American revolution is unique. It occurred at about the same time as the French revolution, and both revolutions were the incubators of constitutions enshrining the political thoughts that were developed in the age of Enlightenment and had gained respectability because of the influence of the political philosophers of the time, men like Voltaire, Rousseau, and Montesquieu.

The difference between the two revolutions, however, is the impact they had on their respective societies. Fifty years after the French revolution, few of France's social structures had changed. Society remained largely feudal and *égalité*, one of the three political goals put into words in the motto of the French revolution (*liberté, égalité, fraternité*), remained elusive.

It was not until the end of the nineteenth century that the political ideals of the French revolution were institutionalized with the birth of the Third Republic (1870). Even then, conservative elements of French society, such as the church, the army, and the elites, fought the restructuring of France's political institutions. France needed two more republics, each with new constitutions, to produce the democratic order that governs the country today.

---

66 Jack Goldstone, "Towards a Fourth Generation of Revolutionary Theory," *Annual Review of Political Science*, 2001

Comparing the evolution of France after the French revolution with the evolution of the United States of America after the American revolution, we find two totally different paths to the democracies the two countries are today.

The reason for the difference is the American Constitution: a brilliant piece of political thought and compromise, a solid political and legal foundation that has guided American political development and its democratic institutions ever since the revolution—a constitution that is still the bedrock of American society today.

Each of France's five republics since the French revolution produced a constitution, yet none lasted more than seventy years before being replaced with a new one. America's Constitution, on the contrary, endured through the centuries.

The reason the American Constitution endured is that the American revolution was owned and directed by learned men—men like George Washington, John Adams, Thomas Jefferson, John Hancock, Benjamin Franklin, James Madison, and Alexander Hamilton, to name a few.

The French revolution, on the other hand, was owned and directed by the mob. The pillars of the Enlightenment, the political philosophers of the eighteenth century, were mostly French. Yet they were not at the table when the French wrote their first constitution.

And therein lies the difference between the success with which France and the United States developed their political institutions after they lived through their respective revolutions: the United States became the world's oldest democracy, stable, enjoying unsurpassed growth, resolving that one gnawing deficiency in its Constitution, slavery, and producing a just and equitable society. In America respect for human rights is paramount, because the Constitution made such rights the DNA of the American character.

Throughout the centuries, the three distinct but equally strong pillars of our society—the legislature, the executive, and the judiciary—have respected and have abided by our Constitution. There has been friction, enormous friction at times, but each time solutions were found within the confines of our Constitution. That we have been so successful in managing our political affairs is in part the result of checks and balances in the system that steered us in the right direction when our ship of state went off course.

The exception to all this is the laws and procedures that have been introduced by elements within our legal system. These laws and procedures have not been in violation of the letter of our Constitution, but they have been in violation of its spirit.

Our Constitution stands for freedom, fairness, and unalienable human rights. As the various chapters in this book have shown, the way our legal system has evolved inhibits some of our freedoms, takes away some of our unalienable rights, and is in many instances inherently unfair. Many of the anomalies of our legal system, such as the contingency fee, class action, and the absence of loser-pays rules, are never mentioned in the Constitution. These legal procedures have been introduced by greedy legal practitioners (both by lawyers as officers of the court and by legislators who write the laws of the land) not to advance fairness and equity but to benefit themselves at the expense of the general welfare. They have created an unregulated fourth branch of government that is not subject to our constitutional checks and balances. Time and again, this fourth branch of government overrides the decisions of the other three branches.

The United States of America is one of the great democracies on the face of the earth. Its enormous wealth, its cherished freedoms, its stellar human rights record, its benevolent influence in world affairs, its boundless energy, its creativity, its refreshing spontaneity, and its cheerful confidence in the future (a confidence my politically more cynical friends in Europe often call naïve)—all of these flow in part from the wisdom of our founding fathers and the manner in which they suggested we conduct our affairs.

Amid these many blessings, America ought not to tolerate a legal system that lingers at the bottom of the ten best legal systems in the world. This great country deserves better than that.

Selected Bibliography

It is customary for a book like this one to provide a bibliography of at least fifteen or twenty books. It is indeed easy to provide the titles of that many books that are critical of certain aspects of the American legal system. If the reader wants to know about ill-conceived sentencing guidelines in our criminal law system, I can suggest a number of books that deal with that subject. If the reader wants to learn more about forum shopping in patent infringement cases, every lawyer can find a number of highly informative texts on that subject. Most of these books, however, resemble law school textbooks, interesting only for the lawyer, the law professor, the judge, the prosecutor, or the law student.

Because law permeates every aspect of our lives and our society, I have attempted to write a book that is hopefully interesting not just to the legal expert but to the lay person as well. Consequently, the books I have chosen for a suggested bibliography are all books that are interesting to the person who does not have a law degree.

I should also mention that few books in my suggested bibliography deal with the anomalies of our criminal law system. Except for some famous fiction, such as Harper Lee's *To Kill a Mockingbird* or the play *Inherit the Wind* by Jerome Lawrence and Robert Edwin Lee (later made into a movie with Spencer Tracy and Fredrick March), which is loosely based on the Scopes trial, there simply isn't much written about that subject, at least for the layman.

The most prolific author dealing with the anomalies of our legal system is Walter K. Olson. His book *The Litigation Explosion* (Plume, 1991) is one of the very first books exploring why, in the latter half of the twentieth century, litigation exploded. It explores who profits from litigation and who loses and how to contain it. The book deals primarily with product-liability and personal-injury cases. The book is somewhat outdated and out of print but still available through Amazon and very worthwhile for those who wish to explore the origins of our litigation explosion.

Olson's two subsequent books, *The Rule of Lawyers* (Truman Talley Books, 2003), which highlights the anomalies of class action, and *The Excuse Factory* (Free Press, 2007), which deals with the incredibly dysfunctional employment law, are highly informative. Olson, who is a senior fellow at the Manhattan Institute for Policy Research, maintains an informative web magazine entitled PointofLaw.com.

Also recommended is Catherine Crier's *The Case Against Lawyers* (Broadway Books, 2002), a book loaded with highly readable examples of legal misconduct, ridiculous rules and regulations, and outrageous jury awards. After stints as a prosecutor and a judge, Crier embarked on a career as a journalist beginning at CNN. She then worked as a correspondent on *20/20* for ABC from where she went to host an issue show on FOX. Crier is today the host of *Catherine Crier Live* on Court TV. As with so many books on the subject, *The Case Against Lawyers* is full of explosive information about the anomalies of our judicial system. It does not, however, explore any of the origins of our judicial problems and regretfully lacks any comparisons with legal systems outside the United States. Only one short chapter in the book deals with criminal law.

A scathing indictment of the ethics of the American lawyer can be found in *The Moral Compass of the American Lawyer: Truth, Justice, Power and Greed* by Richard A. Zitrin and Carol M. Langford (Ballantine Books, 2000).

Anyone wishing to read more about Bill Lerach and his billion-dollar class-action blackmail empire should read *Circle of Greed* by Patrick Dillon and Carl M. Cannon (Broadway Books, 2010). It is a fascinating chronicle of the twenty-year period when Lerach and his partners, under the eyes of judges and prosecutors, built their empire of deceit and fraud, bringing some of America's largest corporations to their knees. The book is a fabulous piece of outstanding journalistic research with probably one shortcoming: the authors seem too enamored with their prey.

The Duke lacrosse players case, a devastating example of prosecutorial misconduct, is admirably chronicled in *Until Proven Innocent: Political Correctness and the Shameful Injustices of the Duke Lacrosse Rape Case* by Stuart Taylor Jr. and K. C. Johnson (Thomas Dunne Books/St. Martin's Press, 2007). Taylor, a graduate of Princeton University and Harvard

Law School, writes for the *National Journal* and is a contributing editor of *Newsweek* and a nonresident senior fellow in Governance Studies at the Brookings Institution. He previously was a senior writer for *American Lawyer Media*, a lecturer at Princeton, a Supreme Court correspondent for the *New York Times*, and an attorney with the Washington DC law firm Wilmer, Cutler and Pickering. K. C. Johnson is a professor of history at Brooklyn College and in 2007–2008 was the Fulbright Distinguished Chair at Tel Aviv University.

The *New York Times Book Review* wrote about *Until Proven Guilty*, "Taylor and Johnson have made a gripping contribution to the literature of the wrongly accused. They remind us of the importance of constitutional checks on prosecutorial abuse. And they emphasize the lesson that ... if you're unjustly suspected of any crime, immediately call the best lawyer you can afford."

A book that is well written, a fascinating read, and highly informative where our criminal law system is concerned is John Grisham's *New York Times* best-selling book *The Innocent Man* (Doubleday, 2006). This book chronicles convicted murderer Ron Williamson's battle with the Oklahoma criminal law system. It describes the entire police investigation and analyzes every court document and every court proceeding in great detail. Grisham examines the exceedingly inadequate defense job by the court-appointed defense attorneys and describes the trial and appeals proceedings document by document and minute by minute.

For readers who are particularly interested in the anomalies of our tort system, I highly recommend *Judge and Jury: American Tort Law on Trial* by Eric Holland and Alexander Tabarok (Independent Institute, 2006). *Judge and Jury* answers the question of whether the American tort system benefits society and examines proposals to reform the system.

Finally, for the reader seriously interested in the shortcomings and pitfalls of our legal system from a historic point of view, I highly recommend a very old book. In 1831, the French government sent a twenty-five-year-old gentleman by the name of Alexis de Tocqueville to the United States to study the American prison system. Why the French thought they might learn something from how Americans treated their prisoners is beyond me. De Tocqueville and his partner, Gustave de Beaumont, spent nine months in the United States not only visiting prisons but also studying every aspect of American society.

De Tocqueville in particular wanted to know everything about the press, class structures and slavery, how the government and the financial and judicial systems functioned, and what role religion played in American society. Upon their return to France, the two gentlemen indeed issued a detailed report about the American prison system, and Beaumont wrote a novel about race relations in the United States.

Four years later, however, de Tocqueville published a treatise entitled *De la democratie en Amerique* (later translated into English under the name *Democracy in America),* a work that is so insightful and so powerful an analysis of American institutions and the culture of the time that it is today as readable and as applicable to many aspects of American society as it was when it was written nearly two centuries ago. *Democracy in America* is a brilliant treatise about life as well as the role of the law and lawyers in America and is a work that has stood the test of time. The Signet Classics edition (2001) is available from Amazon.com.

Appendix I

Child Abuse Cases

There are two cases of child abuse I would like to mention in some detail. The McMartin preschool case was at the time the longest and most expensive legal proceeding in American history. The case began in 1983 and concluded in 1990. It lasted seven years and cost $16 million yet produced no convictions. The Wenatchee case ensnared and jailed more innocent people than any other child abuse case.

McMartin

In 1983 a mentally unstable woman by the name of Judy Johnson enrolled her two-year-old son in the McMartin Preschool in Manhattan Beach, California. Soon thereafter, Judy Johnson, who thought her child had rectal problems, made sexual abuse allegations against Ray Buckey, the only male teacher at the school. After filing her complaint, Judy Johnson was diagnosed with paranoid schizophrenia, her husband left her, and she died of alcoholism before she could testify in the trial.

In the meantime the police, using anatomically correct dolls, began questioning all the children who had ever attended the school. As a result, the entire staff of the school was arrested and indicted. They included Ray Buckey, his mother, Peggy, his sister, Peggy Ann, his grandmother, Virginia, and three teachers. The charges consisted of 208 counts of child abuse and all of the accused except the grandmother were denied bail.

The preliminary hearing lasted nineteen months, during which time the prosecutors began to argue among themselves about the merits of the case. After working on the case in the prosecutor's office for two years and becoming convinced there was insufficient evidence of wrongdoing on the part of the accused, prosecutor Glenn Stevens sought a dismissal of the charges. When his colleagues in the prosecutor's office disagreed, he resigned. He soon went public with the allegation that the prosecutors were putting seven innocent people through a terrible ordeal—he would have no part in it. Soon thereafter, another member of the prosecution team, Christine Johnson, asked to be removed from the case. At the conclusion of the nineteen-month-long preliminary hearing, the prosecution, lacking sufficient evidence, dropped all charges against the defendants except for Ray Buckey and his mother Peggy.

The trial of Ray and Peggy began in April of 1987, almost four years after the original accusations, and lasted an incredible twenty-eight months—imagine the jury, impaneled for twenty-eight months. The trial produced a not guilty verdict for Peggy and a hung jury in the allegations against Ray. As I have said, prosecutors do not give up; they are not supposed to lose. Consequently, five months later a new trial began, this time with Ray as the sole accused. Again the trial produced a deadlocked jury, and all charges against Ray were finally dismissed.

It should be mentioned that in the process, not only was the reputation of the McMartin family and the three teachers destroyed along with their livelihood, but scores of newspapers, including the highly regarded *Los Angeles Times,* for years printed not only the allegations themselves but constant editorial opinions savaging the McMartins and their school. The hysteria reached such epic proportions that scores of preschools in Southern California had to close because parents became paranoid about the safety of their children.

Wenatchee

In 1995 Wenatchee police detective Robert Perez started the ball rolling. His foster daughter Donna told the detective that she had been raped by nearly every adult in the community she had been in contact with. Detective Perez put Donna in his police car and drove her through town. Donna pointed to many houses, twenty-two in all, where she claimed she and her friends had been repeatedly raped and molested over a period of seven years. Donna's sister initially corroborated Donna's accusations. She later testified it had all been made up.

The Wenatchee case is unique in that it did not involve one person accused of sexual misconduct or a small group of teachers and principals in a preschool or daycare center. In the Wenatchee case, a large number of people located in a large geographical area were hauled into court; the Wenatchee case touched, and in many cases destroyed, close to fifty families from the town of Wenatchee and the villages surrounding it. All were allegedly involved in a sex ring.

Forty-three adults were arrested, mostly poor, uneducated parents, some mentally challenged, some Sunday school teachers, all charged with molesting their own children or their foster children. In all, 29,726 charges of child abuse were filed involving sixty children. Hardly any of the defendants could afford a lawyer.

Citizens who objected to the investigative techniques used by the police and Children's Welfare Services were themselves accused of being part of the conspiracy and charged. Social workers who objected were taken off the case or fired. When Pastor Roby Roberson criticized the investigation, he and his wife were arrested. A jury acquitted the Robersons of all charges against them.

No physical evidence was ever presented in court. The evidence was based exclusively on the children's testimony and the admissions of some mentally challenged defendants. Twenty-two of the defendants were convicted, and all served jail time. The children of some defendants were taken away and put into foster care.

Every conviction was later reversed on appeal, primarily because the vast majority of the children recanted their testimony. The town of Wenatchee; the county of Chelan, where Wenatchee is located; and the State of Washington Child Protective Services subsequently paid millions and millions of dollars in compensation for false arrest, police misconduct, misconduct on the part of Child Protective Services, and prosecutorial misbehavior, in which even the judges were implicated.

In 1998, Dr. Phillip Esplin, a forensic psychologist for the National Institutes of Health's Child Witness Project, said that "Wenatchee may be the worst example ever of mental health services being abused by a State ... to control and manage children who have been frightened and coerced into falsely accusing their parents and neighbors of the most heinous crimes."

None of the numerous public officials, police detectives, social workers, and prosecutors who coached and cajoled the witnesses and made up the evidence have ever been indicted.

If you believe that the Fells Acre, McMartin, and Wenatchee cases are so grotesque they must be exceptions, a short description of twenty-eight child abuse cases which took place during the 1980s and 1990s may change your mind. All cases are somewhat similar to Fells Acre, McMartin, and Wenatchee—in all cases innocent people spent five, ten, and in some cases many more years in jail. Moreover, in all cases the convictions of the accused were later reversed.

The twenty-eight cases collectively illustrate a serious lack of fairness in the American criminal justice system. In most of these cases a homophobic, prejudiced, or unbalanced parent accused a teacher in a preschool of sexual abuse or a jealous child or divorced parent sought revenge for an imagined wrong and made a sexual abuse allegation against a former husband or boyfriend.

The police, who usually lack even the most basic training in the investigation of sex abuse cases, coach the children into allegations of abuse by using suggestive and repetitive interrogation techniques. The only too eager prosecutor takes the case and, in closing arguments, reminds the jury that it is their duty to make the world of our vulnerable and innocent children safe from sexual predators. The result? A guilty verdict in nearly all cases. After spending five, ten, fifteen, and sometimes even twenty years in jail, the accused finally proves, often with DNA evidence or through admissions by the now-grown children that they were coerced, that the he or she is innocent and is finally released from jail.

The list has been prepared by using data collected by various organizations, such as victimsofthestate.org, justicedenied.org, truthinjustice.org, and newspaper articles.

- In 1981, Alan Crotzer of Hillsborough, Florida was convicted of kidnapping and raping a thirty-eight-year-old woman and her twelve-year-old daughter. He was convicted despite conflicting testimony during trial. In 2006, after twenty-five years of incarceration, he was released from prison because DNA proved his innocence.
- In 1981, Calvin Willis of Caddo, Louisiana was convicted of raping a ten-year-old girl because his blood type was O (as is

quite common in the male population) and because he wore a cowboy hat, as did the rapist. Exonerating evidence was ignored. In 1981, after twenty-five years of incarceration, he was released from prison because DNA proved his innocence.

- In 1982, James Waller of Dallas, Texas, despite witnesses who testified he was home at the time of the crime, was convicted of raping a twelve-year-old boy because the boy allegedly recognized Waller's voice. In 1992, after eleven years in jail, Waller was paroled. In 2007 DNA evidence proved his innocence.

- In 1983, Larry Youngblood of Pima, Arizona, was convicted of sodomizing a ten-year-old boy on the basis of the victim's testimony that the assailant had a disfigured eye. Larry Youngblood's eye was disfigured. Youngblood appealed, claiming gross negligence on the part of the police in handling DNA samples taken from the victim. The Arizona Court of Appeals agreed that Youngblood had been denied due process and overturned his conviction. The prosecutor appealed the court of appeals' decision to the US Supreme Court, which reinstated the decision, and Youngblood went back to jail. In 2000 DNA samples proved that Walter Cruise, then a Texas inmate, had committed the crime, and Youngblood was finally exonerated.

- In 1983 in Kern County, California, prosecutors promised children of the parents of the Kniffens and the McCuans families that they would be reunited with their parents if they would only testify to having been abused by them. When the parents were convicted, the children recanted. In 1996 the convictions of the four parents were reversed and they were released from prison after fourteen years of incarceration.

- In 1983, Richard McKinley of Homestead in Dade County, Florida received a life sentence for the rape of a minor under twelve years of age exclusively on the testimony of the victim and a police officer who claimed he saw McKinley flee the scene of the crime. McKinley strenuously maintained his innocence. In 2004, after twenty-one years in jail, McKinley was released when DNA proved the semen found on the rape victim was not McKinley's. As is so often the case, prosecutors refuse to admit defeat. In McKinley's case, they demanded that McKinley admit to a lesser charge of attempted sexual battery in order to regain his freedom. McKinley was willing to live with the lesser charge in exchange for his immediate freedom and no probation.

- In 1983, Ronnie Bullock of Cook County, Illinois, was convicted of raping a nine-year-old girl. Bullock was identified by the victim in a line-up, an investigative tool that frequently leads to misidentification. DNA testing exonerated him in 1994, and he was released after eleven years in jail.

- In 1984, John Stoll of Kern County, California, and his two codefendants were convicted of seventeen counts of child molestation involving six children. After five years, his two codefendants won their appeal and were released. Stoll's appeal failed because his defense lawyer failed to introduce exculpatory evidence. Later five of the six kids recanted their testimony and Stoll's conviction was overturned after he had served twenty years in jail.

- In 1984, Edward and Karri LaBois of Hennepin, Minnesota, while running a daycare center, were accused of abusing their four-year-old daughter. After hearing about the accusation, they fled the state with their daughter and, nine years later, were arrested in Salt Lake City, Utah. Not able to find anybody willing to testify against the couple, the prosecutor dropped the charges.

- In 1984–1986 in the Bronx, New York, prosecutor Mario Merola convicted five men (known as the Bronx Five), including Nathaniel Grady, a forty-seven-year-old Methodist minister, of sexually abusing children in daycare centers throughout the Bronx. Grady was accused of sexually molesting six three-year-olds at nap time at the Westchester-Tremont Day Care Center run by his church. He was convicted after a thirteen-week trial. The primary witness against Grady was a three-year-old boy. Showing what a prosecutor can do with a child abuse case in front of a jury, twenty-six character witnesses testified at Nathaniel Grady's trial, including a bishop, a judge, and the Yonkers police commissioner. Nevertheless, the prosecutor won. The minister was convicted on January 20, 1986, and sentenced to forty-five years in prison. Rev. Grady spent ten years in prison before his conviction was overturned and he was released. All the other men won their appeals after having been imprisoned for periods of eight to ten years.

- In 1984, Sylvester Smith of Brunswick County, North Carolina, was convicted of raping two girls aged four and five. Sylvester was released from jail in 2004 when the girls came forward to say they had been coached to accuse Sylvester in order to protect another person.[67]

- Ricky Lynn Pitts and six other defendants from Kern County, California, were convicted of no fewer than 377 counts of child abuse in 1985. All convictions were overturned in 1990 because of prosecutorial misconduct called unprecedented in the court's experience. In the next four years, all of the child witnesses came forward to claim that their testimony was coerced.

- In 1985, Robert Aldridge and Jennifer Wilcox of Montgomery County, Ohio were convicted of child abuse. It became clear eleven years later that the children who had provided testimony during the trial had been forced to do so by the police. John Chronopoulos, then twelve and now twenty-three, testified that the police had charged him with rape, had hand-cuffed him, and taken him to the county's youth detention center, where he had to spend the night. He said he told Detective Jennifer Bazell of the Huber Heights Police Department the next morning that he was willing to tell her "the truth" she had demanded—namely that he had been molested by Wilcox and Aldridge, even though it was a lie. Jason, then ten and now twenty-one, also came forward and testified that he too had agreed to tell Bazell "the truth" after he was placed in a holding cell at the Huber Heights police station. Justin, eight then and now nineteen, said he followed the lead of his brothers because he was told he would also be thrown in jail if he didn't. All three of the brothers said they didn't even know who Wilcox and Aldridge were until they saw them in the courtroom, and they were told where to point when asked

---

67 In 2005 Mike Easley, governor of North Carolina, refused to pardon Sylvester Smith. Reason? In the time-tested tradition of prosecutors not admitting to a miscarriage of justice—it is bad for their careers—Governor Easley happened to be the district attorney when Sylvester was prosecuted back in 1984.

to identify them. Aldridge and Wilcox spent eleven years in jail.

The cases cited below are all variants of the ones mentioned above. They were all the result of prosecutorial misconduct committed by withholding exculpatory evidence, plea bargains with other accused suspects, false identification in a line-up, testimony by a number of young children coached to say what the police or prosecutors wanted them to say, sloppy police work, or juries willing to convict alleged sex offenders based on flimsy evidence.

- In 1986, Arthur Mumphrey of Montgomery County, Texas, was accused of rape. He was released and pardoned in 2006 after eighteen years in prison.
- In 1987, Jimmy Ray Bromgard was convicted of raping of a young girl in Billings, Montana. DNA exonerated him in 2002.
- Dwayne Dail of Wayne County, North Carolina, was accused of raping a young girl in 1987. Dail turned down an offer to plead guilty in exchange for three years of probation. A jury convicted him, and he was sentenced to two life terms plus fifteen years. In 2007, DNA tests proved he could not have been the perpetrator, and he was set free.
- In 1988 in Long Beach, California, Leonard McSherry was convicted of kidnapping and rape. However, DNA testing identified the real culprit as an inmate who was serving a life sentence for assault. McSherry served thirteen years of a forty-eight-years-to-life sentence.
- In 1988, Marvin Mitchell of Suffolk County, Maryland, was convicted of abducting an eleven-year-old girl and raping her. DNA proved him innocent in 1997.
- Kelly Michaels of Maplewood, New Jersey, was convicted in 1988 to forty-seven years in prison on 115 counts of sexual abuse of twenty children. Michaels's conviction was overturned on appeal in 1993, and prosecutors dropped charges against her when the court found one child's testimony had clearly described the taking of rectal temperature and most of the interviews of the children had been "coercive, suggestive, and inept."

- James Love of Hamilton County, Ohio, was accused in 1988–1989 of raping a girl on separate occasions three years, six years, seven years, and eight years earlier. Love attempted to prove during trial that he was in Mexico during the dates of the alleged rapes by producing telephone records of collect calls to his mother during the times in question. Prosecutors claimed the calls could have been made by anyone. Love was sentenced to five consecutive life sentences. When in prison, Love continued to produce proof he was in Mexico at the alleged times of the rapes and was finally released after his conviction was overturned in 2006.
- In 1989, a case involving Little Rascals Daycare Center in Chowan County, North Carolina, is a carbon copy of the Fells Acre Daycare Center and Wenatchee cases discussed above. Ninety children accused twenty adults including a mayor and sheriff of 429 instances of child sexual abuse. A number received very long sentences before the cases were finally settled in 1999, when all charges were dropped.
- In 1989, John Michael Harvey of Tarrant County, Texas, was convicted of molesting a three-year-old who later recanted her testimony with the words, "I am also very angry with the prosecutor. I feel she took advantage of me because she wanted to win her case." John Michael Harvey was declared innocent and released from jail after fifteen years of incarceration.
- In 1990, Guy Randolph of Suffolk County, Maryland, was accused of rape. Randolph was in and out of jail and probation until a judge exonerated him of all charges and declared him innocent.
- Jack Ray Broam, thirty-eight, and Jay Cee Manning, thirty-seven, of Carson City, Nevada, were accused in 1990 by a young man of having sexually abused him, They were convicted to life in prison. The accuser later recanted his story, admitting his mother, Broam's ex-wife, had starved him until he was willing to accuse Broam. Broam was released in 1998 after eight years in jail.
- In 1990, James Bernard Parker of Union County, North Carolina, was accused of rape. He spent fourteen years in jail before he was released when DNA proved he was innocent.

- Robert McClendon of Columbus, Ohio, was also accused of rape in 1990. He spent eighteen years in jail before DNA proved he was innocent and he was released.
- Jimmy Williams of Summit County, Ohio, spent eleven years in jail beginning in 1990 before he was released because of the recantation of a child's accusations.
- In 1991 in Montgomery County, Alabama, Robert Doyle was convicted and spent eleven years in jail before being released because the prosecutor withheld exculpatory evidence.
- Ronnie Mark Gariepy of Hutchinson County, Texas, was sentenced in 1991 to twelve years in jail for the rape of his step-daughter. Although the step-daughter recanted her testimony eighteen months after he was sentenced, Ronnie Mark Gariepy spent another six and a half years in jail before then-Governor George W. Bush of Texas granted him a pardon based on his innocence.
- Peter Rose of Lodi, California, was convicted of rape in 1994. He served nine years of a twenty-seven-year sentence before he was released because DNA proved he was innocent.
- In 1995, Ross Sorrels of Clark County, Washington, was convicted of child rape. Sorrels was freed from prison in 2003 with the help of DNA testing. Ross Sorrels served eight years of a ten-year sentence. In his case there was other evidence in favor of overturning his conviction, and another man was convicted for Sorrels's alleged crime.

Index

Page numbers containing italic "*n*" or "*nn*" (Ex: 58*n*35) indicate references to footnotes

S
Salem (MA) trials, 31
Sample, James, 76, 76*n*38
San Diego, Judicial Panel on
    MultiDistrict Legislation
    hears Toyota plaintiffs
    attorneys pleas in, 139
San Francisco, Police Department
    crime laboratory, 47
San Francisco Examiner, some
    problems at San Francisco
    Police Department crime lab,
    47
Santa Clara County Superior Court
    (CA), shareholder derivative
    suit filed in, 146–147
satanic cults, 27
Satisfaction Guaranteed and Same
    Day Service case, 82–83, 167
SBI (State Bureau of Investigation),
    North Carolina, 48
Scandinavian countries, 55, 83, 144
Scheck, Barry, 23
scheme, as defined by honest services
    law, 9
Schoengold & Sporn PC, 152–153
Scott & Scott LLP, 147–149
Scruggs, Richard "Dickie," 111–113,
    148, 171, 196
Scruggs Class Action Criminal
    Enterprise, 113
Seattle Post-Intelligencer, on
    contaminated DNA test, 46,
    46*n*29
Seay, Frank, 16
Securities and Exchange Commission,
    (SEC), 135–136, 138, 149
Senate. *See also* US Congress
    actions in mining accidents, 7
    appointment of attorney general
        and, 11
    getting pressure about class-action
        suits, 131

lawyer-politicians dominating, xviii
    trial for impeachment of Bill
        Clinton3, 38
Senate Judiciary Committee, hearing
    on contingency fee abuses,
    102
Senator Stevens, US v., 194
sentences
    applying three-strikes-you' re-out
        laws, 8, 13
    in child abuse cases, 27–35,
        215–223
    election of prosecutors and, 13
    judges using discretion in, 8
    long prison, 6
    surveys on average length of, 18
    in US criminal system, 7
settlement mills, 179–184
settlements
    in Alliance Pharmaceutical
        Company case, 128–130
    of asbestos cases, 104, 111,
        137*n*55
    blackmailing targets into, 194
    in BP Gulf Coast case, 139
    budgeting for cost of, 136
    cheap and easy, 181
    cheap and easy settlements,
        181*n*60
    in companies involved with
        mergers and acquisitions,
        136
    contingency fees impact on, 100–
        102, 151
    in cost of products, 152
    in derivative lawsuits, 145–146
    in derivative litigation, 150
    in GM case, 137
    "going rate" for, 111
    largest class-action, 112
    by Milberg Weiss law firm, 135
    from 9/11 World Trade Center
        rescue workers lawsuits,

119–121, 203
Office of Fair Trading supervision
  over, 140–141
out-of-court, 85
process of, 183–184
by Elliott Spitzer as Attorney
  General of New York State,
  23–25
in strike suits, 125
in Toyota case, 139
in Volkswagen of America case,
  152
Seventh Amendment, 87
several liability, 164–165
Severus, Emperor Septimius, 98
sex offenders, alleged, 222
sexual abuse. *See* child abuse cases
sexual abuse allegations, 215, 218
sexual assaults, 41
sexual predators, 28, 218
Shahzad, Faisal, 26
Shall, 116
shareholder derivative suit, 145–150
shareholder lawsuits, 125–126
Sheedy, Barbara, 26
Shingler, Arthur, 147
Shushufindi 61 oil field (Ecuador),
  115
O. J.Simpson criminal trial, 23, 56–
  57, 57*n*34, 90
Singapore
  class-action lawsuits in, 114
  legal system in, 189, 191
  loser-pays rule as common law in,
    81
  shareholders derivative lawsuit in,
    148
Singletom v. Volkswagen, 176
Singleton, Richard, 172
Singleton, Ruth, 172
slip and fall injury, settlements, 181,
  181*n*60
Smith, Michelle, 27–29

Smith, Sylvester, 221, 221*n*67
snitches, 16, 16*n*13
Sorrels, Ross, 224
South America
  class-action lawsuits in, 114
  factions and, xxi
South Carolina (SC), class-action
  suit against Janssen
  Pharmaceuticals and, 106
South Korea
  class-action lawsuits in, 114
  legal system in, 189, 191
  shareholders derivative lawsuit in,
    148
Soviet union, countries born out of,
  factions and, xxi
Spain
  class-action lawsuits in, 140
  legal system in, 191
Spanish civil law system, xx*n*5
Spitzer, Elliot
  as attorney general of New York
    State, 23–24, 39
  as governor of of New York State,
    24–25
  rating by Competitive Enterprise
    Institute as attorney
    generals, 27
Springsteen, Bruce, 69
standard of neutrality, 107
Standard Oil, 69.
StandDown Texas Project, 47
Sta Rite Industries, Lakey v., 157*n*58
state attorneys general
  about, 11–12, 39–40
  Richard Blumenthal in
    Connecticut, 25–27
  class-action suit against Janssen
    Pharmaceuticals and,
    106–107
  imposing interstate and national
    regulations, 12
  imposing penalties on out-of-state